FRITZ LANG

INTERVIEWS

CONVERSATIONS WITH FILMMAKERS SERIES
PETER BRUNETTE, GENERAL EDITOR

Photo credit: Photofest

FRITZ LANG

INTERVIEWS

EDITED BY BARRY KEITH GRANT

UNIVERSITY PRESS OF MISSISSIPPI / JACKSON

www.upress.state.ms.us

The University Press of Mississippi is a member of the Association of American University Presses.

11 10 09 08 07 06 05 04 03   4 3 2 1
⊗
Library of Congress Cataloging-in-Publication Data

Lang, Fritz, 1890–1976.
    Fritz Lang : interviews / edited by Barry Keith Grant.
        p.   cm. — (Conversations with filmmakers series)
    Includes index.
    ISBN 1-57806-576-3 (cloth : alk. paper) — ISBN 1-57806-577-1 (pbk. : alk. paper)
    1. Lang, Fritz, 1890–1976—Interviews.   2. Motion picture producers and directors—Austria—Interviews.   I. Grant, Barry Keith, 1947–   II. Title.
III. Series.

PN1998.3.L36A5   2003
791.43′0233′092—dc21   2002192260

British Library Cataloging-in-Publication Data available

CONTENTS

INTRODUCTION

FRITZ LANG WAS ONE of the giants of the cinema, "the last of the dinosaurs" as he describes himself late in life in his interview with Charles Higham and Joel Greenberg. In Hollywood at one time or another he worked for every major studio except Disney, making films over six decades. Until his death in 1976 his career was virtually synonymous with and a considerably important part of the history of cinema. His work in film spans the silent era almost from its beginnings through the golden era of German Expressionism in the 1920s and the classic studio system in Hollywood to the rise of the international co-production.

In the course of his career Lang directed more acknowledged classics of the German silent cinema than any other director, made the first important German sound film (*M*), and directed some of the most important crime films and films noir of the American studio era. The scale of his work ranged from the German blockbusters to modest Hollywood Bs. Lang directed many great actors, including Rudolf Klein-Rogge, Charles Boyer, Henry Fonda, Sylvia Sidney, Barbara Stanwyck, Glenn Ford, Edward G. Robinson, Randolph Scott, Joan Bennett, Robert Ryan, and Marlene Dietrich. He made Peter Lorre a star with his performance in *M* and was instrumental in launching Spencer Tracy's career with *Fury*. He worked with some of the most illustrious figures of film history, including producers Erich Pommer, Walter Wanger, John Houseman, and David O. Selznick, cinematographers Fritz Arno Wagner, Karl Freund, and James Wong Howe, composers Kurt Weill and Max Steiner, and writers such as Thea von Harbou (his second wife), Dudley Nichols, and Bertolt Brecht. These achievements are all the more impressive when one remembers that Lang experienced several periods of forced inactivity, times when he was unable to find work.

Lang led an exciting life. At one point he was Germany's most famous filmmaker, perhaps the most renowned in all of Europe. He was married at least twice, suspected of murdering his first wife, and a ladies' man who boasted of affairs with a succession of famous and aspiring actresses. Serving in the military during World War I, Lang was wounded in action twice. He witnessed the rise of Nazism in Germany and fled the country shortly after Hitler took power; later in the United States his imperious European manner generated considerable resentment in Hollywood; and then he was stigmatized by the communist hysteria of the McCarthy era. In his later years, after he ceased making films in Hollywood, Lang became a popular speaker on the lecture circuit and a revered figure for the cinéastes of the French New Wave, even appearing as a director named Fritz Lang in Jean-Luc Godard's *Le Mépris* (*Contempt*, 1963).

Film critics and historians have commonly divided Lang's extensive filmography into two major periods, the silent German films and the American studio movies. (*Liliom*, made in France after Lang fled Germany on his way to the U.S., is typically regarded as a curious anomaly, and the final German films an unfortunate coda.) A longstanding and seemingly inevitable matter of debate regarding Lang concerns the relative merits of these two distinct phases of the director's work. Yet this debate in itself does a disservice to Lang's oeuvre, because both periods produced masterpieces as well as misfires and because Lang's distinctive vision is apparent in all his films. Lang himself preferred to think of his career in terms of continuity. In the interview with Higham and Greenberg, Lang admits differences in working methods between Hollywood and Germany but nonetheless refused to offer a comparative judgment regarding the two phases of his career. Asked by Jean Domarchi and Jacques Rivette, Lang responded that he preferred his films of social criticism, examples of which could be found in both periods. As he says to Jean-Claude Philippe, "My life goes on and my films are the most direct expression of what I have seen, of what I have learned and felt. From my point of view, it is an uninterrupted line."

Indeed, the thematic and stylistic consistency in Lang's work across decades, countries, and different production contexts is truly remarkable. His films depict an entrapping, claustrophobic, deterministic world in which people, controlled by larger forces, whether social, metaphysical, or supernatural, struggle vainly against their fate. Lang tells Gero Gandert that "The struggle of the individual against Fate probably is in all my films, (primarily good) people wrestling with a higher, superior power, be it the power of a generally accepted injustice or the power of a corrupt organization, society, or authority. Or be it the power of one's own conscious or unconscious drives." But, he adds, "It is the struggle, the opposition, that is important." "I think that is the main characteristic, the main theme that runs through all my pictures—this fight against destiny, against fate," Lang asserts to Peter Bogdanovich. "Unconsciously, it goes through all my pictures, I suppose: 'hate, murder, and revenge.'"[1] As Lang puts it to Higham and Greenberg, "this has maybe something to do with my so-called philosophy of life."

Nevertheless, Lang insisted that his vision was not a negative one. When asked about the downbeat nature of his films by Axel Madsen, Lang replies that "to tell people there is nothing—no." As he explains to Gretchen Berg, "You get caught in the works, and you can't escape. But aside from that, what I always wanted to show and define is the attitude of combat that must be adopted in the face of destiny. Whether or not the individual wins this fight, what counts is the fight itself, because it is vital." To *Cinema 62* he says that "it is the essence of life to fight for the causes we think are just." Thus he could assert to Peter von Bagh that he was an optimist and not a pessimist, because "People create their own fate and are responsible for it. . . . fate is not what the Gods dictate. Fate is what you do, how you treat certain things, how you develop personally."

Nevertheless, Lang's work is so insistently close, enclosed, closed in, that critics tend to invoke him as the auteur most fully representative of what Leo Braudy calls "the closed style" of cinema, films in which "the frame of the screen totally defines the world inside as a picture frame does" and where "the director is much more autocratic, controlling every detail of production."[2] Braudy opposes Lang to Jean Renoir, whose work represents a more open style, just as for Andrew Sarris "If Renoir is humanism, Lang is determinism."[3] Lang's work, which Sarris describes as "the cinema of the nightmare, the fable, and the philosophical dissertation,"[4] is so distinct that, like "Hawksian," "Hitchcockian," and "Capraesque," "Langian" has become an adjective to describe films with a particularly dark and doomed vision.

But even as the unsympathetic critic Siegfried Kracauer was forced to admit, Lang had the ability to effectively express mood and theme through mise-en-scène. For this reason Lang has been regarded as an important filmmaker from the days of classic auteurism in the 1950s through auteur-structuralism to poststructural auteurism, weathering the vagaries of critical fashion. When the concept of the author was declared dead in the 1980s, Lang became the Lang-text. Following Peter Wollen's famous distinction between Howard Hawks and "Howard Hawks," Stephen Jenkins in 1981 defined Lang as "a space where a multiplicity of discourses intersect, an unstable, shifting configuration of discourses produced by the interaction of a specific group of films (Lang's filmography) with particular, historically and socially locatable ways of reading/viewing those films."[5] Surviving such critical jargon, Lang has yet to be deposed from his prominent position in the auteur pantheon to which Andrew Sarris assigned him in 1968, alongside such other luminaries as Alfred Hitchcock, Howard Hawks, D. W. Griffith, and John Ford.

From a humanist perspective, Lang has often been criticized for being unable to create characters with psychological depth. He is said to convey a coldness toward his characters, the sense that they are merely puppets in a predetermined scenario. To the director's eternal chagrin, Lang's work was singled out by Kracauer, who in his classic study *From Caligari to Hitler* argued that the films revealed an incipient fascist sensibility in their emphasis on ornamentation over character, which he condemned as "Virtuosity alienated from content posed as art."[6] Lang himself, an autocratic workaholic on the set, sometimes acted like the cruel God his films often suggest controls human destiny. According to the accounts of many people with whom he worked, Lang rehearsed actors mercilessly, often testing the limits of their physical endurance, and he frequently insisted upon dictating the details of their blocking and gestures. He kept changes and improvisation on the set to a minimum. As he says to Gretchen Berg, "I like to know exactly what I am going to do when I arrive on the set. I change practically nothing of what I have in my head."

Lang, however, often claims the opposite in his interviews, insisting that collaboration was a more productive method of direction. In the American Film Institute interview, Lang astonishingly asserted that he never had trouble with anybody working on any of his films. He told Jean-Louis Noames that "a director shouldn't show an actor what he should do. . . . The role of the director is, to the contrary, to bring out the best of the actor." In at least three of the interviews in this book Lang says, somewhat defensively, that he didn't want actors simply to obey his directions, because then there would be "twenty little Fritz Langs running around the screen."

It has often been suggested that the dark vision of Lang's films reflected the director's own experiences. As Paul M. Jensen notes, Lang was "twice torn from his peacefully creative life and shuttled between countries; his life was manipulated by forces over which he had no control."[7] Further, Lang was a direct participant in World War I, lived through the uncertainties of the Weimar period, and witnessed the rise of fascism in Germany and conservative demagoguery in the U.S. But when interviewers ask Lang about his personal life, he tends to be guarded, if not secretive. In discussing his past Lang never mentions the fact that he was half Jewish (on his mother's side), for example. Also, he tends to gloss over his marriage and collaboration with Thea von Harbou, who became a Nazi supporter and chose to stay in Germany. In several of the interviews Lang insists that his life generally has nothing to do with his films.

Lang often resisted analyzing his films as well. "I can't explain why I used the sound of bull-frogs' croaking over one of the love scenes in *You Only Live Once*, any more than I can explain the use of rain against the window in a similar scene in *Fury*. . . . It's little more than instinct," he insists. To Gene D. Phillips, Lang explains, "I don't like to dwell on the thematic implications of my films, to explain what they mean. . . . All I have to say I have said in my films and they speak for themselves." The question of unconscious motivation dogged Lang for decades, as if he were afraid that it might mean a loss of artistic control, and he returns to the issue obsessively in these interviews. More than once Lang mentions a screenwriter he knew who went to therapy for his own problems and who as a result could no longer write.

Lang disliked theorizing about cinema. In the interviews Lang frequently says that there are "no theories" for film making and that he has none to offer. To Jean Domarchi and Jacques Rivette Lang flatly says, "I believe that when one has a theory about something, one is already dead." Nevertheless, Lang could provide aesthetic insights into his own films if the inclination seized him. Consider, for example, his explanation of the various uses of sound in *M* in the interview with Gero Gandert and the discussion of movement, action, and emotion in cinema with Jean-Louis Noames. Lang particularly warmed to talking about the special effects and technical problem-solving in his films, as is evident in the lengthy interview with Gretchen Berg.

One issue of style that interviewers inevitably raise with Lang concerns his views on and relationship to expressionism. Lang claims he was influenced by it—"One cannot live through a period without taking some of it in," he tells Domarchi and Rivette—but denies still being one. "I don't know the difference between an expressionist and a non-expressionist mise-en-scène. I produce what I feel," he curtly replies to Jean-Claude Philippe. In the interview with Michel Ciment and others at the 1968 Venice Film Festival, he says simply, "I don't know what expressionism is," although to Berg he explains, "I'm always classified as an expressionist, but I think that I belong to the realists." Lang often claimed that one of the things he learned in Hollywood was that Americans do not like symbolism forced upon them, and so he abandoned the technique in his American films. Sometimes he even asserted that his films were more documentary in spirit. *Mabuse*, for example, he says in Venice, "was a documentary on the post-war period," while on several occasions he argues that the apparently stylized look of the jail cell in *You Only Live Once* was designed with fidelity to real cells in San Quentin. To Peter von Bagh, Lang impatiently asserts that all his films are documentaries precisely because they had "carefully developed screenplays."

Like Hitchcock's films, Lang's often deal with the violent potential lurking within the respectable citizen and suggest that social order requires controlling the beast within. Thus Lang also was often asked questions about violence, both in human nature and its representation in films, his own as well as others. In Venice he says "We can't avoid violence because it is everywhere. It should be present in films." "People no longer believe in Hell or brimstone," he explains to Henry Hart, "So—brutality's now a necessary ingredient of dramatic development and denouement." Lang claims that he preferred to show the results of violence rather than to present violence graphically, arguing that this is a more effective approach. In several interviews he argues that the death of the little girl at the beginning of *M* is more disturbing because it is left to the viewer's imagination, and more than once he makes the same argument about the fatal car explosion that kills Glenn Ford's wife in *The Big Heat*.

Lang could be harsh in judging his own work. He confesses to Higham and Greenberg, for example, that *Human Desire* "was a great success in France, I don't know why. It certainly doesn't deserve it." Sometimes Lang takes responsibility for his failures and mistakes, as he usually does with the unsatisfying ending of *Metropolis*, which he describes in several interviews as embarrassingly naive. More often than not, however, Lang blames producers for his films' shortcomings. Lang tended to see his career as shaped by a conspiracy of studio bosses and uninspired producers more interested in accountancy than art, and in the AFI interview he likens the machinations of producers to the kind of internecine espionage of the Watergate scandal. In the interview with Higham and Greenberg, Lang sketches his career as a series of conflicts with producers and censors, whether Joseph Goebbels in Germany or Will Hays in Hollywood.

As in all the books in the Conversations with Filmmakers series, the interviews collected here are presented in chronological order, in their entirety as originally published. Editing of the interviews conducted in English involved primarily the silent correction of factual errors, as well as the correction of titles and names for consistency and accuracy. However, the interviews published in other languages (French, Swedish, German) presented more of a challenge. Lang never became completely fluent in English; he sometimes spoke awkwardly, and he was fond of idiomatic expressions and American slang, which at times he used incorrectly. Lang's rather idiosyncratic English comes through clearly in Mary Morris's 1945 interview. In some cases the non-English interviews were translated from English into the other language for original publication, Lang's idiosyncratic style of speech inevitably somewhat diluted in the process; then, these essays were translated again back into English for this volume. In some of the French interviews Lang spoke in French, which he spoke no better, and perhaps less well, than he did English. In all the translations for this book the aim was to remain as true to the spirit of Langian discourse as was possible.

Lang was a notoriously difficult interview subject, and he granted relatively few apart from short public relations interviews for the purpose of promoting a new film. He often gave his interlocutors a hard time, sometimes deliberately throwing obstacles in their path, as he did with Gero Gandert and Peter von Bagh, to whom he absurdly denies that there is any violence in his films or that producers ever meddled with his work. Lang's mood in the interviews ranges from ingratiating to hostile, although he tended to be more aloof with male interviewers, more open—sometimes even flirtatious—with female interviewers such as Morris and Berg. The reader will easily discern the interviews in which Lang felt cooperative or kindly disposed toward his interviewer, for whatever reason, and those with whom he had little patience.

Lang was fully aware of his public persona, and always sought to manipulate it to his advantage. He was an ardent self-promoter who carefully constructed myths about himself and his life. Writing about Lang's sartorial elegance and care, for example, biographer Patrick McGilligan says of the director's iconographic monocle that it "was an undeniable facet of his image, alternately attractive and repellent; it never failed to draw people in, giving him the air of a Cyclops with weltschmerz in the eye."[8] Despite his protests, Lang liked being the subject of gossip and the center of attention, laughing to Morris when he describes himself as "the monster of Hollywood."

Readers will notice considerable repetition in both questions and answers in the interviews. To some degree the slight differences in Lang's anecdotes from one interview to the next reveal the inevitable mutability of memory and change of perspective over time, but their overriding similarities reveal as well the director's reserve, if not calculation. McGilligan reports that Lang often reviewed transcripts of his interviews, sometimes revising them, before allowing them to be published. Certain anecdotes appear with regularity in these interviews like jazz riffs on a theme. For example, Lang liked to trot out his disparaging remark about Cinemascope, immortalized in *Contempt*, that it was good only for snakes and funerals (although he admits to Gérard Langlois that "I was wrong, of course, but I said it."). Other stories Lang tells frequently involve his fateful meeting with Joseph Goebbels before leaving Germany and the letter he received from some old cowhands about the authenticity they perceived in *Western Union*. If Lang seems to have been in an uncharacteristically effusive mood in his interview with Gretchen Berg, perhaps the result of alcoholic lubrication, later he threatened court action over its publication.[9]

But it is not just Lang who repeats himself, it is the interviewers as well. Indeed, this was one of the reasons Lang sometimes found doing interviews tiresome. That Lang was doomed to be asked the same questions time and again, imprisoned in the repetitive patterns of these interviews, is a final ironic twist of destiny that is perfectly consistent with the claustrophobic and deterministic vision of his films. If in his movies Lang frequently entraps his viewers by providing misleading clues and encouraging them to make judgments that are later revealed to be untrue, then readers should probably approach these interviews with the same caution.

Still, there are moments in these interviews where Fritz Lang's genuine passion for film shine through. Just as raw emotion and violence sometimes burst forth in Lang's characters, so periodically here does Lang's love for his chosen medium. In several interviews Lang laments that film has evolved from an art form into an industry. Cinema, he tells Michéle Manceaux, "is the art of this century and the people's art." But for Lang film is at the same time an intensely person affair. So to Gero Gandert he describes being caught up by a film idea as being "possessed by it." And to Jean-Louis Noames, Lang ardently confesses that "Making films is for me something like taking a drug. It is a vice that I adore. Without the cinema, I couldn't live."

My sincerest appreciation is due to Glenwood Irons (Department of Applied Language Studies), Jane Koustas and Barry W. K. Joe (Department of Modern Languages, Literatures and Cultures), colleagues at Brock University, and Ms. Bodil Little for their translations of many of the interviews in this book. I am especially indebted to Dr. Will Webster, former Dean of Social Sciences at Brock, for his generous support of my research. Thanks also to Anne Stascavage and Shane Gong at the University Press of Mississippi for their advice and careful attention to the manuscript. The staff in the Brock Library, particularly Phyllis Wright, Pat Longo, Ian Gordon, Annie Relic, and Pat Wilson, were of enormous help in searching out interviews, some of which in the end were not included in this book. John R. Harris, Film Study Center, Museum of Modern Art, and Cindy Stark, Senior Librarian, New York State Library, Albany, both went the extra mile to help track down mysterious interviews with Fritz Lang. Melissa Charlesworth and Gabrielle Grant also provided invaluable research assistance.

Notes

1. Peter Bodganovich, *Who the Devil Made It* (New York: Alfred A. Knopf, 1977), pp. 191, 218.

2. Leo Braudy, *The World in a Frame: What We See in Films* (Garden City, N.Y.: Anchor Doubleday, 1977), p. 48.

3. Andrew Sarris, *The American Cinema* p. 64.

4. *Ibid.*

5. Peter Wollen, *Signs and Meaning in the Cinema*, rev. ed. (London: Secker & Warburg, 1972), p. 168; Stephen Jenkins, "Introduction," *Fritz Lang: The Image and the Look*, ed. Jenkins (London: British Film Institute, 1981), p. 7.

6. Siegfried Kracauer, *From Caligari to Hitler: A Psychological History of the German Film* (Princeton, N.J.: Princeton University Press, 1947), p. 150.

7. Paul M. Jensen, *The Cinema of Fritz Lang* (New York: A.S. Barnes/London: Zwemmer, 1969), p. 10.

8. Patrick McGilligan, *Fritz Lang: The Nature of the Beast* (New York: St. Martin's Press, 1997), p. 59.

9. According to Eisner, Berg's interview with Lang was actually "a skillful confection of statements from Lang's article 'Happily Ever After' and other interviews, articles, and remarks made to Gretchen Berg and her father Herman G. Weinberg in informal meetings." Lotte Eisner, *Fritz Lang* (New York: Da Capo, 1976), p. 397.

CHRONOLOGY

1890   Born December 5 in Vienna, to Paula Schlesinger and Anton Lang, architect.

1913–14   Lives in Paris. With the outbreak of war, Lang returns to Austria and enlists.

1916–17   Lang's first scripts are produced, including *Die Hochzeit im Exzentrikklub (The Wedding in the Eccentric Club)* and *Hilde Warren und der Tod (Hilde Warren and Death)*, both directed by Joe May.

1918   Moves to Berlin, works as story editor for Erich Pommer, head of Decla-Film in Berlin, and as assistant director to Joe May on *Herrin der Welt (Mistress of the World,* 1919).

1919   Lang receives his first four directorial credits: in order of release, *Halbblut (Half Caste), Der Herr der Liebe (The Master of Love), Die Spinnen (The Spiders), Part One: Der Goldene See (The Golden Lake),* and *Harakiri.*

1920   *Die Spinnen, Part Two: Das Brillanten Schiff (The Diamond Ship)* and *Das wandernde Bild (The Wandering Image)* released.

1921   *Kämpfende Herzen (Fighting Hearts)/ Die Vier Um Die Frau (Four Around a Woman)* and *Der Müde Tod (The Weary Death)* released.

1922   Marries co-scenarist Thea von Harbou. *Dr. Mabuse, Der Spieler (Dr. Mabuse, The Gambler): Part One: Der grosse Spieler—ein Bild der Zeit*

(*Dr. Mabuse, The Gambler—A Picture of the Time*) released in April; *Part Two: Inferno—von Menschen unserer zeit* (*Inferno—Men of the Time*) released in May.

1924   *Die Nibelungen, Part One: Siegfrieds Tod* (*Death of Siegfried*) released in February; *Part Two: Kriemhilds Rache* (*Kriemhild's Revenge*) in April. Lang visits New York and Hollywood to study film production.

1927   *Metropolis* released.

1928   *Spione* (*Spies*) and *Die Frau im Mond* (*Woman in the Moon*) released.

1931   Lang's first sound film, *M.*

1933   *Das Testament des Dr. Mabuse* (*The Last Will of Dr. Mabuse*) is released, but banned in Germany. Lang leaves Germany, resides briefly in Paris.

1934   *Liliom*, Lang's only French film, released. Lang signs contract with David O. Selznick and MGM and emigrates to the U.S., in June.

1936   Lang's first American film, *Fury*, is released.

1937   *You Only Live Once* released.

1938   *You and Me* released.

1939   Lang becomes an American citizen.

1940   Lang's first Western, *The Return of Frank James*, released.

1941   *Western Union* and *Man Hunt* released.

1943   *Hangmen Also Die!* released.

1944   *Ministry of Fear* and *The Woman in the Window* released.

1945   Lang establishes Diana Productions with producer Walter Wanger and actress Joan Bennett. Lang's first production for the company, *Scarlet Street*, released.

1946   *Cloak and Dagger* released.

1948   *Secret Beyond the Door* released.

1950   *House by the River* and *American Guerrilla in the Philippines* released.

1952   *Rancho Notorious* and *Clash by Night* released.

1953   *The Blue Gardenia* and *The Big Heat* released.

1954   *Human Desire* released.

1955   *Moonfleet* released.

1956   *While the City Sleeps* and *Beyond a Reasonable Doubt* released. Lang visits Germany for the first time since 1933.

1959   *Der Tiger von Eschnapur* (*The Tiger of Bengal*) and *Das indische Grabmal* (*The Indian Tomb*) are released in Germany.

1960   *Die tausend Augen des Dr. Mabuse* (*The Thousand Eyes of Dr. Mabuse*) released in Germany.

1963   Lang appears as himself in Jean-Luc Godard's *Le Mépris* (*Contempt*).

1976   Lang dies in Beverly Hills, California, on August 2.

FILMOGRAPHY

1917
DIE PEITSCHE (THE WHIP)
Stuart Webbs-Film Co.
Director: Adolf Gartner
Screenplay: **Lang**

DIE HOCHZEIT IM EXZENTRIKKLUB (THE WEDDING IN THE ECCENTRIC CLUB)
May-Film
Director: Joe May
Screenplay: **Lang**
Cinematography: Carl Hoffman
Cast: Harry Liedtke, Magda Magdaleine, Bruno Kastner, Paul Westermeier, Kathe Haack

HILDE WARREN UND DER TOD (HILDE WARREN AND DEATH)
May-Film
Director: Joe May
Screenplay: **Lang**
Cinematography: Curt Courant
Cast: Mia May, Hans Mierendorff, Bruno Kastner, Georg John

1918
LILITH UND LY
Fiat Film

Director: Erich Kober
Screenplay: **Lang**
Cast: Elga Beck, Hans Marschall

1919
DIE RACHE IST MEIN (REVENGE IS MINE)
Decla
Director: Alwin Neuss
Screenplay: **Lang**
Cast: Otto Paul, Alwin Neuss, Arnold Czempin, Helga Molander, Marta
Daghofer (Lil Dagover), Hanni Rheinwald

DIE BETTLER-GMBH (BEGGARS LTD.)
Decla
Director: Alwin Neuss
Screenplay: **Lang**
Cast: Ressel Orla, Fred Selva-Goebel, Fritz Achterberg, Otto Paul, Marta Dagh-
ofer (Lil Dagover)

WOLKENBAU UND FLIMMERSTERN (CASTLES IN THE SKY AND RHINE-
STONES)
Decla
Screenplay: **Lang** and Wolfgang Geiger
Cast: Margarete Frey, Karl Gebhard-Schröder, Albert Paul, Ressel Orla

DIE FRAU MIT DEN ORCHIDEEN (THE WOMAN WITH ORCHIDS)
Decla
Director: Otto Rippert
Screenplay: **Lang**
Cinematography: Carl Hoffman
Cast: Werner Krauss, Carl de Vogt, Gilda Langer

TOTENTANZ (DANCE OF DEATH)
Helios-Film
Director: Otto Rippert
Screenplay: **Lang**
Cinematography: Willy Hameister
Art Direction: Hermann Warm
Cast: Sascha Gura, Werner Krauss, Josef Roemer

DIE PEST IN FLORENZ (PLAGUE IN FLORENCE)
Decla
Producer: Erich Pommer
Director: Otto Rippert
Screenplay: **Lang**
Cinematography: Willy Hameister
Cast: Theodor Becker, Marga Kierska, Erich Bartels, Juliette Brandt, Erner Hübsch, Otto Mannstaedt

HALBBLUT (HALF CASTE, HALF BREED)
Decla-Bioscop
Director: **Lang**
Screenplay: **Lang**
Cinematography: Carl Hoffmann
Cast: Ressel Orla, Carl de Vogt, Gilda Langer, Carl-Gebhard Schröder, Paul Morgan
B & W

DER HERR DER LIEBE (THE MASTER OF LOVE)
Decla-Bioscop/ Helios
Director: **Lang**
Screenplay: Leo Koffler
Cinematography: Emil Schünemann
Art Direction: Carl Ludwig Kirmse
Cast: Carl de Vogt (Disescu), Gilda Langer (Yvette), Erika Unruh, Max Narlinski
35mm, B & W
approximately 58 minutes

DIE HERRIN DER WELT (MISTRESS OF THE WORLD)
PART 8: DIE RACHE DER MAUD FERGUSON (THE REVENGE OF MAUD FERGUSON)
May-Film
Director: Joe May
Assistant Director: **Lang**
Screenplay: **Lang**
Cast: Mia May, Michael Bohnen

DIE SPINNEN (THE SPIDERS), PART ONE: DER GOLDENE SEE (THE
GOLDEN LAKE)
Decla-Bioscop
Director: **Lang**
Screenplay: **Lang**
Cinematography: Emil Schünemann
Art Direction: Otto Hunte, Carl Ludwig Kirmse, Hermann Warm, Heinrich
Umlauff
Cast: Carl de Vogt (Kay Hoog), Ressel Orla (Lio Sha), Lil Dagover (Priestess to
the Sun King), Paul Morgan (an expert), Georg John (Dr. Telphas), Bruno
Lettinger (Terry Landon), Edgar Pauly (Four-Finger John)
35 mm, B & W
approximately 81 minutes

HARAKIRI
Decla-Bioscop
Director: **Lang**
Screenplay: Max Jungk, from the play *Madame Butterfly*, by John Luther Long
and David Belasco
Cinematography: Max Fassbender
Art Direction: Henrich Umlauff
Cast: Paul Biensfeldt (Daimyo Tokuyawa), Lil Dagover (O-Take-San), Georg
John (Buddhist monk), Meinhard Maur (Prince Matahari), Rudolph Lettinger
(Karan), Erner Hübsch (Kin-Be-Araki), Käte Jüster (Hanake), Nils Prien (Olaf
J. Anderson), Herta Hendén (Eva), Loni Nest (child)
35mm, B & W
approximately 108 minutes

1920
DIE SPINNEN, PART TWO: DAS BRILLANTEN SCHIFF (THE DIAMOND SHIP)
Decla-Bioscop
Director: **Lang**
Screenplay: **Lang**
Cinematography: Karl Freund
Art Direction: Otto Hunte, Karl Ludwig Kirmse, Hermann Warm, Heinrich
Umlauff
Cast: Carl de Vogt (Kay Hoog), Ressel Orla (Lio Sha), Georg John (the Master),

Lil Dagover (Priestess of the Sun God), Rudolf Lettinger (Terry Landon), Thea
Zander (Ellen), Reiner-Steiner (Captain of the Diamond Ship), Friedrich
Kühne (All-Hab-Mah, the Yogi), Edgar Pauly (Four-Finger John), Meinhardt
Maur (the Chinese Man), Paul Morgan (the Jew)
35mm, B & W
approximately 95 minutes

DAS WANDERNDE BILD (THE WANDERING IMAGE)
May-Film GmbH
Director: **Lang**
Screenplay: **Lang** and Thea von Harbou
Cinematography: Guido Seeber
Art Direction: Otto Hunte, Erich Kettelhut
Cast: Mia May (Irmgard Vanderheit), Hans Marr (Georg Vanderheit, John
Vanderheit), Rudolf Klein-Rohden [Klein-Rogge] (Will Brand)
35mm, B & W
approximately 87 minutes

1921
DAS INDISCHE GRABMAL (THE INDIAN TOMB)
May-Film
Director: Joe May
Screenplay: **Lang** and Thea von Harbou
Cinematography: Werner Brandes
Cast: Mia May, Conrad Veidt, Lya de Putti, Olaf Fönss, Erna Morena, Bern-
hard Goetzke, Paul Richter

KÄMPFENDE HERZEN (FIGHTING HEARTS)/ DIE VIER UM DIE FRAU (FOUR
AROUND A WOMAN)
Decla-Bioscop
Director: **Lang**
Screenplay: **Lang** and Thea von Harbou
Cinematography: Otto Kanturek
Art Direction: Ernst Meiwers, Hans Jacoby
Cast: Carola Toëlle (Florence Yquem), Hermann Boettcher (Mr. Yquem), Lud-
wig Hartau (Harry Yquem), Anton Edthofer (Werner Krafft, William Krafft),
Rudolf Klein-Rogge (Upton), Robert Forster-Larrinaga (Meunier), Lilli Lohrer
(first maid), Harry Frank (Bobby), Leonhard Haskell (swindler), Paul Rehkopf

(swindler), Gottfried Huppertz (headwaiter), Hans Lüpschütz (hoodlum), Lisa von Marton (Margot), Erika Unruh (prostitute), Paul Morgan (hustler), Edgar Pauly (man), Gerhard Ritterband (newspaper boy)

35mm, B & W

DER MÜDE TOD (THE WEARY DEATH)/ BETWEEN TWO WORLDS (U.S.)/ DESTINY (G.B.)

Decla-Bioscop

Producer: Erich Pommer

Director: **Lang**

Screenplay: **Lang** and Thea von Harbou

Cinematography: Erich Nitzschmann, Hermann Saalfrank (German episode), Fritz Arno Wagner (Arabian, Chinese and Venetian episodes)

Art Direction: Robert Herlth (Chinese episode), Walter Röhrig (German episode), Hermann Warm (Arabian and Venetian episodes)

Music: Peter Schirman

Costumes: Umlauff Museum, Hamburg

Cast: Lil Dagover (young woman, Zobeide, Fiametta, Tiaotsien), Walter Janssen (young man, Frank, Giovanfrancesco, Liang), Bernhard Goetzke (Death, El Mot, archer), Hans Sternberg (mayor), Carl Rückert (vicar), Max Adalbert (lawyer), Erich Pabst (teacher), Paul Rehkopf (sexton), Hermann Picha (tailor), Edgar Klitzch (doctor), Georg John (beggar), Marie Wismar (old woman), Aloisha Lehnert (mother); Rudolf Klein-Rogge (dervish, Girolamo), Eduard von Winterstein (Calife), Erika Unruh (Aisha), Louis Brody (Moor), Lothar Müthel [Mütel] (confidante), Lina Paulsen (nurse), Paul Biensfeldt (A Hi, magician), Karl Huszar (emperor), Max Adalbert (treasurer), Paul Neumann (hangman)

35mm, B & W

122 minutes

1922

DR. MABUSE, DER SPIELER (DR. MABUSE, THE GAMBLER): PART ONE: DER GROSSE SPIELER—EIN BILD DER ZEIT (DR. MABUSE, THE GAMBLER—A PICTURE OF THE TIME); PART TWO: INFERNO—VON MENSCHEN UNSERER ZEIT (INFERNO—MEN OF THE TIME)

Uco-Film/ Decla-Bioscop/ UFA

Producer: Erich Pommer
Director: **Lang**
Screenplay: **Lang** and Thea von Harbou, from the novel by Norbert Jacques
Cinematography: Carl Hoffmann
Art Direction: Otto Hunte, Carl Stahl-Urach, Erich Kettelhut, Karl Vollbrecht
Costumes: Vally Reinecke
Cast: Rudolf Klein-Rogge (Dr. Mabuse), Aud Egede Nissen (Cara Carozza), Gertrude Welcker (Countess Told), Alfred Abel (Count Told), Bernard Goet-zke (Inspector von Wenk), Paul Richter (Edgar Hull), Robert Forster-Larrinaga (Sporri), Hans Adalbert von Schlettow (Mabuse's chaffeur, Georg), Georg John (Pesch), Grete Berger (Fine), Julius Falkenstein (Karsten), Karl Huszar (Hawasch), Julius Herrmann (Schramm), Lydia Potechina (Russian woman), Anita Barber (dancer), Paul Biensfeldt (man with revolver), Karl Platen (Told's servant)
35mm, B & W
120 minutes (Part One), 93 minutes (Part Two)

1924
DIE NIBELUNGEN, PART ONE: SIEGFRIEDS TOD (DEATH OF SIEGFRIED)
AND PART TWO: KRIEMHILDS RACHE (KRIEMHILD'S REVENGE)
Decla-Bioscop/ UFA
Producer: Erich Pommer
Director: **Lang**
Screenplay: **Lang** and Thea von Harbou, based on *Das Nibelungenlied* and the Norse sagas
Cinematography: Carl Hoffmann, Günther Rittau, and Walter Ruttmann (the animated "Dream of the Falcon" sequence)
Art Direction: Otto Hunte, Erich Kettelhut, Karl Vollbrecht
Costumes: Paul Gerd Guderian, Änne Willkomm, Heinrich Umlauff
Music: Gottfried Huppertz
Cast: Paul Richter (Siegfried), Margaret Schön (Kriemhild), Rudolf Klein-Rogge (Etzel, King of the Huns), Georg August Koch (Hildebrand), Theodor Loos (Gunther), Bernhard Goetzke (Volker von Alzey), Hans Adalbert von Schlettow (Hagen Tronje), Georg John (Mime, the smith, Alberich, Blaodel), Gertrude Arnold (Queen Ute), Hanna Ralph (Brunhild), Rudolph Ritter (Rüdi-ger), Fritz Alberti (Dietrich), Hans Carl Müller (Gerenot), Erwin Biswanger

(Giselher), Hardy von Francois (Dankwart), Frieda Richard (lecturer), Georg
Jurowski (priest), Iris Roberts (page), Grete Berger (Hun)
35mm, B & W
Part One, 130 minutes; *Part Two*, 95 minutes

1927
METROPOLIS
UFA
Producer: Erich Pommer
Director: **Lang**
Screenplay: **Lang** and Thea von Harbou
Cinematography: Karl Freund, Günther Rittau
Art Direction: Otto Hunte, Erich Kettelhut, Karl Vollbrecht
Special Effects: Eugen Schüfftan
Costumes: Änne Willkomm
Music: Gottfried Huppertz
Cast: Alfred Abel (Joh Fredersen), Gustav Fröhlich (Freder), Rudolf Klein-
Rogge (Rotwang), Brigitte Helm (Maria, robot Maria), Heinrich Georg (Fore-
man), Fritz Rasp (Slim), Theodor Loos (Josaphat), Heinrich George (Grot, the
foreman), Erwin Biswanger (No. 11811), Olaf Storm (Jan), Hanns Leo Reich
(Marinus), Heinrich Gotho (master of ceremonies), Margarete Lanner
(woman in car)
150 minutes

1928
SPIONE (SPIES) (U.S.)
Fritz Lang-Film-GmbH/ UFA
Producer: **Lang**
Director: **Lang**
Screenplay: **Lang** and Thea von Harbou, based on her novel
Cinematography: Fritz Arno Wagner
Art Direction: Otto Hunte, Karl Vollbrecht
Music: Werner R. Heymann
Cast: Rudolf Klein-Rogge (Haghi), Gerda Maurus (Sonia), Lien Deyers (Kitty),
Craighall Sherry (Police Chief Burton Jason), Willy Fritsch (No. 326), Lupu
Pick (Matsumoto), Fritz Rasp (Jullusic), Louis Ralph (Hans Morrier), Paul Hör-

biger (Franz), Julius Falkenstein (hotel manager), Georg John (train conductor), Paul Rehkopf (Strolch), Hertha von Walther (Lady Leslane)
35mm, B & W
85 minutes

1929
DIE FRAU IM MOND (WOMAN IN THE MOON) (BY ROCKET TO THE
MOON) (U.S.)
Fritz-Lang-Film-GmbH/ UFA
Producer: **Lang**
Director: **Lang**
Screenplay: Thea von Harbou, based on her novel
Cinematography: Curt Courant, Oskar Fischinger, Otto Kanturek
Special Effects: Konstantin Tschetwerikoff
Art Direction: Otto Hunte, Emil Hasler, Karl Vollbrecht
Music: Willy Schimdt-Gentner
Technical Advisors: Hermann Oberth, Willy Ley, Gustav Wolff, Joseph Danilowatz
Cast: Gerda Maurus (Frieda Venten), Willy Fritsch (Wolf Helius), Fritz Rasp
(Walt Turner), Klaus Pohl (Prof. Georg Manfeldt), Gustav von Wangenheim
(Hans Windegger), Gustl Stark-Gstettenbauer (Gustav), Margarete Kupfer
(Mme. Hippolt), Max Maximilian (Grotjan), Alexa von Porembsky (flower
vender), Gerhard Dammann (foreman), Heinrich Gotho (second floor tenant), Karl Platen (technician), Alfred Loretto and Edgar Pauly (spectators),
Tilla Durieux, Hermann Valentin, Max Zilzer, Mahmud Terja Bey and
Boprwin Walth (financiers)
35mm, B & W
146 minutes

1931
M
NERO Film
Producer: Seymour Nebenzal
Director: **Lang**
Screenplay: Thea von Harbou
Cinematography: Fritz Arno Wagner, Gusav Rathje
Art Direction: Karl Vollbrecht, Emil Hasler

Editing: Paul Falkenberg
Cast: Peter Lorre (Hans Beckert), Gustav Gründgens (Schränker), Otto Wernicke (Chief Inspector Karl Lohmann), Theo Lingen (Baurenflänger), Theodor Loos (Commissioner Groeber), Georg John (blind peddlar), Ellen Widmann (Frau Beckmann), Inge Landgut (Elsie), Ernst Stahl-Nachbaur (Police Chief), Paul Kemp (pickpocket), Franz Stein (minister), Rudolf Blümner (defense attorney), Karl Platen (watchman), Gerhard Bienert (police secretary), Rosa Valetti (servant), Hertha von Walther (prostitute), Fritz Odemar (the Cheater), Fritz Gnass (burglar)
35mm, B & W
117 minutes

1933
DAS TESTAMENT DES DR. MABUSE/THE TESTAMENT OF DR. MABUSE (THE LAST WILL OF DR. MABUSE) (U.S.)
NERO Film/ Constantine/ Deutsche Universal
Producer: Seymour Nebenzal
Director: **Lang**
Screenplay: **Lang** and Thea von Harbou, based on characters from a novel by Norbert Jacques
Cinematography: Fritz Arno Wagner, Karl Vass
Art Direction: Karl Vollbrecht, Emil Hasler
Music: Dr. Hans Erdmann
Cast: Rudolf Klein-Rogge (Mabuse), Oskar Beregi (Dr. Baum), Otto Wernicke (Detective Karl Lohmann), Wera Liessem (Lilli), Gustav Diessl (Thomas Kent), Klaus Pohl (Müller), Karl Meixner (landlord), Theodor Loos (Dr. Kramm), Georg John (Winkler), Theo Lingen (jeweller), Camilla Spira (Anna), Paul Oscar Höcker (Bredow), Rudolf Schündler (Hardy), Paul Henckels (lithographer), Ludwig Stössel (employee), Hadrian M. Netto (Nicolai Grigoriew), Paul Bernd (blackmailer), Henry Pless (Dunce), A.E. Licho (Dr. Hauser), Karl Platen, Anne Goltz, Heinrich Gretler (sanitarium assistants)
35mm, B & W
122 minutes

1934
LILIOM
S.A.F./ Fox Europa
Producer: Erich Pommer

Director: **Lang**
Screenplay: Robert Liebmann and Bernard Zimmer, based on the play by
Ferenc Molnar
Cinematography: Rudolph Maté, Louis Née
Art Direction: Paul Colin, René Renoux
Music: Jean Lenoir, Franz Waxman
Cast: Charles Boyer (Liliom), Madeleine Ozeray (Julie), Florelle (Madame
Muskat), Robert Arnoux (strong man), Antonin Artaud (knife-grinder),
Roland Toutain (sailor), Alexandre Rignault (Hollinger), Henri Richaud
(commissioner), Richard Barencey (Purgatory policeman), Raoul Marco
(detective), Pierre Alcover (Alfred), Leon Arnel (clerk), René Stern (cashier),
Maximilienne (Madame Menoux), Mimi Funès (Marie), Viviane Romance
(cigarette girl), Mila Parély (secretary in heaven)
35mm, B & W
120 min.

1936
FURY
Metro-Goldwyn-Mayer
Producer: Joseph L. Mankiewicz
Director: **Lang**
Screenplay: **Lang** and Bartlett Cormack, based on the story "Mob Rule" by
Norman Krasna
Cinematography: Joseph Ruttenberg
Art Direction: Cedric Gibbons, William A. Horning, Edwin B. Willis
Costumes: Dolly Tree
Music: Franz Waxman
Editing: Frank Sullivan
Cast: Spencer Tracy (Joe Wilson), Sylvia Sidney (Katherine Grant), Walter
Abel (district attorney), Bruce Cabot (Kirby Dawson), Edward Ellis (sheriff),
Walter Brennan (Bugs Meyers), George Walcott (Tom Wilson), Frank Albert-
son (Charlie Wilson), Arthur Stone (Durkin), Howard Hickman (governor),
Jonathan Hale (defense attorney), Leila Bennett (Edna Hooper), Morgan Wal-
lace (Fred Garrett), George Chandler (Milton Jackson), Roger Gray (stranger),
Edwin Maxwell (Vickery), Esther Dale (Mrs. Whipple), Helen Flint (Franc-
hette), Frank Sully (dynamiter)
35mm, B & W
94 minutes

1937
YOU ONLY LIVE ONCE
Wanger/ United Artists
Producer: Walter Wanger
Director: **Lang**
Screenplay: Gene Towne, Graham Baker, based on a story by Towne
Cinematography: Leon Shamroy
Art Direction: Alexander Toluboff
Costumes: Helen Taylor
Music: Alfred Newman, Song "A Thousand Dreams of You" by Louis Alter
and Paul Francis Webster
Editing: Daniel Mandell
Cast: Sylvia Sidney (Joan Graham), Henry Fonda (Eddie Taylor), Barton
MacLane (Stephen Whitney), Jean Dixon (Bonnie Graham), William Gargan
(Father Dolan), Jerome Cowan (Dr. Hill), Warren Hymer (Buggsy), John Wray
(warden), Jonathan Hale (district attorney), Ward Bond (guard), Charles
"Chic" Sale (Ethan), Margaret Hamilton (Hester), Guinn Williams (Rogers),
Wade Boteler (policeman), Henry Taylor (Kozderonas), Jean Stoddard (ste-
nographer), Ben Hall (messenger)
35mm, B & W
86 minutes

1938
YOU AND ME
Paramount
Producer: **Lang**
Director: **Lang**
Screenplay: Virginia Von Upp, based on a story by Norman Krasna
Cinematography: Charles Lang, Jr.
Art Direction: Hans Dreier, Ernest Fegté
Costumes: Edith Head
Editing: Paul Weatherwax
Music: Kurt Weill, Boris Morros; songs "The Right Guy For Me" by Weill and
Sam Coslow, "You and Me" by Ralph Freed and Frederick Hollander
Cast: Sylvia Sidney (Helen Roberts), George Raft (Joe Dennis), Robert Cum-
mings (Jim), Barton MacLane (Mickey), Harry Carey (Mr. Morris), Roscoe
Karns (Cuffy), Warren Hymer (Gimpy), Guinn Williams (taxi driver), Cecil

Cunningham (Mrs. Morris), George E. Stone (Patsy), Vera Gordon (Mrs. Levine), Carol Paige (torch singer), Bernadene Hayes (Nellie), Egon Brecher (Mr. Levine), Joyce Compton (Curly Blonde), Willard Robertson (Dayton), Roger Grey (attendant), Adrian Morris (Knucks), Harlan Briggs (McTavish), Paula de Cardo and Harriette Haddon (cigarette girls), Matt McHugh (newcomer), Paul Newlan (bouncer), Margaret Randall (clothes thief)
35mm, B & W
90 minutes

1940
THE RETURN OF FRANK JAMES
Twentieth-Century/ Fox
Producer: Darryl F. Zanuck
Director: **Lang**
Screenplay: Sam Hellman
Cinematography: George Barnes, William V. Skall
Art Direction: Richard Day, Wiard B. Ihnen
Costumes: Travis Banton
Music: David Buttolph
Editing: Walter Thompson
Cast: Henry Fonda (Frank James), Gene Tierney (Eleanor Stone), Jackie Cooper (Clem), Henry Hull (Major Rufus Todd), John Carradine (Bob Ford), J. Edward Bromberg (George Runyan), Donald Meek (McCoy), Eddie Collins (station agent), George Barbier (judge), Ernest Whitman (Pinky), Charles Tannen (Charlie Ford), Lloyd Corrigan (Randolph Stone), Russell Hicks (prosecuter), Victor Kilian (preacher), Edward McWade (Col. Jackson), George Chandler (Roy), Irving Bacon (bystander), Frank Shannon (sheriff), Barbara Pepper (Nellie Blane), Stymie Beard (Mose), Davidson Clark (officer), William Pawley, Frank Sully (actors), Louis Mason (watchman)
35 mm, color
92 minutes

1941
WESTERN UNION
Twentieth Century-Fox
Producer: Harry Joe Brown
Director: **Lang**

Screenplay: Robert Carson, based on the novel by Zane Grey
Cinematography: Edward Cronjager, Allen M. Davey
Art Director: Richard Day, Albert Hugsett
Costumes: Travis Banton
Music: David Buttolph
Editing: Robert Bischoff
Cast: Robert Young (Richard Blake), Randolph Scott (Vance Shaw), Dean Jagger (Edward Creighton), Virginia Gilmore (Sue Creighton), Barton MacLane (Jack Slade), John Carradine (Doc Murdoch), Slim Summerville (Herman), Chill Wills (Homer), Russell Hicks (governor), Victor Kilian (Charlie), Minor Watson (Pat Grogan), George Chandler (Herb), Chief Big Tree (Chief Spotted Horse), Chief Thundercloud (Indian leader), Dick Rich (Porky), Harry Strang (henchman), Charles Middleton (stagecoach rider), Addison Richards (Capt. Harlow), Irving Bacon (barber)
35mm, color
95 minutes

MAN HUNT
Twentieth Century-Fox
Producer: Kenneth Macgowan
Director: **Lang**
Screenplay: Dudley Nichols, based on the novel *Rogue Male* by Geoffrey Household
Cinematography: Arthur Miller
Art Direction: Richard Day, Wiard B. Ihnen
Costumes: Travis Banton
Music: Alfred Newman
Editing: Allen McNeil
Cast: Walter Pidgeon (Capt. Thorndike), Joan Bennett (Jerry), George Sanders (Quive-Smith), John Carradine (Mr. Jones), Roddy McDowall (Vaner), Ludwig Stössel (doctor), Heather Thatcher (Lady Risborough), Frederick Walcock (Lord Risborough), Roger Imhof (Capt. Jensen), Egon Brecher (Whiskers), Lester Matthews (major), Holmes Herbert (Farnsworth), Eily Malyon (postmistress), Arno Frey (police lieutenant), Fredrik Vogeding (ambassador), Lucien Prival (man with umbrella), Herbert Evans (Reeves), Keith Hitchcock (bobby)
35mm, B & W
102 minutes

1943
HANGMEN ALSO DIE!
Arnold Productions/ United Artists
Producer: **Lang**
Executive Producer: Arnold Pressburger
Director: **Lang**
Screenplay: **Lang**, Bertolt Brecht, and John Wexley, from a story by **Lang** and Brecht
Cinematography: James Wong Howe
Art Direction: William Darling
Costumes: Julie Heron
Music: Hanns Eisler, Song "No Surrender" by Eisler and Sam Coslow
Editing: Gene Fowler, Jr.
Cast: Brian Donlevy (Franz Svoboda), Anna Lee (Mascha Novotny), Walter Brennan (Prof. Novotny), Gene Lockhart (Emil Czaka), Alexander Granach (Alois Gruber), Margaret Wycherly (Ludmilla Novotny), Dennis O'Keefe (Jan Horak), Nana Bryant (Mrs. Novotny), Billy Roy (Beda Novotny), Hans von Twardowski (Reinhard Heydrich), Jonathan Hale (Dedic), Lionel Stander (cabby), Sarah Padden (Miss Dvorak), George Irving (Necval), Tonio Selwart (Haas, Gestapo chief), Byron Foulger (Bartos), Virginia Farmer (landlady), Louis Donath (Shumer), Edmund MacDonald (Dr. Pilar), James Bush (worker), Arno Frey (Itnut), Lester Sharpe (Rudy), Arthur Loft (Gen. Vortruba), William Farnum (Viktorin), Reinhold Schünzel (Inspector Ritter)
35mm, B & W
140 minutes

1944
MINISTRY OF FEAR
Paramount
Producer: Seton I. Miller
Director: **Lang**
Screenplay: Seton I. Miller, based on the novel by Graham Greene
Cinematographer: Henry Sharp
Art Direction: Hans T. Dreier, Hal Pereira
Costumes: Edith Head
Music: Victor Young
Editing: Archie Marshek

Cast: Ray Milland (Stephen Neale), Marjorie Reynolds (Carla Hilfe), Dan Duryea (Costa), Carl Esmond (Willi Hilfe), Hillary Brooke (Mrs. Bellaire), Percy
Waram (Inspector Prentice), Alan Napier (Dr. Forrester), Erskine Sanford (Mr.
Rennit), Mary Field (Miss Penteel), Byron Foulger (Newby), Thomas Louden
(Mr. Newland), Helena Grant (Mrs. Merrick), Aminta Dyne (first Mrs. Bellaire), Lester Matthews (Dr. Morton), Eustace Wyatt (blind man)
35mm, B & W
84 minutes

THE WOMAN IN THE WINDOW
Christie Corp./ International Pictures/ RKO
Producer: Nunnally Johnson
Director: **Lang**
Screenplay: Nunnally Johnson, based on the novel *Once Off Guard*, by J. H.
Wallis
Cinematography: Milton Krasner
Art Direction: Duncan Cramer
Special Effects: Vernon Walker
Costumes: Muriel King
Music: Arthur Lange
Editing: Marjorie Johnson
Cast: Edward G. Robinson (Richard Wanley), Joan Bennett (Alice Reed), Ray-
mond Massey (Frank Lalor), Dan Duryea (Heidt), Edmond Breon (Dr. Bark-
stone), Thomas E. Jackson (Inspector Jackson), Arthur Loft (Mazard),
Dorothy Peterson (Mrs. Wanley), Frank Dawson (steward), Carol Cameron
(Elsie), Bobby Blake (Dickie)
35mm, B & W
99 minutes

1945
SCARLET STREET
Diana Productions/ Universal
Producer: Walter Wanger
Director: **Lang**
Screenplay: Dudley Nichols, based on the novel and play *La Chienne* by
Georges de la Fouchardière
Cinematography: Milton Krasner

Special Effects: John P. Fulton
Art Direction: Alexander Golitzen
Costumes: Travis Benton
Music: Hans J. Salter
Editing: Arthur Hilton
Cast: Edward G. Robinson (Christopher Cross), Joan Bennett (Kitty March), Dan Duryea (Johnny), Rosalind Ivan (Adele Cross), Jess Barker (Janeway), Russell Hicks (Hogarth), Margaret Lindsay (Millie), Vladimir Sokoloff (Pop Lejon), Charles Kemper (Homer), Samuel S. Hinds (Charles Pringle), Arthur Loft (Dellarowe), Anita Bolster (Mrs. Michaels), Cyrus W. Kendell (Nick), Fred Essler (Marchetti), Edgar Dearing, Tom Dillon (police officers), Chuck Hamilton (chaffeur), Gus Glassmire, Howard Mitchell, Ralph Littlefield, Sherry Hall, Jack Stratham (workers), Rodney Bell (Barney), Byron Foulger (landlord), Will Wright (cashier)
35mm, B & W
102 minutes

1946
CLOAK AND DAGGER
United States Pictures/ Warner Bros.
Producer: Milton Sperling
Director: **Lang**
Screenplay: Albert Maltz and Ring Lardner, Jr., based on a story by Boris Ingster and John Larkin
Cinematography: Sol Polito
Art Direction: Max Parker
Special Effects: Harry Barndollar, Edwin DuPar
Costumes: Leah Rhodes
Music: Max Steiner
Editing: Christian Nyby
Cast: Gary Cooper (Prof. Alvah Jasper), Lilli Palmer (Gina), Robert Alda (Pinkie), Vladimir Sokoloff (Dr. Polda), J. Edward Bromberg (Trenk), Dan Seymour (Marsoli), Marc Lawrence (Luigi), Marjorie Hoshelle (Ann Dawson), Ludwig Stössel (the German), Helen Thimig (Katherine Loder), James Flavin (Col. Walsh), Pat O'Moore (the Englishman), Charles Marsh (Enrich), Larry Olson (Tommy), Don Turner (Erich)
35mm, B & W
106 minutes

1948
SECRET BEYOND THE DOOR
Diana Productions/ Universal International
Producer: **Lang**
Executive Producer: Walter Wanger
Director: **Lang**
Screenplay: Silvia Richards, based on the story "Museum Piece No. 13" by
Rufus King
Cinematography: Stanley Cortez
Production Designer: Max Parker
Costumes: Travis Banton
Music: Miklos Rosza
Editing: Arthur Hilton
Cast: Joan Bennett (Celia Lamphere), Michael Redgrave (Mark Lamphere),
Anne Revere (Caroline Lamphere), Barbara O'Neil (Miss Robey), Paul Cava-
nagh (Rick Barrett), Mark Dennis (David), James Seay (Bob Dwight), Natalie
Schafer (Edith Potter), Anabel Shaw (society girl), Rosa Rey (Paquita), Donna
De Mario (gypsy), David Cota (her lover), Mark Dennis (David)
35mm, B & W
99 minutes

1950
HOUSE BY THE RIVER
Fidelity Pictures/ Republic
Producer: Howard Welsch
Director: **Lang**
Screenplay: Mel Dinelli, based on the novel *Floodtide* by Sir Alan P. Herbert
Cinematography: Edward Cronjager
Art Direction: Boris Leven
Special Effects: Howard and Theodore Lydecker
Costumes: Adele Palmer
Music: George Antheil
Editing: Arthur D. Hilton
Cast: Louis Hayward (Stephen Byrne), Lee Bowman (John Byrne), Jane Wyatt
(Marjorie Byrne), Dorothy Patrick (Emily Gaunt), Ann Shoemaker (Mrs.
Ambrose), Howland Chamberlain (district attorney), Will Wright (Inspector

Sarten), Jody Gilbert (Flora Bantam), Peter Brocco (coroner), Margaret Sed-
don (Mrs. Whittaker), Sarah Padden (Mrs. Beach), Kathleen Freeman (Effie
Ferguson), Leslie Kimmell (Mr. Gaunt), Effie Laird (Mrs. Gaunt)
35 mm, B & W
88 minutes

AMERICAN GUERILLA IN THE PHILIPPINES
Twentieth Century-Fox
Producer: Lamar Trotti
Director: **Lang**
Screenplay: Lamar Trotti, based on the novel by Ira Wolfert
Cinematography: Harry Jackson
Special Effects: Fred Sersen
Art Direction: Lyle Wheeler, J. Russell Spencer
Costumes: Travilla
Music: Cyril Mockridge
Editing: Robert Simpson
Cast: Tyrone Power (Chuck Palmer), Micheline Presle [Prelle] (Jeanne Marti-
nez), Jack Elam (Spenser), Bob Patten (Lovejoy), Tom Ewell (Jim Mitchell),
Tommy Cook (Miguel), Robert Barrat (Gen. Douglas MacArthur), Juan Tor-
ena (Juan Martinez), Carleton Young (Col. Phillips), Miquel Anzures (Philip-
pine traitor), Eddie Infante (Col. Dimalanta), Orlando Martin (Col. Benson)
35mm, color
105 minutes

1952
RANCHO NOTORIOUS
Fidelity Pictures/ RKO
Producer: Howard Welsch
Director: **Lang**
Screenplay: Daniel Taradash, based on the story "Gunsight Whitman" by
Silvia Richards
Cinematography: Hal Mohr
Art Direction: Robert Priestly, Wiard B. Ihnen
Costumes: Joe King, Don Loper
Music: Emil Newman, songs "The Legend of Chuck-a-Luck," "Gypsy Davey"
and "Get Away, Young Man" by Ken Darby

Editing: Otto Ludwig
Cast: Marlene Dietrich (Altar Keane), Arthur Kennedy (Vern Haskell), Mel
Ferrer (Frenchy Fairmont), Jack Elam (Geary), Dan Seymour (Commanche
Paul), George Reeves (Wilson), Gloria Henry (Beth Forbes), William Frawley
(Baldy Gunder), Lisa Ferraday (Maxine), John Raven (Chuck-a-luck dealer),
Frank Ferguson (preacher), Francis MacDonald (Harbin), John Doucette
(Whitey), Stuart Randall (Starr), Rodric Redwing (Rio), Charles Gonzales
(Hevia), Jose Domingues (Gonzales), John Kellogg (salesman), Stan Jolly
(Deputy Warren), Frank Graham (Ace Maguire), Fuzzy Knight (barber), Roger
Anderson (Red), Felipe Turich (Sanchez), Lloyd Gough (Kinch), Russell John-
son (croupier)
35mm, color
89 minutes

CLASH BY NIGHT
Wald-Krasna Productions/ RKO
Producer: Harriet Parsons
Director: **Lang**
Screenplay: Alfred Hayes, based on the play by Clifford Odets
Cinematography: Nicholas Musuraca
Special Effects: Harold Wellman
Art Direction: Albert S. D'Agostino, Carroll Clark
Music: Roy Webb, song "I Hear a Rhapsody" by Joe Gasparre, Jack Baker and
George Fragos
Costumes: Michael Woulfe
Editing: George J. Amy
Cast: Barbara Stanwyck (Mae Doyle), Paul Douglas (Jerry D'Amato), Robert
Ryan (Earl Pfeiffer), Marilyn Monroe (Peggy), J. Carroll Naish (Uncle Vince),
Keith Andes (Joe Doyle), Silvio Minciotti (Papa D'Amato)
35mm, B & W
105 minutes

1953
THE BLUE GARDENIA
Blue Gardenia Productions/ Gloria Films/ Warner Bros.
Producer: Alex Gottlieb
Director: **Lang**

Screenplay: Charles Hoffmann, based on the story by Vera Caspary
Cinematography: Nicholas Musuraca
Special Effects: Willis Cook
Art Direction: Daniel Hall
Music: Raoul Kraushaar, song "Blue Gardenia" by Bob Russell and Lester Lee
Editing: Edward Mann
Cast: Anne Baxter (Norah Larkin), Richard Conte (Casey Mayo), Ann Sothern (Crystal Carpenter), Raymond Burr (Harry Prebble), Jeff Donnell (Sally Ellis), Ruth Storey (Rose Miller), George Reeves (Capt. Haynes), Richard Erdman (Al), Ray Walker (Homer), Celia Lovsky (blind woman), Frank Ferguson (drunkard), Nat King Cole (himself)
35mm, B & W
90 minutes

THE BIG HEAT
Columbia
Producer: Robert Arthur
Director: **Lang**
Screenplay: Sidney Boehm, based on the novel by William P. McGiven
Cinematography: Charles Lang, Jr.
Art Direction: Robert Peterson
Costumes: Jean Louis
Music: Daniele Amfitheatrof
Editing: Charles Nelson
Cast: Glenn Ford (Dave Bannion), Gloria Grahame (Debby Marsh), Jocelyn Brando (Katie Bannion), Alexander Scourby (Mike Lagana), Lee Marvin (Vince Stone), Jeanette Nolan (Bertha Duncan), Peter Whitney (Tierney), Willis Bouchey (Lt. Wilkes), Adam Williams (Larry Gordon), Howard Wendell (Commissioner Higgins), Dorothy Green (Lucy Chapman), Robert Burton (Gus Burke), Chris Alcaide (George Rose), Michael Granger (Hugo), Carolyn Jones (Doris), Ric Roman (Baldy), Dan Seymour (Atkins), Edith Evanson (Selma Parker)
35mm, B & W
90 minutes

1954
HUMAN DESIRE
Columbia
Producer: Lewis J. Rachmil and Jerry Wald

Director: **Lang**
Screenplay: Alfred Hayes, based on the novel *La Bête Humaine* by Emile Zola
Cinematography: Burnett Guffey
Art Direction: Robert Peterson
Music: Daniele Amfitheatrof
Editing: Aaron Stell
Cast: Glenn Ford (Jeff Warren), Gloria Grahame (Vicki Buckley), Broderick
Crawford (Carl Buckley), Edgar Buchanan (Alec Simmons), Kathleen Case
(Ellen Simmons), Peggy Maley (Jean), Diane DeLaire (Vera Simmons),
Grandon Rhodes (John Owens), Dan Seymour (bartender), John Pickard
(Matt Henley), Paul Brinegar (brakeman), Dan Riss (Prosecutor Gruber), Vic-
tor Hugo Greene (Davidson), John Zaremba (Russell), Carl Lee (John Thur-
ston), Olan Soule (Lewis)
35mm, B & W
90 minutes

1955
MOONFLEET
Metro-Goldwyn-Mayer
Producer: John Houseman
Director: **Lang**
Screenplay: Jan Lustig and Margaret Fitts, based on the novel by John Meade
Falkner
Cinematography: Robert Planck
Art Direction: Cedric Gibbons, Hans Peters
Costumes: Walter Plunkett
Music: Miklos Rozsa
Editing: Albert Akst
Cast: Stewart Granger (Jeremy Fox), George Sanders (Lord Ashwood), Joan
Greenwood (Lady Ashwood), Viveca Lindfors (Anne Minton), Jon Whiteley
(John Mohune), Liliane Montevecchi (gypsy dancer), Sean McClory (Elzevir
Block), Melville Cooper (Felix Ratsey), Alan Napier (Parson Glennie), John
Hoyt (Magistrate Maskew), Donna Corcoran (Grace), Jack Elam (Damen),
Dan Seymour (Hull), Ian Wolfe (Tewkesbury), Lester Matthews (Major Hen-
nishaw), Skelton Knaggs (Jacob), Richard Hale (Starkill), John Alderson

(Greening), Ashley Cowan (Tomson), Frank Ferguson (coachman), Booth
Colman (Capt. Stanhope), Peggy Maley (tenant)
35mm, Cinemascope, color
87 minutes

1956
WHILE THE CITY SLEEPS
Thor Productions/ RKO
Producer: Bert E. Friedlob
Director: **Lang**
Screenplay: Casey Robinson, based on the novel *The Bloody Spur* by Charles
Einstein
Cinematography: Ernest Laszlo
Art Direction: Carroll Clark
Costumes: Norma
Music: Herschel Burke Gilbert
Editing: Gene Fowler, Jr.
Cast: Dana Andrews (Edward Mobley), Rhonda Fleming (Dorothy Kyne),
Sally Forrest (Nancy Liggett), Thomas Mitchell (Griffith), Vincent Price (Wal-
ter Kyne), Howard Duff (Lt. Kaufman), Ida Lupino (Mildred), George Sanders
(Mark Loving), James Craig (Harry Kritzer), John Barrymore, Jr. (Robert Man-
ners), Mae Marsh (Mrs. Manners), Robert Warwick (Amos Kyne), Vladimir
Sokoloff (George Palsky), Larry Blake (police sergeant), Ralph Peters (Meade),
Edwin Hinton (O'Leary), Sandy White (Judith Fenton), Celia Lovsky (Miss
Dodd), Pit Herbert (bartender)
35mm, SuperScope, B & W
100 minutes

BEYOND A REASONABLE DOUBT
RKO
Producer: Bert E. Friedlob
Director: **Lang**
Screenplay: Douglas Morrow
Cinematography: William Snyder
Art Direction: Carroll Clark
Music: Herschel Burke Gilbert, song "Beyond a Reasonable Doubt" by H. G.
Gilbert and Alfred Perry

Editing: Gene Fowler, Jr.
Cast: Dana Andrews (Tom Garrett), Joan Fontaine (Susan Spencer), Sidney
Blackmer (Austin Spencer), Philip Bourneuf (Thompson), Barbara Nichols
(Sally), Edward Binns (Lt. Kennedy), Shepperd Strudwick (Wilson), Arthur
Franz (Hale), Dan Seymour (Greco), Rusty Lane (judge), Robin Raymond
(Terry), William Leicester (Charlie Miller), Joyce Taylor (Joan), Carleton
Young (Kirk), Trudy Wroe (hat-check girl), Joe Kirk (clerk), Charles Evans
(governor), Wendell Niles (announcer)
35mm, RKO-Scope, B & W
80 minutes

1959
DER TIGER VON ESCHNAPUR/DAS INDISCHE GRABMAL (THE HINDU
TOMB)/ JOURNEY TO THE LOST CITY (U.S.)/TIGER OF BENGAL (G.B.)
CCC-Films/ Artur Brauner/ Gloria Film/ Regina Films/ Criterion Films/ Riz-
zoli Films/ Imperia Films Distribution
Producer: Artur Brauner
Director: **Lang**
Screenplay: **Lang** and Warner Jörg Lüddecke, from the novel by Thea von
Harbou and the original scenario by **Lang** and von Harbou
Cinematography: Richard Angst
Art Direction: Helmut Nentwig, Willy Schatz
Costumes: Claudia Herberg, Günther Brosda
Music: Michel Michelet (*Tiger*), Gerhard Becker (*Grabmal*)
Choreography: Robby Gay, Billy Daniel
Editing: Walter Wischniewsky
Cast: Debra Paget (Seetha), Paul Hubschmid [Alan Burton in the American
version/ Henri Mercies in the French version] (Harald Berger), Walter Reyer
(Chandra, the Maharajah of Eschnapur), Claus Holm (Dr. Walter Rhode),
Sabine Bethmann (Irene Rhode), René Deltgen (Prince Ramigami), Valery
Inkijinoff (Yama), Jochen Brockmann (Padhu), Jochen Blume (Asagara),
Luciana Paoluzzi (Bahrani), Guido Celano (Gen. Dagh), Angela Portulari
(peasant), Richard Lauffen (Bhowana), Helmut Hildebrand (Ramigani's servant), Panos Papadopoulos (messenger)
35mm, color
101 minutes (*Tiger*), 102 minutes (*Grabmal*)

1961
DIE TAUSEND AUGEN DES DR. MABUSE (THE THOUSAND EYES OF DR.
MABUSE)
CCC Filmkunst/ Criterion Films/ Cei-Incom-Omnia Distribution
Producer: Artur Brauner
Director: **Lang**
Screenplay: Heinz Oskar Wuttig and **Lang**
Cinematography: Karl Loeb
Art Direction: Erich Kettlehut, Johannes Ott
Costumes: Ina Stein
Music: Bert Grund
Editing: Walter and Waltraute Wischniewsky
Cast: Dawn Addams (Marion Menil), Peter Van Eyck (Travers), Wolfgang
Preiss (Jordan), Lupo Prezzo (Cornelius), Gert Fröbe (Commissioner Kras),
Werner Peters (Hieronymous P. Mistelzweig), Andrew Cecchi (hotel detective
Berg), Reinhard Kolldehoff (clubfoot), Marie Luise Nagel (blonde woman),
Howard Vernon (No. 12), Nico Pepe (hotel manager), David Cameron (Par-
ker), Jean-Jacques Delbo (Deiner), Werner Buttler (No. 11), Linda Sini (Corin-
na), Rolf Moebius (police officer), Bruno W. Pantel (reporter)
35 mm, B & W
103 minutes

FRITZ LANG

INTERVIEWS

The Monster of Hollywood

MARY MORRIS / 1945

UNLESS YOU MAKE A POINT of watching credit titles on movies, Fritz Lang may be an unfamiliar name. Nevertheless, he's a man on your side—if you like pictures that say something as well as entertain. He is an expert on psychological thrillers, but he also knows the sort of place this world should be. And some of this knowledge usually creeps in among his nerve-jerking chills.

In Germany, before Hitler, Lang directed *M, Siegfried, Destiny,* and some other films that are now preserved as classics by the Museum of Modern Art Film Library. In this country he has made a number of memorable pictures, among them *Fury,* a bold indictment of lynching, *You Only Live Once, Man Hunt, Hangmen Also Die.*

When I asked around town what Fritz Lang was like, newspapermen and people who had worked with him told me he was good at conversation—that he talked with his mind not his mouth. They said he had learned a lot about America in the eleven years he'd been here, that he eagerly watched political and social events and was liberal in his political thinking. They said also that he was a despot, egocentric and cruel.

Gossip is easy in Hollywood and you've got to keep your doubts sharpened. Nonetheless, what I heard about Lang—added to what I knew of his pictures—made me eager for a meeting with him.

I called Lang at the Beverly Wilshire hotel and he said he'd be happy to talk to me—would even take me to dinner.

From *PM*, 4 February 1945.

"Darling," he said, Hollywood-confidential-style, but heavy with the Austrian accent, "do you like dry Martinis?" I said yes. "All right, come at six and we have a long talk before dinner. I mix a *real* Martini with *real* Noilly Pratt vermouth."

The Beverly Wilshire, one of the country's plushiest hotels, was quiet and dignified and the people I saw in the elevator had been tailored by the best. When I knocked at Lang's apartment, Lang himself—wearing a monocle—opened the door.

I had been told that Lang had a stiff, military bearing, and in the photographs I'd seen his face was stone-like. But here in his comfortable, cluttered quarters he was gracious and easy. He smiled benevolently.

This place was the most lived-in looking hotel suite I'd seen. He must have lived there for some time, for books, papers, and manuscripts were stacked and scattered everywhere. Card tables had been set up to catch the overflow.

We went into the kitchen right away to see about the Martini. He worked and I watched, trying to size him up. The monocle, which he kept in his eye all the time, had me fascinated—I wondered why he wore it. Then I decided it was his most distinguished feature—and I felt I had probably answered my question. He was rather large, solid; every move he made yelled confidence. His manner was very continental. He played the role of a man tending to *my* comforts and tastes but I noticed *he* made the decisions.

Preparing the Martini, he said, "Let me know if this isn't perfect." His manner implied that of course it was. I said it was too warm. He took it from me graciously and stirred it against the ice again.

He had complained of being tired, so when we returned to the living room I dropped into a deep easy chair and told him to stretch out on the couch. "No, no, no," he said pulling me out of the chair and depositing me on the couch, "this is the way." I protested, but it did no good. I remained on the couch; he took the chair.

It was then that I noticed the cup of coffee in his hand—no Martini. He explained that he would not take a drink while being interviewed.

I said he needn't be afraid of me.

"Oh yes, darling," he said, "you could do me much harm—I could do myself much harm. That one moment off guard!"

He was serious and dramatic about this and I was impressed with his point. For the next hour, his coffee and my Martini were the symbol to me of the struggle beneath our free-wheeling conversation. Much later, during dinner, it came out inadvertently that he wasn't drinking because of doctor's orders. There were elements of truth, I suppose, in his first explanation, but I think his real purpose in saying it had been to dramatize our situation. And that amused him. Also, it brought us conveniently to his pet subject.

"The one moment off guard. That is my hobby," he told me. "For everybody there is this moment—a moment of weakness when he may make a mistake. It is one of the inevitable rules of life. If you like it there is a preaching here—the one moment—watch out!"

He stood up, considering his thoughts; I waited. He was wearing a silk shirt with fine blue checks. No jacket. I watched him rub his hand carefully across his chest, feeling the texture of his shirt. "You see, this is why I am making so many pictures about criminals. They interest me so very much. It is so easy, even the most law-abiding citizen, to become a criminal in that one offhand moment. I am very much believing that once you make the step down, the abyss opens and you take the next step. There is the saying—give the devil your little finger and he takes the whole hand. Criminals are just the ones who are giving in, getting caught. I only try to have an understanding of them—I am not condemning. I want to see the causes—why they are giving in."

"You believe one can tell what ails our social system by examining our criminals?"

"That is it. I am hoping people will learn to look deeper for the causes of crime. I am studying, reading the papers all the time—there is very much interesting about crimes in the papers. Unfortunately, in pictures there are so many kinds of crimes we cannot touch."

We talked then for a while about a recent double murder in Los Angeles. A man had picked up a woman one evening, taken her to a hotel room and cut her to pieces with a knife. Then he had picked up another woman, taken her to a hotel room, and cut *her* to pieces. People I knew had been too revolted to read much about it; Lang had devoured every printed word and gotten unprintable, inside information from reporters. Among other things he'd discovered that the murderer had had a pillar-to-post kind of bringing up.

Lang sat down and we were silent again. He made these pauses felt because they were timed just right. I couldn't tell what he was going to say next. I know he didn't want me to ask any questions—he was leading the conversation. "I try very, very much to know about the people I make movies about. In everybody, I think, one can see patterns caused by their weakness and strongness. People keep making same faults all through life. It is so rational—you can always see this thing. Especially in criminals.

"I am often thinking what kind of a shock a murderer wakes up with the morning after and finds out the people he murdered are no more alive. The let-down. How the impulse, the fury or jealousy is gone. The anger, the hatred. Now horrible despair—now he knows in a day or two, 90 to 100, they will catch him. For a while he will concentrate on not being caught but sooner or later will again come that moment off guard. He betrays himself by going back to let us say his passion for good food. The police are watching for him in these places because they know his passion."

He paused and rolled his tongue carefully around his lips. Then he said, "In the end his life was nothing but waiting for this rendezvous with the electric chair."

I asked him if he had difficulty getting the studios to let him make serious pictures. Instead of answering directly, he said:

"Since the first year I was here I have been trying to say, in pictures, what I think about the Nazis. I suppose I have a social conscience—a bloody word. It means really that I think I have something to say. I know what I think and I myself would turn down telling certain stories at this time. This is not the time, for instance, to preach that there are good Germans!"

Was he thinking of *The Seventh Cross,* a recent picture about the German underground?

He nodded. "As our army is coming into Germany we have not seen many German people helping us. Have we? And what goes on in the German mind since these war years is something I doubt anybody who has been away from Germany the last five years can know. What I know is not enough—even if I use my imagination."

Had his interest in politics been increased by the advent of Hitler and the necessity of changing his country in middle life?

He stood up, walked around, came back toward me. The timing of his silences made what he said seem more important. I waited expectantly. "Honeybunch," he said, "my viewpoint has not changed so much. I have always been interested in these things. But I have become—a little more of the fighting qualities, I suppose."

"But you were one of the most famous film directors in Europe."

"You see, darling, Hitler comes to power. One night Herr Goebbels of the Propaganda Ministry ordered me to come to him and there is asking me to head the whole industry for the Nazis. I am acting pleased but when I leave I catch a train—fortunately my papers are in order—and I go to France. I give up my fortune, my fine collection of books and paintings. I must begin over again. It is not so easy. But, yes, it was good. I was *arrivé*—fat in my soul, fat around the heart. Darling, too much success . . . oh, it is not good for the man."

Had he found the change in language a handicap?

"Look darling," he said, "I get so much beauty out of this language I speak so lousy, but it is a great handicap. When I am talking ideas, it is so impossible to convey—to get exact understanding and I am getting so tired searching for the right word. When I am working on a picture—at end of the day I am all pumped out, my tongue is so tired it does not properly form the words.

"I am going home at night, reading for relaxation but even here is work. I am reaching for the dictionary—like with a mystery story the other evening I read, '*scallops* on the edge of a brandy glass.' I must find out what meaning has scallops here. Then I am reading five or six papers every day—the funnies, *PM* and the Republican newspapers, too."

He got up to answer the phone then and I looked over his books and other possessions. They turned out to be a sort of index of the range of his interests. On the mantel were most of the new, solid books on world affairs and a sprinkling of the best novels. Near me, a card table held a potted orchid surrounded with a great collection of pipes, stacked boxes of expensive cigars, a book of nursery tales for children, a pocket-sized edition of Lincoln's addresses and speeches, a book of American folk songs, The Bible, some expensive chocolate candies. A book, *Basic Radio,* was turned down on a chair.

On the coffee table in front of me I saw old copies of many different newspapers. I picked a book off the top—*Stronger Than Death (Stories of the Russians at War).* Under it I was somewhat surprised to see the gaudy cover of *True Detective*—turned face down. Under a stack of *PM*'s was a copy of *Better Homes and Gardens.*

When he came back from the phone I asked Fritz what subjects he thought best suited for the screen or stage today.

"No more shooting. Everybody today is writing scripts about Johnnie comes marching home and don't give him a gun. We've seen all that a thousand times before.

"What we are doing must be information disguised as good entertainment. It doesn't make any sense to make plays that depress people. You are doing no good if the audiences are coming out of the theaters feeling down. This is not the time to be negative—it's time to be constructive. There is always this problem when you have something serious to say. But I am always racking my brain for some new way to keep the audience from boredom."

What subjects did he think one could get away with? What ideas did he think should be dramatized?

"We should be making pictures that make people think about Allied unity, about how close our American history is paralleling what happens in Europe today. We should be telling how the war was on Saipan.

"But all this is so very difficult. I am always thinking—how can one arrange to tell about these things and make them tasty to the masses? Movies is the art of our century—the art of the people. I am on the side of the people."

Then why wasn't he making stories that faced up to the problems of our times? (His newest picture, *The Woman in the Window,* is a murder thriller.)

"In Hollywood it is not always possible to find people who will back you while you experiment. Anyway, you cannot always and constantly preach."

"Yes, I said, "but if Fritz Lang does not keep shoving against Hollywood tradition—who will? People who have followed your work expect it of you."

"I have an honest life and refuse to contribute to fascism!"

"Guess you're not a crusader at heart," I said.

"A crusader makes one thing but if he is killed by his opponent—it accomplishes nothing. I wish to stay around longer—to do what I can for good—longer."

I started to argue but thought better of it when I saw his face. He wasn't looking benevolent now. I abandoned the subject and he suggested we get out to dinner.

Outside, we climbed into my car and drove to The Players, a celebrity hangout owned by Preston Sturges, the famous writer-director. I snapped on the car radio and we heard a lilting, old-fashioned tune. I said something about it being romantic.

"What do you think means romance?" said Fritz.

I asked what he was driving at. I'm not good at definitions. We struggled around for a bit with concepts—love, love-affairs, romance, infatuation, etc.

I remember Fritz saying: "Everybody is looking for love, something unknown. They feel something with a person, and darling—they lie to themselves. They talk themselves into something. It is perhaps just infatuation. Mixup number one is sex. It is a game perhaps—with the illusion of love—to fill their leisure time, to escape boredom."

"You fellows with the continental manner are the menaces," I said.

"On the contrary," he laughed and leered a bit. "Look darling, it is just my European tick you are referring to—they say we Europeans understand women better than American men. American males, if they are not making love, want to be with other men. Europeans enjoy the company of women; but let's face it, I don't think any man understands everything about women.

"I'll tell you something, darling. About Joan Bennett, a very good friend of mine. One day a well known writer said to me, 'I like Joan a lot but I'm uncomfortable with her—she's so female, 100 per cent female.' Well darling, women are an unknown quantity such men have not explored—they do not know women unless they are making love."

"You aren't married?" I asked.

"Long ago," he said. I knew he had been married in Germany to a woman who wrote the scripts for his films, Thea von Harbou. I asked what had happened.

"It was a case of two characters growing apart," he said. "In the beginning we were interested in the same thing, German culture—books, music, movies. My honey, it is so often that way in the beginning. But life is fluctuant. Time passes and things change. Have you found anything is lasting love—eternal love?"

He paused. "I didn't. For some people it is only a matter of adjustment to maintain a certain comfort. It is not easy to change. I do not kick out my cook—do I?" He took a long wait. "My wife became a Nazi."

We were quiet a few moments and then I said I guessed now he was only interested in flirting with the girls. He smiled and said that he had been looking around for a long time. "You know, Don Juan, I think was not a philanderer—just a perfectionist. He was only looking for the perfect counterpart for himself. It is so hard to find the perfect counterpart.

"If I am really loving a girl, I am wanting to share everything with her—

skiing, swimming—damn it, there is a word in German for which there is no translation." He asked me for my pencil and for the next half mile occupied himself carefully printing it out: *Mitteilungsbeduerfnis.*

"You must have it with the one you love—and it is basic element in any creative person. The word says a man has need, a passion to give his experiences to others. He is needing to tell to another person his experiences, the beauty he sees and is touching. But it is not an easy affair like chewing the rag over a glass of wine. With this feeling, if you are in love with somebody you want to share everything. You want to convey things—all the gamut. Now if I'm in love it's a very, very lousy love if I cannot share from top down to hell with my girl. I am not in love only when we are happy. Is that correct?"

"Right," I said.

We were in the restaurant now. The captain showed us to a table. It was some table! Gary Cooper was at our left and Humphrey Bogart and Lauren Bacall to our right. B&B called greetings and then Bogart came over to relate a few more of those simple-minded jokes he and Bacall had started telling me a few weeks before when I had visited them on their set.

Suddenly a young woman walked down the aisle in front of the tables and all eyes swept with her. What caused the commotion was her brilliant red silk shirt draped over a spectacular up-tilted front. When she had disappeared, Lang was the first to speak. "I would like to make a cut here on her, gently, with a knife." He ran his finger down my back.

"Why?"

"It is becoming such a fraud, what these girls are doing—I would like to see it all fall down to normal."

When Bogart had gone back to Bacall I asked Fritz to tell me why he had such a reputation as a meanie.

"Darling, I am the monster of Hollywood—the demoniacal man. You must not spoil this legend they are making." We laughed a bit. He was being sophisticated. Underneath, I figured he must have other feelings; I urged him to be serious.

"Now look, I think I know my business. I have strong opinions—know exactly what I want—always, about everything. Nobody, darling, likes a wise guy. That is how it is. I think I am perhaps more difficult than many directors. Directing, I think, is not simply being a traffic cop—giving stop and go signals to people on the set. Darling, I am so often having dissatisfaction—I feel so strongly about every line in the script, the acting, all the architectural values of the picture, each camera move. I study for weeks and make notes and plans about how I will do everything. If for some reason I cannot, for instance, make a camera move the correct way—it is physical pain for me."

I said I understood—that I knew a lot of perfectionists and they were usually hard to get along with.

"It is the content of my life—my work," said Lang. "It is easy to talk about this but—well, I can't help it. I make no compromise. People are talking—I know."

I suggested that he'd probably got off to a bad start in Europe where it is a tradition that directors are imperious. (Mike Curtiz, a Hungarian, once told me he had been brought up in that tradition but had learned he got more from Hollywood actors by being kind.)

"I am never on purpose being unkind to anybody," said Fritz with an affronted manner. "You never reach anything that way. Oh, I am absolutely sure I have made mistakes—stepping on other people's toes. In the early days I was not realizing how it was here in Hollywood. I am working on a scene—I do not want to stop until I am finished. But actors in America are very particular about eating at regular hours.

"Out of these things certain reputations are made," he said.

On the way back to his hotel Fritz told me he was worried. "These nights I sleep without rest," he said. "If I should wake up there is no hope. I must turn on the light and read—cannot go back to sleep. Every day I am talking, talking, talking—pondering, rolling in my head, ideas. I do not recognize people in the studio or I am not remembering names. I cannot clutter my brains with such memorizing—sometimes I think people do not understand."

I said that was a quick way to get a high-hat reputation.

"But how do I count my life? Everything is my work—how my pictures are made."

From one who talked so well about love, I said, that was a surprising statement.

We stopped at Lang's hotel.

"I have just bought myself a house with a view and I go there soon with my dogs—as soon as I get a telephone," he said. "I have some good paintings, a library of five or six thousand books. I have spent a lot of money to give myself comfortable surroundings."

I asked why, after eleven years in this city of beautiful women, he hadn't found a wife.

He reached for the door handle.

"Do you think, darling, I would be good to make marriage with?"

Fritz Lang Today

HENRY HART / 1956

FRITZ LANG IS A TALL, broad-shouldered, loose-limbed man of
sixty-three whose large gray face is what the Scots call craggy. It is a strong
face, full of non-symmetrical planes which form odd angles. The nose is
somewhat like a predatory bird's. The rock and beak implications in Lang's
face would set the imagination off toward Mount Caucasus and Prometheus
were it not for the monocle Lang wears in his left eye. He says he is blind in
his right one.

The monocle makes one remember that Lang was born in Vienna and that
the kind of drama he is most familiar with occurs in cities—modern ones.
His father was an architect and Lang himself studied painting in Vienna,
Munich and Paris. He served in the Austrian Army in World War I and was
wounded three times. While in the hospital he began writing stories and
scenarios. Erich Pommer gave him his first job in movies with Decla in Berlin. Lang was soon directing for UFA—*Destiny* in 1921, *Dr. Mabuse, the Gambler*
(1922), *Siegfried* (1923), *Metropolis* (1926).

Lang's opinion today of some of these films is the distillation of his very
complicated psychology, which has been fabricated by such social upheavals
as War I, the Russian revolution, post-war German nihilism, and the rise and
fall of Nazism, and by such personal upheavals as emigration to the US in
1933.

Lang says he has found that the pictures he was sure were good when he
made them, have withstood time, but that time has exposed the faults of

---

From *Films in Review,* 7:6 (June/July 1956).

those films he was not sure about at first. This sounded a bit pat, but Lang seemed to believe it as he said it.

Lang is disinclined to talk about *Siegfried,* and shrugged disinterestedly when I said it contains things which are still effective. I had the feeling the subject matter of *Siegfried* had become distasteful to him. And he repudiated the subject matter of *Metropolis,* though not its sets and decor. At least he repudiated *Metropolis'* thesis that just as the heart mediates between the brain and the hand, so the tenderer emotions will mediate between a proletariat and a managerial oligarchy of the future.

I remarked that that was the stock Communist disparagement of *Metropolis.* Lang shrugged.

"Where today do you see the heart mediating anything?" he asked bitterly, and with melancholy.

"Collectively, perhaps not," I replied. "But individually—"

"Ah, individually, yes," said Lang, in agreement, but also morosely, as though he were mindful that the individual's valor is as nothing in the midst of the madness of men in the mass.

M (1931) is the Lang picture Lang likes most. He said he had not seen the recent re-make of it, which is incredible, and he added, with what passes over his face as a smile: "I never got such good notices as in the reviews of that picture." I asked how he had discovered Peter Lorre and he replied that it had been in a small Berlin theatre where the fare was a kind of commedia dell' arte. He then volunteered the fact that he had done considerable work on the script of *M.*

"I took no credit for it," he said in an odd tone. I was surprised to see him bow his head. "The script credit went to my wife [Thea von Harbou]," he said softly, and he added, with ever so slight a break in his voice: "She went over to the Nazis."

Lang quoted Dudley Nichols to the effect that "a script is a blueprint." "It's a little more, a little more," he said, without much conviction. Lang regards a director as more "a captain of a ship than a dictator." He thinks up the "touches" in his films the night before a scene is to be shot "in the dark of my library, with coffee and a cigar, neither of which I should have." He is aware of and deprecates his "greed for money." He does not like the wide screen, and he sees no need in movies for electronic tape—"if you know what you're doing you don't need anything to show you the result instantly."

Of the pictures he has made in Hollywood he most often mentioned *Fury* and *You Only Live Once*. He thinks he supplied plausible reasons for the actions of the characters in his most recent film, *While the City Sleeps*. The murderer in it, he contended, wanted the feeling of importance which followed the act of murder. I reminded Lang of his erstwhile predilection for emphasizing the responsibility of society for crime. He said quickly: "Yes, it's half the man, half society, fifty fifty."

This led to a discussion of brutality in current films. Lang thinks it is necessary—dramatically. "People no longer believe in hell and brimstone, or even retribution," he said. "But they fear physical pain. So—brutality's now a necessary ingredient of dramatic development and denouement."

Lang defended Otto Preminger for making *The Man with the Golden Arm*. When I remarked that Preminger had changed the book and given a false picture of the possibility of cure, Lang said Preminger had shown that when an addict has a reason, such as love, for curing himself, he can do it. This surprised me, for I could tell by the look in Lang's eye that he was as aware as I that less than two per cent of the addicts who are cured, even with medical help, stay cured.

It is impossible to look into Lang's eyes—the monocled one and the blind one—without seeing much of the travail of the twentieth century.

"Do you think man is getting better?" I impulsively asked.

He did not at once understand the question. Then he said quickly: "Oh, yes!" And knocking on wood, as he had often done in the course of the interview, he added: "Otherwise one would commit suicide."

Interview with Fritz Lang

JEAN DOMARCHI AND JACQUES RIVETTE/1959

Passing through Paris on the occasion of a retrospective of his work organized by the Cinémathèque Francaise, Fritz Lang really was impatient to give us an interview we had been waiting for. Despite his haste and his fatigue, he tried to express himself in French, relying on the kindness and the competence of Mme Lotte H. Eisner for the translation into our language of the English or German terms which he used from time to time in order to add nuance to certain aspects of his thoughts.

Q: *We begin by asking what period of his work he prefers.*
LANG: That's very difficult. It isn't a question for me of an excuse. I don't know what I should say. Do I prefer the American films or the German films? It isn't for me to say, you know. One believes that the film one is making will naturally be the best. We are simply men, not gods. Even if you don't believe it will be less important, even the mise-en-scène, than this or that earlier film, you still try to make your best work.

Q: *Of course. Also, within the different periods, German or American, are there certain films to which you feel more attached?*
LANG: Yes, naturally. Listen. When I make blockbusters ["*superproductions*"], I am interested in people's emotions, in the audience's reactions. That's what happened in Germany with *M*. In an adventure film or a crime film like *Dr. Mabuse* or *Spione*, there is only pure sensation; the development

From *Cahiers du cinéma*, 99 (September 1959), pp. 1–9. Copyright © *Cahiers du cinéma*. Reprinted by permission of *Cahiers du cinéma*. Translated by Glenwood Irons.

of character doesn't exist. But, in *M* . . . I began something quite new for me, something that I followed in *Fury*. *M* and *Fury* are, I believe, the films I prefer. There are others as well, which I made in America, *Scarlet Street, The Woman in the Window, While the City Sleeps*. These are all films based on a social critique. Naturally I prefer that, because I believe that critique is something fundamental for a director.

Q : *What exactly do you mean by social critique, that of the system or that of civilization?*
LANG : One can't really differentiate. It is the critique of our "environment," of our laws or our conventions. I will admit to a project. I must make a film where I put all my heart. It is a film which shows modern man as he is: he has forgotten the true meaning of life, he works only for things, for money, not to enrich his soul, but to gain material advantages. And because he has forgotten the meaning of life, he is already dead. He is afraid of love, he simply wants to go to bed, make love, but he doesn't want any responsibilities. He only wants to satisfy his desire. I think it is important to make this film now. *While the City Sleeps* shows the hard competition of four men inside a newspaper office at the beginning. My personality refuses the personal satisfaction of being a man. Because each of us, these days, is looking for position, power, money, but never anything inside. You see, it is very difficult to say, "I like this or that." When one begins a film, maybe one doesn't even know exactly what one is doing. There are always people to explain what I want to do, and I say to them, "You know more than I." When I undertake a work, I try to translate emotion.

Q : *In fact, is what you are critiquing in your films a sort of alienation in the German sense of the word "Entfremdung" (Estrangement)?*
LANG : No, it is the fight of the individual against circumstances, the eternal problem of the ancient Greeks, the fight against the gods, the fight of Prometheus. It's the same today, we fight against laws, we fight against imperatives which don't seem just or good for our times. Perhaps it won't be   *Beyond* necessary thirty or fifty years from now, but it is now. We are always fighting.

Q : *Is that the case for all your films, for* Rancho Notorious, *for* While the City Sleeps?
LANG : Yes, for all my films.

Q: *Even for* Die Nibelungen?

LANG: Exactly, but I think that film has become too big to go into its minutiae.

Q: *All the same, in* Metropolis, *that subject is already very clearly indicated.*

LANG: I am very severe about my work. One cannot say now that the heart is the mediator between the hand and the brain, because it is a question of economics. That's why I don't like *Metropolis*. It's false, the conclusion is false, I don't accept that I made that film.

Q: *Was that imposed on you?*

LANG: No, no.

Q: *That surprises us, that seems to be an addition, and not part of it.*

LANG: I believe you are right.

Q: *As for the end of* Fury, *you don't reject it?*

LANG: No the end of *Fury* is an individual ending, not a general conclusion. One cannot give recipes for living. It is impossible.

Q: *Finally, the lesson of your films will be that each man must find his own solution.*

LANG: I think so. Man can revolt against things that are bad, that are false. One must revolt when one is "trapped" by circumstances, by conventions. But I don't believe murder is a solution. Crimes of passion do not solve anything. I love a woman, she betrays me, I kill her. What is left? I lost her love and she is dead. If I kill her lover, she will hate me and I will still lose her love. Killing is never a solution.

Q: *What then for you is a solution? For example, for the heroes in* While the City Sleeps, *what is the solution for them, because the conclusion of the film appears to be very pessimistic, even full of bitterness.*

LANG: I don't believe life is very easy. [Laughs] But my conclusion isn't pessimistic. We see the fight between four men over social position, one for money, another for power, the third, I don't remember, the last because he liked to do that. But the man who wins against the others is the one with an ideal. Which means that, if you always do what you must do without detesting it, if you never need to spit in the mirror in the morning, you get what you want. Where is the pessimism in that?

Q: *We have the impression that the sympathetic hero is not as sympathetic as that.*
LANG: That's something else, that's something else.

Q: *No, we would like to say that the tone of the film. . . .*
LANG: The tone of this film is perhaps a glimpse of a film that I want to undertake now, a critique of our contemporary life, where no one lives one's personal life. We are always under work-related obligations that are very important. After all, money is important. Often critics ask me why I made such and such a film. The truth is that I need money. [Laughs] Somerset Maugham wrote that even artists have the right to make a living.

not Brecht

Q: *In the meantime, are there films which you made for money and in which you had no interest?*
LANG: No, of course. I have never made a film solely for money, never. But certain films, I admit, I would have preferred to make something else. When I conceive of a film, I am interested in it, but certain adventure films interest me less than *M* or *Fury* or *The Woman in the Window,* the films that critique society.

Q: *What brought you to make a Western like* Rancho Notorious?
LANG: First, I wanted to show that there could be a woman who could lead a gang, and a man who could be a celebrated hold-up man, but because he is too old, and because he doesn't draw his gun as quickly, he was no longer a hero. Along comes a young man who shoots more quickly than the older man. The eternal story. Then there was an interesting technical element: to introduce a song as a dramatic element. With six or eight lines of the song, I arrived more quickly at the conclusion, and I avoided showing certain things which would be more boring for audiences, and which weren't very important for the film.

Q: *At that time, did you see, and do you now watch many Westerns?*
LANG: Yes. I like Westerns. They have an ethic that is very simple and very necessary. It is an ethic which one doesn't see now because critics are too

sophisticated. They want to ignore that it is necessary to really love a woman and to fight for her. When I was making *Der Tiger von Eschnapur,* I argued with my screenwriter because I wanted the Maharaja to say, "If you give me your word of honor, I will let you free in my palace," and the screenwriter answered, "Listen, everyone will laugh. What is a word of honor worth today?" Admit that that is very sad. [Laughs] There are today no contracts which I cannot break or which my partner cannot break. What is one hundred pages worth? If he refuses to give me the money, I am obliged to go to court and spend five years. Same for me. If I refuse to honor my contract, no one can force me to. That's idiotic. Whereas, if I give my word of honor, that binds me more. These are fundamental ideas that should be repeated to young people because each year there is a new generation. In Berlin, I saw a German anti-war film. The reviews were terrible, under the pretext that the film did nothing original, that it brought out old themes. But what new things can we say against war? The important thing is that one repeats these things again and again and again.

Q: *Do you consider cinema a medium of persuasion and education?*
LANG: For me, cinema is a vice. I love it infinitely. I've often written that it is the art form of our century. And it should be critical.

Q: *What circumstances led you to make* Human Desire, *and for what reasons did you change the ending and what led up to it?*
LANG: In a review, your *Cahiers* gave me an answer. Why?

Q: *But you liked that film, or would you prefer not to speak about it?*
LANG: I would very much like to speak about it, but Renoir's film is better. First, I had a contract. If I had refused, they would have said, "Perfect, but if we have another film for you, because you've made money on this one, you won't make any more." That could last one or two years. So I am inclined. Then the producer says to me, "That's understood, we like the Renoir film very much, but we can't make 'perverse sex.' We need a young, clean-cut American." In fact, he was right because censorship would be opposed to someone like [Jean] Gabin. You couldn't imagine the difficulties that we had in finding a rail line that would authorize takes under the pretext that we would show a murder. They said to me, "On our line, a murder, but that's

impossible." And they were right, absolutely right. Could you believe that the authorities for the Santa Fe Railroad would be very happy to see a film with a murder on one of their trains? [Laughs]. Who could make a film on the human beast if he doesn't follow the book? My film isn't *La Bête Humaine*. It was called, in English, *Human Desire*. It was inspired by a book, a film. I wonder why you gave it a good review in your *Cahiers*.

Q : *Formally, your film is very good.*
LANG : Thanks very much, you are very kind, but it wasn't *La Bête Humaine*.

Q : *To return to your ideas on the Western, you have frequently addressed an objection from numerous critics, one that we don't share, that reproaches you for your taste for melodrama. Do you not like this so-called melodrama, as much in your Westerns as in your* policiers, *as in your films with romantic triangles, in the measure that they permit stronger situations, where people, men, are more revealed?*
LANG : I don't care that it's a melodrama, I don't know. The truth is what I often see in my observations about murderers, I am frequently in places where a crime has been committed. I don't think that what I've seen is melodrama. As well, it's not up to me to critique critics. I make a film, it's a child which I put out to the world. Everyone has the right to critique it. That's all. Permit me the only vanity that makes me happy: public approbation. I don't work for the critics but for audiences whom I hope are young. I don't work for people of my age because they should already be dead, me too. I don't want to come to Paris. This cocktail, these few words in front of the public at the Cinémathèque, I told Mme Lotte Eisner, this reminds me of a monument for an unhappy man who isn't yet dead. She is right. A young public has really responded. I was very moved, very moved, because that proved that I hadn't worked for nothing.

Q : *You told us earlier that the director's goal was to critique. Couldn't that be the definition of mise-en-scène?*
LANG : All art, I believe, should critique something. It isn't enough to say it's good, it's enticing, it's marvelous. In any case, what can one say of a woman who is good? She's a good mother, a good wife. But what can one recount about a bad woman? One can speak for hours about her, she is interesting [Laughs]. Yes or no? You say about one that she is good, but the other. . . . The question is, "Why is she bad?", "Is she really bad?", "What right has

she?", "What were the circumstances?", "Weren't men responsible?" One could talk all night. And we could talk all night with her. [Laughs] I saw, here in Paris, an English film called *Room at the Top*. There were two women, one very frank, the other very bad. Simone Signoret was the most interesting, not because she was the better actress, but because her sentiments were the more passionate.

Q: *In what way were you influenced by or have you worked against the Expressionist current?*
LANG: I was very influenced by it. One cannot live through a period without taking some of it in.

Q: Die Nibelungen *seems expressionist in the best sense of the term, whereas* Caligari *seems expressionist in the very worst sense.*
LANG: You are wrong. Because *Caligari* is an interesting attempt, it was the first attempt. When Wiene tried again with *Genuine,* that didn't work. The cinema is a living art. It is necessary to take all that is new, not without examination, but all that is good for you, all that enriches you.

Q: *What seems to you to be good in the Expressionist movement, what did you use in your films?*
LANG: That is difficult to tell you; that which I take is my emotion. I try to create something. In this type of interview, one asks me to explain what I would like to have done. One day, in America, some admirers showed me what I thought when I made *M.* I said to them, "That's very interesting, but that's the first time I realized it." I can't really answer you, these are emotions. When young directors come to ask me, "Could you give us rules for directing," I tell them "There are no rules." Today I see that something is good, I should go in that direction, tomorrow I say it isn't right, I should take a different direction. I used the train and now I use a plane, but it is impossible to pretend that the train is bad. I can't say what I found in Expressionism. I used it, I tried to absorb it.

Q: *Certain of your colleagues like to develop theories of art, in particular Eisenstein, who wrote a number of theoretical articles. Aren't you also tempted to develop theoretical considerations about your work in the same sense as Eisenstein about his own work, and then generalize those theories to all cinema?*

LANG: I believe that when one has a theory about something, one is already dead. I don't have time to think about theories. One should create emotions, not create under rules. To work with rules is to work with one's experience, is to fall into routine. I know a man named Mr. Kracauer who wrote a book called *From Caligari to Hitler*. His theory is absolutely false. He used all his arguments to prove a false theory. I therefore feel forced to dissuade today's youth from believing in a book that is full of idiocies. I told him. He was very angry. [Laughs] You know I have a language, I simply use it and I can prove anything. But it isn't necessary for my truth. A theory is nothing for an artist, it serves only for people who are already dead.

Q: *Did you know Murnau in Germany?*
LANG: Yes, but not very well. He left very early for America, and was already dead when I arrived there. He had made his excellent works. He was a very interesting personality. He made *Nosferatu,* very, very good. *Tabu,* and even a *Faust* where we find very, very passionate things.

Q: *Since you often go to the cinema, are there directors whom you admire more than others, or would you rather not answer?*
LANG: Naturally I won't tell you the names, but I prefer certain actors and certain directors.

Q: *Do you admire Renoir?*
LANG: I told you that *La Bête Humaine* is better than *Human Desire*. One can't compare the two films.

Q: *What do you think of Orson Welles, of Nicholas Ray?*
LANG: I've seen two or three of Ray's films that I like very much. *Rebel Without a Cause* is a very good film.

Q: *His first film,* They Live By Night, *was inspired by your films.*
LANG: I accept that. Listen, I've stolen things from other directors, and I am very content and very proud if someone steals something from me. What does that mean, steal? One takes an idea that one admires and one tries to make it one's own.

Interview with Fritz Lang

JEAN-CLAUDE PHILIPPE/1961

''HELLO, MR. FRITZ LANG.''

A man who incarnates forty years of cinema stands before me. He gives me his trademark courteous, benevolent and noble smile.

A monocle placed precisely in the fold of his eyelid, he talks about his films, his life, with disarming ease. At the end of a few minutes, he has put you completely at ease.

He almost takes over the interview. Refusing to be lead off track by some theory or another, he goes straight for the simple, the essential.

"You know, I am not a mysterious man," he says mischievously.

When he thinks, searches for the words in French (he speaks French but thinks in English), his bright eyes, paled further by experience, are of a rare beauty.

The man gives off an impression of honesty, of moral integrity. That is the only explanation for his permanent youthfulness and constantly renewed knowledge of cinema.

When I spoke to him about the solid technique and topicality of some of his old films, he says, "When a film is made well and with great honesty, it does not date. On the other hand, things that were done approximately collapse entirely with age."

"Mr. Lang, the major interest in your work lies in its appeal to three generations of film lovers. There was the expressionist period, the American period and once again the German period with *The Tiger of Bengal, The Indian Tomb*

From *Télérama*, 9 July 1961, pp. 29–30. Translated by Jane Koustas.

and the new version of Doctor Mabuse. Which one of these periods is the most important in your opinion?"

"I don't like to talk about periods. Film is my life. I was born in Vienna. I had a German education and I turned quite naturally to film. It was a great shock to me when Mr. Hitler arrived on the scene. Once, Dr. Goebbels received me and offered to put me at the head of the German film industry. I was to become the sort of official film maker of the Nazi regime. I told him that I was thrilled by his offer. Then (fortunately I had a passport), I left the country. First I shot a film in France, *Liliom,* and I left for the United States.

"No, really, I can't say a new period. My life goes on and my films are the most direct expression of what I have seen, of what I have learned and felt. From my point of view, it is an uninterrupted line.

"Of course, you know, in Hollywood there were ups and downs. We saw, for example, actors who were very successful on Broadway finding themselves out of work later. It's normal; it's America. What interests me the most is the desire to be free. I hate contracts. It gives me the liberty to not do what I don't want to do. I hate being tied down."

"What is the most important theme in your films?"

"Certain things interest me because they are eternal. One always has to fight evil in all its forms. It is important to fight even when the outcome is uncertain."

"From this perspective, which of your films do you think are the most important?"

"*M* firstly and *Hangmen Also Die.*"

"Hasn't evil taken on a particular narrative form? I am thinking, of course, of *Hangmen.*"

"I think you have to denounce it in all its forms. It can be Nazism, a corrupt government or police force, parents who do not understand their children."

"You've turned several times to the subject of Dr. Mabuse, the latest version of which is coming out this week in Paris."

"The character interests me above all. He is evil incarnate, a drive for power that ends by destroying itself."

"In America, you took on a new genre, the Western."

"Let me tell you something. You are Parisian. If we were to visit Paris together, certain things would strike me and not you because you are used to them. That is what happened to me with the Western. For six months, I lived for my own pleasure with the Indians in Arizona, the Navajo. When I made my Western, *Western Union,* I got a letter from some men who had actually lived in the wild west. They told me that the film was just like their memories. I think I showed things the way people wanted to remember them."

"Does the moral aspect of the Western interest you as well?"

"Yes, because of its simple moral code. All the simple morals are important for the success of a film. Even in Shakespeare, the morals are simple. The fight between good and evil is as old as the world itself and I think will go on for a long time."

Suddenly Fritz Lang says, "Don't ask me if man is good or evil. I won't answer because I don't know."

"You've also tackled the detective film with *The Big Heat* and *While the City Sleeps.*

"Through the detective film, I was looking for a form of social criticism. *The Big Heat* shows corrupt policemen and the subject of *While the City Sleeps* is the power struggle within a major newspaper."

"With respect to the latter, you seem to judge the characters harshly."

"I believe that I showed people as they are. When I first started, I would not have tried to explore the psychology of my characters as I did in *While the City Sleeps.* Life showed me to look at things and people with humility and understanding."

"What do you think of the film *Beyond a Reasonable Doubt?*"

"I don't like it at all. I made it, let's face it, because I was bound by a contract. I think it is impossible to place the audience in the presence of a hero for an hour and a half and then reveal in the last five minutes that he is an assassin."

"Do you place great importance on the audience?"

"I make my films for a large audience. I like and respect the audience. But I don't let myself be driven by what I am told about the audience. Sometimes I am told that the audience does not understand something. I refuse to believe it. The audience understands far more than we think."

"Could you tell me how you go about direction? Your style has evolved since expressionism."

"It is hard for me to give you an answer. I don't know the difference between an expressionist and a non-expressionist mise-en-scene. I produce what I feel.

"When I write a scene, sometimes I close my eyes and sketch out the movements, the faces. Things and characters come to life in my imagination. Sometimes I let myself be guided in previously unexplored directions by my characters. I live a long time with my characters before I begin shooting.

"To direct the actors, I need to have my characters' past in mind even if this past does not influence the actual plot of the film. I help the actors by describing their past.

"In any case, there is no foolproof recipe for direction or for working with actors. If there were such a recipe, all films would be good and would be successful."

"Which directors do you admire the most?"

"William Wyler, Billy Wilder, George Cukor, and John Ford."

"And in Europe?"

"I consider Fellini's *La dolce vita* a very great film."

"Finally, I am going to ask the fatal question, the one that divided film lovers. Should *The Tiger of Bengal* and *The Indian Tomb* be classified with Lang's masterpieces or are they minor films?"

"I'm starting to get tired of that question. The problem for me was making a big budget film for a worldwide audience."

"Did you shoot it seriously?"

"Yes. Furthermore, I wouldn't know how to make a film offhandedly. I can't imagine treating offhandedly an enterprise that goes on for five or six months and about which one thinks daily. Those who say they made a film offhandedly are simply looking for an alibi."

"What are your projects?"

"To shoot a film in India and in Italy but I can't say any more. I hope too that the upcoming remake of *Hangmen Also Die* will be a success." (Fritz Lang touches wood with the modesty of a novice.)

We hope so too and we will be discussing it.

Fritz Lang Speaks

CINÉMA 62/1962

I CONSIDER THE DIRECTOR to be a sort of psychoanalyst. He must get under people's skin. Some time back, the idea that a critic is also a type of psychoanalyst came to me. He finds in a man's work certain things that the man himself isn't aware of. I'm in the habit of laughing when people tell me what I am trying to say in my films; but later I think that there are things I do unconsciously and that super-intelligent critics find significant, even if I am not quite sure myself of what I wanted to say.

There were certain things at the beginning of *Metropolis* that bothered me. While I was filming *Metropolis*, I really enjoyed the drama of the film; then, a few years later, I began to find faults with it. For example, the symbolism was too strong. Recently, during interviews and discussions with critics, it occurred to me that what seemed like symbolism then—36 years ago—could have been my unconscious way of exploring something.

One of my next films, which greatly interests me, treats the problem of youth. Someone said that there is no place today for individualism. Lindberg's solitary flight across the Atlantic has no place in today's world. [John] Glenn or [Yuri] Gagarin only symbolize the end work of thousands of men. When in *Metropolis* I showed in a symbolic way that man has become part of the machine, I wondered whether that was simply an unconscious manifestation of something real. When we look at the pictures of [John] Glenn, we see that he is practically a living part of the machine. The destiny of the

From *Cinéma 62*, 70 (1962): 70–75. Translated by Glenwood Irons. Reprinted with permission.

Greeks and Romans was their God. Actually it was something more—either a dictatorship or a battle against a society which in some instances tried to suppress or devour the individual. That struggle appears throughout my work, and is an essential part of it.

I think of one of my American films, *The Big Heat*, with Glenn Ford, on the subject of corruption in large cities. He must leave the police force in order to mount his personal fight against the enormous parasite which threatens to devour everyone. It is always the same subject. Or my film about prisons, *You Only Live Once*, where again a man (what Americans call a "three-time loser") tries to follow his destiny. He is hunted and he fights all alone against the power that menaces society, but he must fight. That fight is important. If we think we have even the slightest chance of success, we must continue to spread [*"propager"*] what we think is just. Maybe one might become a martyr—though I don't believe so—but it is the essence of life to fight for the causes we think are just.

Something very disconcerting once happened to me. You probably remember my film *Hangmen Also Die* (filmed in 1943 from a Brecht screenplay), a film on the crimes of Hitler in Czechoslovakia. That film was poorly received: people said that it reminded them too much of the war. Now, 19 years after the film first appeared, it was recently shown in Paris. I went to see it. It seemed to me that the film showed the people's battle against the invasion of Prague by fascist soldiers. But, during the 19 years, nothing has really changed, the battle hasn't ended: "Ce n'est pas la fin" is rather prophetic, since now the same thing is happening, only the invaders come from the other side.

At this moment in Paris and Rome there is the desire to do something new in films. We can like or dislike these initiatives. That is unimportant. These men are working towards a new cinema. That is important.

When we make films which cost ten or twenty million dollars, with well-known actors, etc., that has nothing to do with cinematic art. That is simply a consumer product. Cinematic art has little to do with liking a film—*Last Year At Marienbad*, for example. We should keep in mind that such films are trying to do something completely new with limited resources.

Many years ago, we in America were in the habit of saying, "Listen, we're not going to film shots, we're not going to film a script; we're simply filming an outline." Nothing has changed.

I have begun preparation for my next film. It will be based on a personal idea. I have never seen a film where the problem of youth has been honestly treated. It is either black or white. Whether we call these youths "Teddy Boys" with black jackets, juvenile delinquents, or as in Germany, *die halbstarken,* it is far too easy simply to criticize them or to say they are bad; rather it is necessary to find out why they are bad. It is necessary to find a comparison. What happened to us during our own youth? What help did we have? My film will focus on a history of crime, but it will also show the problems of youth and how they try to resolve problems. It will try to clearly understand the relations they have with their parents and with their future. And there will be this aspect: there are no longer any individuals.

We can't ignore facts. It is the same as those who say, "Don't regret the fact that, after the typewriter has been invented, people forgot the art of calligraphy." Television cuts down on the time we spend reading books, but we can't change that, we imply that we must adapt to this new situation. We always regret when something we thought eternal turns out not to be. But nothing is eternal. Everything changes and changes.

I would like to have made this new film in England. When working in Europe, one must make co-production arrangements between two countries. Everything depends on knowledge of the arrangements in them. But in Europe one has the advantage of making films which one could never make in the United States because of the high costs. In my films, I am most interested in the destiny of the individual. I don't believe that subject requires spending millions and millions of dollars. If one wants to make grand spectacle films like those in America, obviously one must suppress the problem of the individual. What we see instead are big battles and generalities about the "human condition." One cannot give you a "spectacle" without the "human condition." Such films end up becoming animated posters.

Unfortunately, a large number of American directors work in television because there isn't enough work in the cinema. I live in Beverly Hills, where there are seven television stations. The seven stations broadcast from six in the morning until two in the morning. Who could—and how could they?—create enough good programming? I have seen a few good television programs, but to maintain good quality is impossible.

All men have a certain amount of vanity. Because it has been often cited, *M* has become an important film. I certainly didn't know that at the outset. The subject of *M* has been in other films directed in the United States and Germany. In the United States, they have even copied the music which the character in *M* whistled. Nonetheless, no one has improved the quality of the film. There is nothing new to say about a person who, victim of certain mental afflictions, must fight as the central character in *M* does. But, is *M* a work of art? No. Who can say what a work of art is or what it isn't? Actually, we have a tendency to say, "This is art, this isn't art." But isn't it up to time to decide what is a work of art?

When a film has been around for a very long time, and then is re-released in 1960 and runs for 18 weeks with exceptional ticket sales (as was the case in Paris with one of my films), isn't that proof of the wide audience for the film? That film was the realization of a dream, since commercial success is very important. One doesn't make films for two or three devoted art-lovers, but for all those who go to the cinema.

There are films which are simply for escape. When I was making *Western Union,* I lived with the Indians for a certain time, before which I knew nothing of the Far West. As I had just arrived in the United States, I saw much more than other directors because they had become jaded by living there. My film certainly wasn't an actual documentary of the Far West as it was during its time; in other words, it wasn't the *old* Far West. But I received letters from old-timers who had known the Far West during the pioneer era. They said that *Western Union* presented things "realistically," as they were; but what is reality? I didn't show the Far West *as it was*. The film made the public dream that the Far West was like that. I won't say that the dream and the story are better in the movies than in life. But they both have the right to exist.

For me, it is important to have the widest possible audience. For the simple reason that I always try to "say" something in my films. When I made *M,* I was against capital punishment—I am still against it—but I didn't expect that capital punishment would be abolished everywhere ten days after the film was released. All we can do is show things for what they are.

When I made *Fury,* on the subject of lynching, I couldn't hope for the abolishment of hanging. I simply wanted to put my finger on the subject. Otherwise, I would have become a politician. I am not a miracle worker. I can simply show certain things and say, "I think this is right," or "I think this is wrong," "look at these things, one after the other." When I do what we generally call crime films, there is a critique of certain aspects of reality. That doesn't mean I have a formula for stopping crime. That's not my affair.

Personally, I believe that democracy is not a particular form of government. We call it a form of government, but in reality it is the result of certain forces in equilibrium. It is marvelous that democracy allows us to say what we want to say.

I think that certain people overestimate the power of a director. A film is the result of teamwork. But the director has certain powers. Permit me to tell you a story. When *Fury* was finished, the producer asked me into his office after a private viewing of the film. He accused me of changing the screenplay. I asked him how I could have done that since I didn't speak a word of English. He demanded a copy of the screenplay, and after reading it he exclaimed, "Hell, you're right. But it seems different on the screen!" And perhaps it was different—for him!

Fritz Lang on *M:* An Interview

GERO GANDERT/1963

GERO GANDERT: *How in fact did you arrive at the theme for* M? *Was it current in 1931? Is it true that there were contemporary models for your child murderer Beckert, like Haarmann, Grossmann, Kürten?*

FRITZ LANG: I am a more than attentive newspaper reader, I read not only the papers of *one* country and I endeavor, above all, to read between the lines. I have been interested in a thousand things in my life, and out of these interests in a thousand things came one primary interest: *mankind.* And not only what he does—in innocence or in guilt[1]—but what moves him to act, *what makes him tick!* And with the attempt to identify this, there grows not only personal awareness, but much more important, sympathy. Through this one's own sphere of thought is enriched; as a reaction to it, associations with all things one has occupied oneself with for a lifetime are expanded.

Who can honestly say how one arrives at a theme? What influenced him? It could be a falling leaf from a tree in Autumn, a sudden lull in the wind, a sudden thunderstorm. . . . Once I believe in a theme—"am possessed by it"—then I do a great deal of research. I like to know as much as possible about every significant thing (nothing is insignificant), right down to the finest detail. And since, at the time that I decided on the theme for *M,* so many serial murderers were performing their dastardly deeds—Haarmann, Grossmann, Kürten, Denke—I of course asked myself the question: What induced these people to their actions? Contemporary "models," as you call

From Gero Gandert, *M: Protokoll* (Hamburg: Marion Von Schröder Verlag, 1963). Translated by Barry W. K. Joe. Reprinted with permission of Gero Gandert.

them, they certainly were not, none of them was a child murderer. But in Breslau around this time, there were some dreadful crimes committed against children, without their perpetrators being caught.

In *M* it fell to me not only to examine what drives a person to such a horrible crime as the murder of children, but also to roll out the pros and cons of capital punishment. The tenor of the film, however, is *not* the sentencing of the murderer, but rather the warning to the mothers: "Ya gotta watch out fer yer kids better." This human accent was particularly close to the heart of my wife at the time, the writer Thea von Harbou; she wrote, in collaboration with me, the screenplays of almost all my German films before 1933 and naturally also had a significant role in the development of this material. For many years she was my most important collaborator and assistant. . . .

G G : *Was there a real life model for Inspector Lohmann? Did you work together with the homicide squad at all? Did you have advisors? Were psychoanalysts or doctors consulted?*

F L : I can't in fact answer your question of whether there was a model for Lohmann with a simple "No," that is, as far as his human qualities are concerned, his joviality and his humour. But certainly I was advised and instructed by members of the criminal investigation squad (by "Alex") about the methods of the police in their search for a criminal. Likewise, I had long conversations with psychiatrists and psychoanalysts about the mental state of compulsive murderers.

G G : *Critics have stated that your films contain romantic elements. In this regard they have referred particularly to* M *and the scenes in the beggars' market. Would you concur with such an observation?*

F L : I find this reference, in fact like many critiques, to be pretty superficial. I do not believe that romantic elements are contained in *M* or in *Fury* or in other films that I made in America, such as *The Woman in the Window* (1946), *Scarlet Street* (1945), *While the City Sleeps* (1956), *The Big Heat* (1953)—perhaps picturesque elements, but not romantic.

On the other hand, whenever one treats a "romantic theme," for example in *Der müde Tod* (*The Weary Death*, 1921) or in the film that is set in the 17th Century, *Moonfleet* (1955), one must be true to this romanticism in the staging, which does not mean that one falsifies the emotions of the characters in the "romantic" (negative) sense.

If the scenes in the beggars' market are considered romantic, one can respond that this beggars' market existed in Berlin. There was even a crime magazine, the name of which I unfortunately cannot recall, that used to publish articles and photographs about this beggars' market.

G G :   *Criticism always refers to the influence of Bert Brecht's* Threepenny Opera *that is supposedly evident in* M. *Is there such an influence, in your opinion?*
F L :   Did Bert Brecht influence me? Of course. Which of his contemporaries did he not influence? Can you simply ignore a genius such as Brecht? Which is, however, not to say that one must simply adopt his views as one's own. One develops not only under the influences that one encounters.

G G :   *The treatment of sound as a dramaturgical medium in* M *is often praised. One almost gets the impression that we were further along in this area in the early days of sound films than today.*
F L :   *M* was my first film with sound. At that time you could count the number of sound films available for viewing on the fingers of one hand. Naturally I attempted to come to terms with this new medium: *sound.* I found, for example, that when I was sitting alone in a sidewalk cafe, of course I heard the noises from the street, but that when I was immersed in an interesting conversation with a companion, or when I was reading a newspaper that totally captured my interest, my organs of hearing no longer registered these noises. Hence: the justification to represent on film such a conversation without laying down the aforementioned street noises as background to the dialogue.

At that time I also came to the realization that not only could one use sound as a dramaturgical element, but in fact absolutely had to. In *M,* for example, when the silence of the streets (I deliberately omitted the optional street noises) is sliced in shreds by the shrill police whistles, or the unmelodic, constantly recurring whistling of the child murderer, that gives mute expression to his compulsive urges.

I also believe that in *M* was the first time I had sound overlap sound, one sentence from the end of one scene overlapping the beginning of the next, which not only accelerated the tempo of the film, but also strengthened the dramaturgically necessary association in thought of the two juxtaposed scenes.

For the first time, as well, the dialogue of two contrapuntal scenes (the questioning of the gang members with the aim of finding the child murderer, and the questioning of the detectives assembled in the police station for the very same purpose) was handled in such a way that the entire dialogue forms, to a certain extent, a whole. That is to say, for example, one of the criminals starts a sentence, and one of the detectives is shown finishing a sentence, and both parts make sense. And vice-versa. Both techniques were later used generally.

When, on the other hand, the blind street vendor hears the dissonant melody of a barrel organ, stops up his ears so as not to hear it any more and suddenly the sound of the barrel organ is cut, although the audience would actually have to be able to hear it, then that is an attempt that certainly has a justification. Which does not mean that such an attempt establishes a rule.

I certainly do not believe that a film is bound by any rules. It is always new and a principle that is right for one shot can already be all wrong for the next.

GG: *Siegfried Kracauer writes in* From Caligari to Hitler *that M was supposed to be released under the title* Mörder unter uns (The Murderer Among Us). *Georges Sadoul reports in his* History of Film *that a representative of the Nazi party threatened a boycott of the film because of this "title that is an insult to all Germans." You are said to have thereupon given in. Are these reports accurate?*

FL: For once, Siegfried Kracauer is not wrong, apart from his assertion that *M* is a film about Kürten, the child murderer of Düsseldorf. First, Kürten was not an admitted killer of children, second, the screenplay for *M* was finished before Kürten was apprehended.

What Georges Sadoul writes is plucked out of thin air.

I changed the original title *The Murderer Among Us* during the filming of *M*, influenced by the scene in which one of the pursuers draws an M on his palm with chalk so that, should he strike the murderer on the shoulder, the murderer will be marked with the chalk mark for the other pursuers. Other than that, I just thought *M* was a more interesting, more effective title.

GG: *Certain motifs and fundamental tones seem to recur in your films: an inexorable fate prevails; the guilty/the innocent are persecuted; protagonists are delivered*

from their dark drives and instincts; death is stronger than they are. Can you offer
an explanation for this?
F L :   The struggle of the individual against Fate probably is in all my films,
(primarily good) people wrestling with a higher, superior power, be it the
power of a generally accepted injustice or the power of a corrupt organization, society or authority. Or be it the power of one's own conscious or
unconscious drives.

If you say that my films show that "Death is stronger" than everything
else, then I have to say that you are wrong. As far as Death is concerned, I
think that it is sometimes preferable to a life under conditions unworthy of
life, and that one must fight for that which one has accepted as "right," even
against superior powers, even if death threatens to be the final outcome. It is
the struggle, the opposition, that is important.

I. On the one hand, innocence with all the external appearance of guilt, as
in *Fury* (1936) or *You Only Live Once* (1937), on the other hand, guilt with all
the appearance of innocence—is there anyone who must not admit that they
are both one and the same? Beyond appearance, what is guilt and innocence? Can one indeed be innocent or guilty? If there is an answer in abso-
lute terms, it can certainly be only a negative one. Every single person has
the responsibility to find his reality that is valid for him, regardless of how
tenuous that reality might be. These thoughts were first expressed by Jacques
Rivette. I believe a good director must be a kind of psychoanalyst and Jacques
Rivette apparently carried out a thorough psychoanalysis of me and my
films. [Note in the original—ed.]

With Fritz Lang

MICHÈLE MANCEAUX/1964

M M : *Are you enjoying yourself at Cannes?*
F L : Enjoy, enjoy! That's a big word. It interests me.

M M : *For how long have you been making films?*
   The white-haired gentleman counts with his fingers. It takes an entire hand, each finger representing a decade, to arrive almost at the total.
F L : You don't have any gentlemanly questions to ask? I am in a hurry.

Fritz Lang barely smiles. He constantly wavers between irony and anger. Rarely does Cannes have the honour of having such a prestigious and competent jury chair.

M M : *Do you think holding the Cannes Festival is important?*
F L : Things would not be better if it were not held.

M M : *Is that a gentlemanly answer?*
F L : No. There are many films seen here by the world press that would have not gone beyond their own borders otherwise.

M M : *What criteria do you use to judge a film?*
F L : The problem is not to decide if I like fish or not. Even if you do not like fish, you can taste it and decide if it is well cooked or not. It is the same in film. I try to be as objective as possible and to forget that I am a filmmaker

From *L'Express*, 673 (7 May 1964): 27–28. Translated by Jane Koustas.

myself. Of course, huge battle scenes do nothing for me. I can figure it out ahead of time and there are no ideas there. But as soon as it is not lions but human beings who are moving, it's fascinating.

M M : *Intelligence, sensitivity, taste, strength, imagination. Which is the most important for a director?*
F L : He has to know life. [Fritz Lang laces his sentences with German or English to be more specific.] He has to know the straits of life, *schiften.* How do you say it?

M M : *The layers of life, the slices. . . .*
    Fritz Lang becomes annoyed, picks up a pencil and draws overlapping layers.
F L : He has to have experience. No, it is not a matter of age.

M M : *Should a director be cultured?*
F L : Of course! He must also read newspapers. I take a lot from newspapers.

M M : *How has film changed since you've been making films?*
F L : There is only one real change, that's sound. During the silent movie era we were forced to prefer action. Now, I don't think that action is superfluous, quite the opposite, but one can also explore character. In a film one must find everything.
    Did you see *M?* Many say that it is an adventure film. Others say that is psychological. And for others still it is the defence of a criminal who wonders how he was able to commit his crime and by what force he was pushed. In the silent era, investigation was limited.

M M : *Do you think that today's film offers as many possibilities as literature?*
F L : You would never compare painting to music or sculpture. It is different. Every art form has its purpose and its techniques and these cannot be confused. As for cinema, it is the art of this century and the people's art.

M M : *Do you think adaptations of novels can result in good films?*
F L : I think that a true auteur should create an original film and conceive it himself. But why be tied down? There are no rules. Everything interesting is allowed. The only thing not allowed is length.

MM: *Do you want to end this conversation?*
FL: No. Continue.

MM: *When films are very long, do you leave before the end?*
FL: Never. A question of honor among thieves.

MM: *What interests you in life?*
FL: Life.

MM: *Yes, but what in particular? Man, nature, reading, trips?*
FL: Everything. Martinis, light, a leaf falling from a tree. For a director, nothing is ever lost. Even films devoid of interest are interesting. You can see what you should not do.

MM: *How do you work?*
FL: Like everyone else, by trying to make a vague vision real. It is very difficult, my dear. Now we have to finish.

Fritz Lang gets up. It seems as if he has talked a lot and that he does not like explaining himself. Too bad! It was the best moment of the week.

It is not that the festival is mediocre. There are even signs of an honest search for quality, which is rare, an honest quality but no sparkle. Conscientious, humanist films, slices of life served up just right to move you.

New Interview with Fritz Lang

JEAN-LOUIS NOAMES/1964

We have been waiting for an occasion to publish a new interview with Fritz Lang. Cannes gave us the opportunity. More than an "interview," this is a conversation with his friend Gene Fowler, Jr., and Jean-Louis Noames, our correspondent, around a microphone in August 1963, at Fritz Lang's Hollywood estate. Hence Lang's recollection of memories: he had just returned from Italy where he participated in the shooting of Le Mépris [Contempt]. *Hence as well the uncustomary demonstrations of mise-en-scene played out by the filmmaker who delighted in showing both how directing draws on rhetoric and how this happens in his own films.*

NOAMES: *In your last interview with* Cahiers du cinéma, *you said that, for you, the cinema is a vice. . . .*

LANG: Making films is for me something like taking a drug. It is a vice that I adore. Without the cinema, I couldn't live. I love this art form, which alas, has become, in the majority of countries, an industry. But I've never wanted to say that the cinema was a drug to aid the artist, or the creator of films, to overcome certain inhibitions, as for example Fellini showed in 8½. I simply wanted to say that, to love the cinema, I am given over to it in the same manner as an individual gives himself over to drugs.

NOAMES: *But doesn't the cinema have a beneficial influence on certain directors?*

From *Cahiers du cinéma*, 156 (June 1964): 1–8. Copyright © by *Cahiers du cinéma*. Reprinted by permission of *Cahiers du cinéma*. Translated by Glenwood Irons.

LANG: I really couldn't say. . . . But I think you are touching on something important: perhaps, in effect, all artists need to create, and in some way find a way of expressing their sentiments, their thoughts. I believe, for example, I will not kill anyone, nor steal—perhaps I could rape ["*violer*"], I don't know. Only a psychoanalyst could really answer that question. I'll tell you a story that, perhaps, sheds some light on this problem. Eight years ago, someone here in Hollywood said to me, "I could tell you exactly what you were thinking when you made *M* and why you made it." And he began to explain it all! I responded, "All that you are saying is very kind, but I think you are entirely wrong. I know exactly why I made *M*: I was interested in showing film-monsters which were in style; after *Metropolis* or *Woman in the Moon,* I wanted to make a more intimate, deeper film, and I was very interested in particular by the mind of a child murderer: but that didn't stop me from being completely against him."

On another occasion, in Paris, someone, I don't know who or for what magazine, interviewed me: we spoke of my profession as a director, and in relation to my work with actors, we came up with the same problem. I told him that, in my opinion, a director shouldn't show an actor what he should do: in a word, I in no way want the actor to ape me. The role of the director is, to the contrary, to bring out the best of the actor. For that reason, he should, each time, be a sort of psychoanalyst, explain his role to the actor, help him to discover the character he should create or recreate out of the script. At that moment, I ask myself if the role of the critic is perhaps also to psychoanalyze the director: to discover the depth of his films. In a certain sense, that answers the question you have asked me: perhaps, if you wish to do that type of psychoanalysis and that would certainly take a long time you would find out why a director needs his films in order to live, and why I have myself made such and such of my films . . .

The question, moreover, comes back to what a critic should be: a film critic, a critic of the creative process. And it would be, in effect, fascinating to discover why the creator does certain things. But I am afraid of that: I know a very good writer, very talented, who underwent psychoanalysis. Two years later, he couldn't write anything. Because, I believe, our work as creators is the result of certain . . . frustration no, not frustration: moreover (we should pay close attention to the choice of words), the result of an "abnormality." In a certain sense, we are different . . . finally, it is necessary to be crazy to want to make movies. To return to the case of that writer, he became too lucid about himself: he didn't ask questions about the world, what was going on, about his place in the world, about the why of things. That was of no interest to him: his problems were resolved; but he couldn't write any more. That's what we do in our films, give our own commentaries on unresolved problems.

NOAMES: *Let's take the case of Antonioni: in his films, he repeats the impossibility of living, of communicating, of loving, and yet, it doesn't seem to me that this helps him to live. . . .*

LANG: I don't know that his films don't help him to live. . . . Perhaps they do. Perhaps, also, but I don't know whether it is true, he is incapable of living and he tries to prove to himself that life is impossible—which, in any case, I can't believe.

NOAMES: *Do you think that his problems as a director are translated in his style or his manner of directing: one can see, for example, a rapport between certain difficulties in communication and certain uses of dialogue?*

LANG: I don't know. As it happens, I discussed with certain writers and directors the use and abuse of cinematic dialogue. The cinema, we are in agreement, is the image of movement, and not simply filmed theatre. Now, how do we show, for example, without using dialogue that a husband and his wife are still on good terms but no longer have that initial great love?

Here's what I would suggest: suppose the scene occurs in a hotel, where the couple is in an elevator, going up to, let's say, the 17th floor. The husband and his wife are both very likeable, neither too old nor too young. And the husband has his hat on his head. At the tenth floor, the elevator stops and a young woman gets on: the husband removes his hat, and the elevator continues up. You have the perfect expression, and without pronouncing a single word, that the love between the couple is no longer what it was, that there is no longer the fascination between the lover and his beloved. It is simply natural politeness which makes you take your hat off when in the company of a young woman in an elevator, which the man doesn't think of doing for his wife, but only for another woman. That's how we can express something so precise in a silent scene. But, as Antonioni has done, showing a woman who walks, walks, and walks down a street, that could signify anything, there is no dramatic content.

Or else, it is necessary to consult a film critic to understand what one has seen. But what is very dangerous about this attitude, about our era, moreover of *your* era, is that it leads us to find this type of film as an excuse. . . . One says: life is thus. And even though these films help us to live in a certain way, at the same time they persuade us that it is useless to fight in life, that, in any case, we have lost in advance. And no one will make the effort.

N O A M E S :   *But in your films, aren't people also always pursued by their destiny?*
L A N G :   That is the problem that has always interested me, not to say obsessed me, that is, is all, in one way or another, *inevitable.* Once one has started something, one cannot escape from it. But, despite that, I have always wanted to show and define the attitude of *struggle* which people should adopt in the face of fatal events. It is not important or essential to be victorious in the fight, it is the fight itself which is important and vital. Some time ago, Gene Fowler and I had a conversation where the subject was happiness. And the value of this happiness. We tried to define its situation, its content, and we couldn't imagine a state of constant happiness: that implies that there is no desire for anything, that one lives like an angel of paradise, playing on one's harp. . . .

That which I call "happiness" is the pursuit of this happiness. For me, for the director, happiness is not what comes once the film is completed, when one says one has done something. Happiness for me—and this is what constitutes my "vice"—is when I am in the process of making a film. Even if the conditions of making the film are very, very difficult, I forget everything: and only at that moment am I perfectly happy. The fight for something, there is something that is important, not the result. One must, certainly, fight for a result, but a result is never definitive, is not the end of the struggle. If you have attained something, that is no reason to stop. Because life doesn't stop either. Like life, you have to incessantly start again from the beginning. That is why my "pursued characters," as you call them, don't fight (as in Greek drama) against God or Destiny, but against the circumstances of life, against, who knows?, the opinion of their neighbors, against stupid laws and other similar things.

When you fight for your love, for example, and when you come to defeat the obstacles . . . (Lang interrupts himself for an instant, before carrying on suddenly): that is when the real struggle begins, when you are finally married—and live with her!

NOAMES: *This struggle, is it translated in your films by a certain opposition between movement and immobility?*

LANG: I don't know if that is right. . . . That would be, if I have understood, a little like what we said earlier: that when someone—one of my characters— abandons the struggle, he ceases to move forward. That never happens to my characters: they never stop the struggle. But to answer your question, it is necessary to ask first how it could be possible to film an action—a drama, a movement—that could, however, be *static*. . . . (To film immobility, that comes back to Corneille: "It is logical that illogic goes against logic"). Well then, when, on the occasion of some shock, you realize that your fight for something appears to have arrived at its final point, or that you are at an impasse, you should stop for a second, under the effect of the shock. If, for example, you see a man in a film walking back and forth in a room, and he suddenly stops, you, the spectator, you say, "He has an idea," then the fellow starts walking, right? Then, at the moment when he receives the shock, instead of running around like an animal stuck in a cage, he stops: it is then that something violent has happened inside, and that the drama is translated by a stop in movement, that this immobility is full of action. Which is to say that a "static action" is not inaction.

In one of my films, we see a man who escapes and runs for his freedom: but, at the corner of a street, he sees a policeman: he stops brusquely, and we see him in close-up. But this stop, this close-up, lasts only a second: immediately, the reaction of the man is to turn around and run.

NOAMES: *But isn't the action interrupted by this close-up?*

LANG: No, because this isn't an instant of reflection which I show on his face in close-up: I'm showing only the shock itself, the experience of surprise. I believe it isn't reflection but instinct that makes him turn so quickly in the opposite direction: which is why I don't show him looking right, then left, which would suggest hesitation and dead time in the action, here is a reaction to a dramatic emotion. Let's take again the example of a man condemned to death, and who is on the electric chair: it isn't possible that he is immobile, that he could be calm, that he shows no emotion, under the pretext that he knows himself to be already dead. No! In truth, he fights like a beast, he hasn't yet abandoned the struggle. Without doubt, this final fight will do nothing for him, but this doesn't prevent him from an animal instinct that makes him refuse to see himself attached to the chair to die.

Of course, it is easier to resolve these contradictions if we treat them, as in silent films, as stylized situations. It is fashionable today to avoid showing people immobilized while they are speaking: but if they are eating, we can't make them continually get up and sit down while they speak! Moreover, there are very dramatic situations where neither movement nor action are necessary. A couple is eating dinner in an apartment, and the wife says to her husband that she has been unfaithful: I can understand that he gets up and yells. But if that same scene takes place in a restaurant, he couldn't get up and yell without attracting attention: imagine this man, sitting across from his wife who announces coldly that she was unfaithful the day before: and he can't make a single gesture, nor say a single word, he can't stand up to slap her. Isn't this scene much stronger due to the fact that this forced inaction has gained in interest and dramatic intensity? The emotion is much larger when such sentiments are *contained,* and the audience feels them at least as much as if they had been manifested graphically.

Perhaps that is because we worked on silent films, because we come from the Silent Cinema, that we like above all the action, movement. However, I have the impression that your cinéastes hold to this as well. I haven't seen Godard make many stationary shots . . . but there is a difference: in our silent films, we were obliged to express ourselves *across* the action: whereas Godard, for example, seems less interested by action itself than by its result, its effect. Perhaps that allows him to go further with his actors, to make them give everything they have. To see him make that would interest me greatly. As well, I like him a great deal: he is very honest, he loves the cinema, he is just as fanatical as I was.

In fact, I think he tries to continue what we started one day, the day when we began making our first films. Only his approach is different. Not the spirit. He has the same desire to advance this new art form, the art form of our century where the money-makers have made an industry: in trying too hard to make money, they have only succeeded, in most countries, in killing the goose who laid the golden egg. . . . What Godard is trying to find is, first, a form which is his own, and which can best express his personality. As for me, more occupied by the content of a film (which to me seems more important than the form): what I want, above all, is that the ideas on which I work, the phrases on which I work, will find an audience.

But perhaps it is simply in the way we conceive the mise en scène where the difference resides: Godard loves to improvise, whereas I like to know exactly what I will do when I arrive on the set. Of course, I give my actors the maximum liberty, but Godard goes further: he only gives his actors the idea of what they are supposed to be saying, letting them use their own vocabulary.

NOAMES: *But don't you believe that a director from the school of silent film comes to the conclusion that in the absence of dialogue, more ingenuity is required, in order to create character more rapidly?*

LANG: More rapidly, no. And don't forget that we also had intertitles which allowed us to express, from the moment a character opened his mouth, what *we ourselves* would like to do. . . . Godard, who never had the experience of silent cinema, comes, however, to improvise at all levels, and not simply with dialogue: he invents scenes at the moment he films them! And they don't correspond to anything: for example, to conclude a scene, he needs a phrase that we can't find. I had the opportunity to utter a phrase that he used: "Death isn't a solution." But that gave him another idea: When Bardot is in the bathtub, she is holding a book, and on the cover we can read "Fritz Lang." In the book is a phrase that I once said about death: which established a relationship with the situation that occurs in the next scene. Godard improvised and at the same time made it better.

NOAMES: *Didn't you say that a film above all should be shaped during editing?*

LANG: Yes, but only if one has a great deal of footage at one's disposition. There is a phrase that I like very much: "To make a film is to rewrite." We cut certain things and we modify others. . . . But for Godard, all that isn't necessary, he doesn't have to do that. He films very little in close-up, whereas I do that often. *Le Mépris (Contempt)* was done in technicolor and widescreen (what do you call that? Oh yes, Cinemascope, about which I have an answer: "Cinemascope isn't for human beings, it's for snakes and funerals." They'll love me after that.) But, if I had made the film, there would have been many close-ups.

Godard, he didn't have this problem. He fights to give a very personal form to his films: and for that reason, he has problems with his producers. Moreover, these people always want to change something. There are very few "real" producers. A real producer should be a great friend of the director:

but most are jealous of him. One time, in one of my films, there was a scene which a producer didn't like, and which I found very good, very funny. For a week, I argued with him, I said to him, we have previews precisely to get the public's reaction. The producer gave me the possibility to verify, during a private projection, that I was wrong. But the audience, which liked the scene, laughed and applauded a lot. Despite that, the producer dug in his heals, and said: "I will show the film enough times until I find an audience that doesn't like the scene." That's so stupid! These are probably frustrated people. You have seen *Rancho Notorious,* haven't you? Well, it was originally called *Chuck-a-Luck* because the ranch was called that, and there was also a game of that name. As well, the film's song worked around "chuck-a-luck." But, Mr. Howard Hughes called the film *Rancho Notorious!* When I asked him why, he said that in Europe no one knows what "chuck-a-luck" means. But, in Europe, do we know what "Rancho Notorious" means? You see, there isn't a "copyright" for a director, nor for anything else in this industry of misfortune! A playwright, he has all sorts of rights, and if he refuses, one doesn't have the right to change even a comma in his play. In the USA, I've told you, we have a system unknown in Europe, the "preview." If those whom we call producers were human beings, and honest, they would recognize that it is only there where one can judge if the film is good or not, know whether people like it or not. Perhaps then there will be a sort of understanding between producers and directors, and then directors will accept to change certain things which producers don't like. But if producers feel themselves to be always right, understanding isn't possible. Now, I call the cinema an industry, and it could be an Art. We have made an industry and killed the Art: but also killed the industry.

There is only one country where it is still possible to consider cinema as an art form, and that is France. But even there, the money invested is at the base of all the problems. I argued with the producer of *Le Mépris,* a charming man, I might add, Beauregard, and I asked him why he made one scene in a very small, uncomfortable projection room. He answered that it was cheaper to use real décor, because studios are very costly. I then said to him: "Yes, but here you film at most three or four shots per day, and when you want to change the lighting, it is very difficult." But, at the end of filming, I understood his reasons, I will not make any more films that are not entirely in natural décor. Of course, there are large inconveniences: in *Le Mépris,* we had to film in a room where there were four immense windows! We had to film a long scene, but the time taken to work out the lighting, to put down rails for travelling shots, to complete takes: the light had changed, the sun had moved. Whereas, in the studio, we have all the time, the effects which permit us to compensate for the absence of natural décor: we can even create the sea, with its advancing waves . . .

The Viennese Night: A Fritz Lang Confession, Parts One and Two

GRETCHEN BERG/1965

Part One

The words of Fritz Lang that we're going to read have nothing to do with an interview. This is rather a long monologue, collected by the tape recorder of Miss Gretchen Berg during a number of evenings in New York with Lang and some friends at the St. Moritz Hotel. Present were Willy Ley (technical advisor of *Woman in the Moon*), a rocket expert, a young wife of his friend, Tonio Selwart (who played the adjutant Heydrich in *Hangmen Also Die*), and finally Herman G. Weinberg and his daughter Gretchen, whom we thank very much. In other words, none of Lang's statements were provoked by questions. This is a "confession" of a filmmaker, the first which he has made. This "Viennese night" is therefore haunted with memories, filled with evocations, more than it is dedicated to reflections. The director, if allowed—something which is impossible during an interview—at the will of his memory, of his humor; his caresses, and again his deceived dreams, awakens his unfinished projects; almost at the end of his career, he plows through in all senses and as if by chance, he invites us to his own "vagabondage." We have also respected his disorder. The digressions, the repetitions, even the asides which are of themselves a long digression in the margins of a work, create—in our eyes at the very least—the most interest, and are, for the most

Part One from *Cahiers du cinéma*, 169 (August 1965): 42–61. Part Two from *Cahiers du cinéma*, 179 (June 1966): 50–63. Copyright © by *Cahiers du cinéma*. Reprinted by permission of *Cahiers du cinéma*. Recorded and transcribed by Gretchen Berg. Originally translated from English by Jacques Bontemps. Translated from French by Glenwood Irons.

part, in the emotions shared by this intimate flashback. Neither does it escape us that Fritz Lang, even if he dwells for a moment here on his past, has lost nothing of his pride, his enthusiasm—is it even necessary to say?—of his youth. No matter how advanced in age he is, he doesn't believe he has already stopped, and he continues to expect everything from cinema, and from mankind.

FRITZ LANG: I haven't seen a single post-war German film which pleased me, except *Des Teufels General [The Devil's General]*, directed by Helmut Kautner, which was magnificent. After 14 months of work there, two years ago, I finally and definitively abandoned the idea of making another film in Germany. The people with whom one works are really insupportable. Not only do they not keep promises—written or not—but even the film industry (if it is still possible to call it that, which once gave the country a world-wide name in film production) is now run by ancient men of the law, ancient SS, or exporters of God knows what. They work in an effort to organize production conditions so that their account books are already in the black before the film begins. That's why making good films doesn't interest them, because why bother worrying about it when only the writing of Great Books assures all the money you need? The film industry in Germany is very much behind the American film industry. Who would have believed that a people such as the Germans, who had so much advanced film technique, could now be so retrograde? For example, the organization which financed *The Thousand Eyes of Dr. Mabuse* also said, "I have seen the death of the enterprise in terms of art." The producers harvested so much money from my two first *Mabuse* films that they wanted to continue. I said to them, "What would you like me to do now?" Mabuse is dead! Then I learned in a magazine about the American army's experimental bullet, which leaves no trace. I then wanted to make a brutal and realist film in a style which evoked the news. I finally dove into this project, and I had to keep going. You know that the film had an enormous financial success in Germany, and received the Wetvoll Prize, meaning that it was far above present production and artistic quality. This is a sort of German Oscar—which has the advantage of being accompanied by a considerable reduction in taxes. Do you remember, Herman, what you said of the absence in *The Thousand Eyes* of the marvelous demonic resonance in *Last Will?* I don't believe that you were speaking entirely just about the film. Listen, don't forget that the first takes place in an insane asylum, where the

ghost of Dr. Mabuse visibly takes hold of the brain of a schizophrenic professor who directs the asylum, and the other takes place in the cold reality of
today—where there is no place for ghosts or apparitions, and where the real
fear of atomic war is there every instant. There no longer is this unknown
fear, there no longer are these disquieting mind games, but the Death's Head
of annihilation which, each morning, smiles with lovely teeth on the front
page of every newspaper. I remember very well that, when, after almost 25
years, I reviewed a print of *Last Will* in East Berlin, I found the apparition of
the ghost of Mabuse—or of that which professor Baum imagined to be the
ghost of Mabuse—very much out of style. But I think that beauty and friend-
ship means one should mutually respect the opinions of the other. And you
will very much deceive me, angel, if you don't honestly tell me your deepest
thoughts. I think that friends' quarrels are excellent things. It is very agreeable to be sitting here, drinking and talking. . . .

The film I really wanted to make in Germany was based on an idea of
mine; I had never seen a film—even *Rebel Without a Cause* by Nicholas Ray,
no matter how good—in which the problem of youth had been correctly and
honestly shown. What we call Teddy Boys, black shirts or, in German *"die
Halbstarken,"* it is very easy to criticize them and to say they are bad, but it is
necessary to discover why they are like that. In any case, how can you speak
of a missing demonic resonance in *Last Will* after what the Nazis did during
the Second World War? After that, anything I can do pales in comparison. In
the meantime, the government of West Germany in Bonn gave me the greatest honour for a filmmaker: the "Pellicule d'Or." This blessed event took a
few months to sink in.

Oh, I was very satisfied with *The Thousand Eyes,* not least because I avoided
the disaster of two tear-jerker (*"Schnulzen"*) *Indians.* It was very painful to
work with the climate near New Delhi, a very humid climate, even though
we avoided the monsoons. But I didn't sense any Oriental lassitude stopping
me: I wouldn't permit it. I had an indescribable homesickness, I missed the
United States. *The Tiger* and *The Tomb* were originally shown in Germany on
two different evenings during two hours each. But in America, they were
both reduced to 90 minutes and called *Journey to the Lost City.* They worked
well everywhere, but personally I detested them. People have said to me,
now, they were horrible, the continuity was completely disrupted. We are
completely without defenses when our work is broken into pieces.

In 1957, I was in the United States on New Year's with friends who had emigrated from Germany like me. We were talking about Germany when someone called me. Artur Brauner of CCC Films in Germany wanted me to do the remake of the two Indian films which I had written with Thea von Harbou in 1919 for Joe May's Decla Bioscop company. Originally, I wrote them to make my debut as a director, but when the screenplay was finished, a few problems got in the way, among which was the death of my mother. We were in the mountains when Thea von Harbou, who wasn't yet my wife, came to me and said, "Look, they have decided to make it themselves." They had no confidence in me. You could never know how much that bothered me at the time. In 1957, I hadn't seen Germany for 24 years. The Indian films were made only because the producer demanded I make a German film on a popular subject for 4 million marks, which would allow for a certain international success—America included. It was a challenge which was amusing and agreeable. The subject lent itself to many possibilities, so I accepted. But, when I read the screenplay which they gave me, I cried, "I can't do this!" In the first place, this sort of stupid sentimentality doesn't interest me, and it isn't even good melodrama! That's why I rewrote the script.

Oh, I've had numerous ideas for films which have never been made. One, *Behind Closed Doors,* was about the lack of human space today. We're prisoners of money, and because of this we have lost all contact with real life, real love; we do nothing but look to satisfy our needs, forgetting our families, our children. . . . This, if you will, in a word, is the man who has lost his soul. I believe this is not only true of Germany, but of the entire world. Another project, *The Running Man,* which I had in 1953, recounted the story of a man taken with amnesia who goes through the film from street to street, effectively running from his responsibilities. But that doesn't reveal his repressed desires which he satisfies by committing, for example, some crime, or by living an adventurous life, which makes him into a Jekyll and Hyde personality type. He ends up escaping himself in the middle of his amnesia. This was a remarkable story which was exploited just in this minimum of possibilities—they were numerous, they were passionate. The story was based on something I read in *The New Yorker,* which was titled "Lost." Then there was *The Devil's General,* from Ernst Udet, the German pilot who refused to fly for the Nazis and crashed his own plane. David Selznick contacted me in 1951 to make that film. I was very interested in this project because I liked the Carl Zuckmayer play very much, but I had just that day signed with 20th Century Fox to make *American Guerilla in the Philippines.* When I returned from

Manila, Selznick had given up on the idea. But I had to ask myself honestly if the subject still interested me by then. Having fled Hitler, and being a Catholic German, I was naturally concerned by such a subject, but would it interest the American public? I also had a project about Canaris. This individual had always interested me. In 1955 CCC Films had asked me to direct a film on the revolt of this general against Hitler on July 20, 1944. But that coincided once again with something else: *While the City Sleeps,* with which I had to be careful because that was a story about the press, and we didn't want to be attacked by journalists all over the world.

You know, Herman! Herman! (A loud noise from the next room, where five other people with a tape deck, listening to the sound track of *Contempt* by Jean-Luc Godard, hearing Lang, make a considerable noise. He asks that they lower the volume.)

Herman! You know, I've read many stories in the newspapers on the things people wanted me to do. Don't believe everything you read in the papers. There was *Mistress of the World,* which I refused because our experiences of the last few years have made many of the premises of intrigue laughable, and the public doesn't accept them. Unperturbed, producers announced the film in the papers. They suggested *Die Nibelungen.* I firmly maintained it was impossible. Where will you get the actors? As for legendary individuals, where will they go, how will they speak? What will they say? They announced it again, and again I didn't do it. Then I heard that they wanted to film at the actual place of the action. But where is it? This is a legend! "How fancy can you get?" Next, the same Artur Brauner came to find me, and said he had bought the name of Dr. Mabuse from Norbert Jacques, author of the original novel. Then, why not do a remake of *Last Will?* At first I refused. Then, little by little, an idea grew in my thoughts, because I had read Nazi documents which had recently been published, giving information about Joseph Goebbels. Four hotels were to have been built in Berlin after the German victory in order to allow diplomats from beaten states to visit. In every room there would be a hidden microphone centrally connected so that the government could learn exactly what happened in each room. Taking the idea to the point where television cameras were hidden behind a mirror gave me a point of departure for a post-war Mabuse. In the German version, it was a fanatic who profited from a world gone chaotic by putting into practice the ideas of Mabuse. In the French version—to my great horror—we created the son of Mabuse. I suppose we could have given him a daughter as well. "How fancy can you get?" Seymour Nebenzal, producer of *Last Will*—who still owes me money for *M*, the dog—presented *Last Will* as a probable commercial success, especially given the success of the original. At first I refused, since I had left Mabuse in an asylum at the end of the last film, and I didn't know how to get him out. I only accepted when I realized that there was the possibility of a commentary on Nazism in the subject of an asylum director hypnotized by his own sickness. I was at that time very interested in mental illnesses, having earlier spent eight days in an asylum (for scientific research!). Goebbels of course banned the film on the 29th of March, 1933, and above all, private screenings. But, in my opinion, he had an astonishingly sophisticated vision. There was nothing unpleasant in this intrigue, he said, it is simply the need of a Führer who challenged Dr. Mabuse in the end, and who would save the world from those who would destroy and pervert the true ideal of real values. Goebbels told me elsewhere that years earlier Hitler and he saw *Metropolis* in a small village, and that Hitler wanted me to make Nazi films.

When I tried to make *M* in 1931 (its original title was *The Murderer Among Us*), I received menacing anonymous letters, and I was then told that the main studio at Staaken was off limits. "But why such an incomprehensible conspiracy against a film about a child killer in Dusseldorf?," I asked the studio director. "Ah, I understand," he said, and with a big smile, he gave me the keys to the studio. But I had already seen the Party insignia on the back. I then understood that the Nazis thought the title applied to them. When they found that the film was based on Peter Kürten, the killer of Dusseldorf (whom I knew personally), they consented to let me make the film. The title had to be changed to *M*, for murderer. I have never seen the remake produced by Nebenzal and directed by Joseph Losey. I am certain that you are right when you say that it was ruined. It might interest them to know that I don't think that Nebenzal ever had the rights to remake *M*. They told me that after the last war, he sent some Greek or other Balkan diplomat to Berlin to get the rights from my ex-wife, Thea von Harbou. She sold him the rights (in my opinion she shared them 50/50), for about $4000; she sold the rights to this scoundrel because at that time no American had the right to buy anything on a German subject. But I couldn't contest this because my personal papers were left in Berlin when I fled Hitler, and my business office had been bombed.

In fact, I have never thought that a remake of *M* was possible or desirable. The original was entirely set in the strangeness of the 1930s in Berlin, and around the not so curious situation of crime in the social structure of Germany in the '30s, a situation which is impossible to transpose to the United States. As well, I think that the value of the original film, in that it reveals the interior life of a child killer, has been researched and developed by other directors. I don't think that the second *M* can cause me any blame. In fact, I used real criminals for the part concerning the dregs of society. There were 24 actors arrested during filming.

I read in the papers, a few years ago, that the East Germans hoped to make a film on a Russian lunar landing. They had a print of *Woman in the Moon,* and the production company was told by the authorities that the film had better be scientifically as correct as mine. Walt Disney once made a TV documentary on rocket ships, and asked me permission to insert my scene of the rocket launch. The launch scene used a small plastic model. Experts from Cape Kennedy asked me a few months ago to come for a talk on rocket ships, and they recognized me as their elder. During 1948, I tried to convince some major studios to make a film with rocket ships, a film of the immediate future, in which rockets have not yet reached the moon. I didn't manage to convince any of them, and I believe they had some regrets, much later, to have missed such a commercially certain idea. As I hadn't written a single line on this project, but simply proposed the idea, I had never spoken with Luc Moullet about his book on me because that would have been wrong to let people think I wanted to remake my *Woman in the Moon.* I was shocked to read the advertisements for two American films, *Rocketship XM* and *Destination Moon,* because both films were sold as the first films on rocket ships ever made!

Oh, I received a large number of scripts during my years in the United States, but honestly, I am so lazy that sometimes I didn't even read them. Instead, I went to Palm Springs, where I lived in a small house, made my own meals, watched the impressive street traffic and the women sitting around the pool. . . .

Also in 1948, there was the *Corruption* project, but it didn't go further than a few conversations. *Winchester '73* was also a project for Diana Inc., the production company I ran with Walter Wanger and Joan Bennett. They had an option on the original story by Stuart Lake, but it expired before financing could be arranged. Universal International, which had the rights, didn't

want to extend my option, and wanted to produce the film itself. That's why
I eventually abandoned the idea. They made it under the direction of
Anthony Mann, and had considerable success, but they didn't keep the original idea I had prepared for their script. The subject interested me greatly: a
westerner lost his rifle, a Winchester '73, which was for him the only reason
for living, and the symbol of his strength. He needed to find the rifle or else
find new reasons to live, he needed to find his lost strength. . . .

Don't ask me, baby, if man is good or bad. I think he should get better—
you, you, you! (During the conversation in French, Lang hits the wooden
part of the coffee table)—because, if not, he should destroy himself. If you
can get up in the morning, look in the mirror and shave or put on your
make-up without spitting at that face, then you are "still a good person" (a
phrase found in *The Return of Frank James*).

Yes, I like Westerns. They have a simple but necessary moral. I made three:
The Return of Frank James, Rancho Notorious and *Western Union*. I lived with
the Indians during the filming of the latter, but I knew nothing of the Far
West. Since I've been in America, I've seen many things which American
cineastes haven't seen, because they are too used to seeing them. My film
certainly wasn't a view of the West as it was at the time; in other words, I
didn't show the "old" Far West, but I received letters from older people who
knew the west as pioneers, and they told me that *Western Union* presented
things as they were. But what is reality? I didn't have the intention of showing the Far West as it had been, but the film made the public dream and gave
it a sense of how things had been then. I don't want to say that dreams and
stories are better in films than in reality, but they both have the right to be
used.

You know, I'm having trouble sleeping. Can you sleep? My God, how I
envy you. But when, by chance, I sleep, I dream. Do you dream as well? Yes,
I know the "counting sheep" thing, but I can't imagine sheep and if I can, I
can't get them to jump over the fence!

Yes, the rifle in *Winchester '73* is the symbol of the man's strength. If there
are symbols in films, they should always be motivated by the requirements
of the action. I don't believe films should be made as we make an equation.
For my part, I first have the idea of a silhouette, then people and characters
draw themselves. They live for me . . . I observe different characters in the
darkness of my office, with a coffee and a cigar, neither of which I touch.
When I write a scene, I close my eyes and see the movements, the faces.

Things animate themselves, the people take on bodies in my imagination. I am guided by them in directions which I haven't envisioned in the first place. I live a long time with them before filming. I don't know what happens in my subconscious, that's up to you to discover, and no doubt you have the right to the point of view you adopt.

It would be an error to constantly see symbols in the objects one shows in films. In my films, objects are signs, but very concrete signs. If, for example, Brian Donlevy, in *Hangmen Also Die,* brings a bouquet of flowers, that's because he found a way of meeting the young woman without attracting attention. I believe that Expressionist symbolism is absolutely *passé* (in French during the conversation). I also believe that in *M,* the young girl's rolling ball is not a symbol. And in *Hangmen,* when Alexander Granach's hat, which has been stuffed under a pile of laundry, falls to the ground, that isn't an Expressionist symbol. It signifies the death of Granach, but it is above all an image of a concrete fact. I am always questioned about my "Expressionist period." I respond with: "I don't understand what you mean by that. I am always counted among expressionists, but I personally place myself among the realists. In films, it is too easy to associate ideas and images with things that don't necessarily belong in the film in question. Paying respect to the sign allows it to be perceived with more clarity in the cinema as opposed to the theatre. If you want, one could say the rolling hat in *Hangmen* isn't a symbol in the ordinary sense, but a symbol by association.

In any case, I am now a long way from Expressionism. It is out of style. Just as, when I began to work in the United States, I was rid of symbolism. The Americans said, "We are intelligent enough to understand: it is useless to add symbols." But I was very influenced by Expressionism. One cannot live through an epoch without being influenced by something. In fact, *Caligari* was one of the films which I should have made in 1919 and which I had to abandon because of Erich Pommer, my producer, to make the second part of *Die Spinnen: Das Brillanten Schiff [The Diamond Ship].* The idea of a realist story built around Mayer and Janowitz's original story, that is to say, to tell that story in an insane asylum, that was mine.

In any case, angel, I don't believe in theories. I think that when you have a theory about something, you are already dead. I don't have the time to think about theories. We should create emotions and not follow rules. There are no rules. That's what I answered to someone who reminded me of a phrase of Nietzsche: "I am no one's phrase, I am a man!" As for Nietzsche, his idea of the superman is very strong in Germany, but not in France or the United States.

A director should always have a psychiatrist at his side to tell him what he is doing. Recently, in France, a question was sent to certain directors, asking them how they direct a scene. How do you respond to such a question? This is a moral affair. Today, I would say it is good to do this or that; tomorrow, I would say it is necessary to do things differently. I once travelled by train and now I take a plane, but I couldn't now say trains aren't worth anything. I can't say what I found in Expressionism; all I can say is that I used it, that I tried to master it. I believe that the more we tend towards simplicity, the more we progress.

Which brings me back to the Western. It is a genre full of simple ideas. Each year, there are new ones for the young, because each year there is a new generation. Critics say that in today's war films there is nothing new. But what can one say about war that is new? The important thing is that we repeat it again and again.

I don't work for critics but for youth. I don't work for people my age, because they should already be dead and me with them! One cannot deny the facts, angel: television has eaten away the time we should spend reading; it serves nothing to regret that, better to adapt to it. One always regrets the loss of something one hopes will last forever, but nothing lasts forever, everything changes. . . .

Who wants a whiskey? Some cake? Some milk? What about the people who are with me? Water? Water isn't only illegal here, it is immoral. Don't you agree?

GRETCHEN WEINBERG: *Agreed, Fritz Lang.*
FL: Sometimes I think directors who don't drink, the day the drink they'll make the best film in the world. Don't you think?

GW: *I think so, Fritz Lang.*
FL: You know, angel, sometimes I imagine you speak solely to give me pleasure. You know, when I was young and studying at L'Ecole des Beaux-Arts in Munich, between courses, I had to live, and to pay for the courses. Well, I drew for newspapers, fashion drawings and advertisements. I even painted a fresco for a bordello! Tonio, where are you going? Sit down!

GW: Ja, gnadige Herr, kuss Hande! [Yes sire, your grace, I kiss your hand!] (12:30am. Lang and Tonio Selwart start telling anecdotes about the "old days" which throw them into laughter. Willy Ley begins to talk.)

LEY: One of the most important scientific articles I ever wrote, perhaps the most important of the century, was on something which hadn't yet happened: the flight to Mars of the American spaceship Mariner D4. That flight hadn't yet happened; they hadn't had that success. I haven't yet finished the book which I wrote on that flight. The last page is white. How will it finish? Who knows? (Lang listens attentively.) With today's technology, we can go to the moons of Jupiter. Not in five or six years, but today.

"Who said that," asks Lang?

LEY: Wernher (von Braun) said it. I am 95% certain about the rocket to Mars.

"Put the television on," says Lang, "perhaps that news is already on."

LEY: Not yet. In three months we'll know.

FL: At the time I made *Woman in the Moon,* the sets were made based on the opinions of well-known astronauts who had studied the moon for years and who were qualified to give opinions on its surface. In 1959, we saw the dark side of the moon. A Soviet photo showed the entire world something which no one had ever seen. It was the most sensational event of the year, remember? Whoever doubted photography would be part of progress couldn't any longer. The camera on a lunar rocket recorded, transmitted, confirmed. But what had really happened? What was brought to us in those pictures of the dark side of the moon? The question is still unanswered.

I believe we need to continue to make rocket ships because we are still a young country. But Willy, my dear ["*mein Liebchen*"], I believe there is no place in the world for individualism. The solo flight of Lindbergh across the Atlantic, this effort of a lone man, can't happen today. The astronauts, Glenn or Gagarin, are not symbols of individualism, but of the work done by thousands of men. Man is just a part of a larger mechanism. One minute, Wilhelm, let me say this again: as I showed in *Metropolis,* in a very symbolic way, man has become almost a part of the machine, so I ask myself now if this isn't an unconscious manifestation of something which really exists today. When we look at the pictures of John Glenn, we see that he is practically a living part of the machine. The destiny of the Greeks and the Romans were controlled by their gods. Today, there is something more: you must fight at every instant those aspects of society which tend to devour the individual. *You Only Live Once* is also the story of a man who tries to live an honest life. He is pursued, fighting alone against the menacing power of a society which he must fight. To fight, that is what counts. If we think there is the smallest chance to succeed, we must continue to do what we believe is good. Perhaps this is a sort of martyrdom, even if I don't believe it, but it is the essence of life, fighting for the causes we believe to be right. That is truly the problem that has always interested me—not obsessed or possessed me, because I was possessed only once—that's all, in one way or another it is inevitable. You get caught in the works, and you can't escape. But aside from that, what I always wanted to show and define is the attitude of struggle that must be adopted in the face of destiny. Whether or not the individual wins this fight, what counts is the fight itself, because it is vital.

"You were speaking of Greek Tragedy," said Willy Ley. "That reminds me of what I would have done if I hadn't become a scientist: write a study of *The Odyssey* to try to discover a new 'route' for heroes, taking into account the point of view of Odysseus, a man of his time, thinking of the terms at work in his time. I've always thought, as well, of a similar manner of Bible study, a line by line commentary by a man of science. Do you remember *The Odyssey*, Fritz?

I just then turned to Capri, my dear ["*mein Liebchen*"]. In fact, scenes in *Contempt* which show my version of *The Odyssey* weren't filmed by me.

(Ley cites some lines in German from *The Odyssey*.)

"I remember the route of *The Odyssey*," Lang says. I have been from Tarsus to Phoenecia, from there to the islands. We studied it in school."

"Yes," says Ley, "and on the inside cover is a map of the voyage."

"Fritz, my preferred genius," says Tonio Selwart, "I recently saw *Hangmen* again. It is extraordinary. You really are a genius. Everyone remembers me in the role of the Gestapo officer who picks a pimple on his cheek. People I don't know have come to see me by plane, have stopped me in the street, I am famous because of that friendly Nazi. Hangmen also die!

F L : They should die! The other films which use scripts I wrote but didn't direct were: the third and fourth episodes of *Die Spinnen* in 1919, for Decla-Bioscop. An organisation of super criminals wanted to take over the world thanks to a fabulous Inca treasure. The idea of a master criminal anarchist with supreme power was to become one of my favorite themes. Parts 3 and 4,

Das Geheimnis der Sphinx [*The Secret of the Sphinx*] and *Um Asiens Kaiserkrone* [*About the Imperial Crown of Asia*], were never filmed.

In 1933 I hoped to go to Vienna, where I was born, to make "Die Legende vom Letzen Wiener Fiaker" ["The Legend of the Last Viennese Fiacre"] after an original story, but events didn't permit, so it was never made. It was the story of an 'idyl' in the "Hauptallee"; where cars weren't admitted, only graceful carriages. At the fall of the Hapsburg dynasty, a decree appeared: Cars would now be admitted in the "Hauptallee." The heart of a coachman, in one moment, was broken, and he went to heaven with his horse and carriage. But St. Peter stopped him at the gates. "You can't bring them here," he said. "If I can't bring them, I won't enter either," said the coachman. They asked God to arbitrate, and He said, "That's a charming horse, but I can't break the laws." But the coachman made such an eloquent plea for his horse which had served him so well that God smiled and said, "Very well, you will be my one and only coachman, you will drive me." Happily, the coachman and his horse entered Paradise and the wheels of the carriage were transformed into stars, the stars of the coachman who drove God's special carriage.

The Man Behind You in 1934. An original story by me based on *Dr. Jekyll and Mr. Hyde,* but retold in modern psychiatric terms. I wrote it for MGM without ever making it. I've always kept the rights.

Hell Afloat was the same, in the same year. An original story by Oliver H.P. Garrett and me, on the disaster at S.S. Morro Castle. It was also written for MGM. We didn't make it because David Selznick, who was supposed to produce it, left to found his own production company.

Men Without a Country in 1939. It was an original story by Jonathan Latimer and me for Paramount, the first anti-Nazi story written for the screen. Paramount still owns it. Three spies: one Japanese, one Nazi, and one "international" were looking for the secret of a horrible invention of war. The head of the spy network worked for a beauty institute which served as headquarters for the network. His adversary is a member of the American G-2, navy intelligence. The head of the spies found the secret armament: a blinding ray (I was, as you know, briefly blinded during WW I). The spy also met the inventor, who is himself blind, but who moves around his laboratory as though he can see. The inventor blinds the spy with his ray and the last scene would have shown takes of these two blind men colliding with one another. Paramount used that last scene for another of its films. A few years ago in Hollywood, I was shown another film: *Dillinger.* During the screening,

I said to myself that I had already seen that somewhere. In fact, the producer had bought one of my films and used certain scenes in *Dillinger*. But I didn't remember having directed these scenes myself before leaving the screening room. This reminds me of a situation that took place after a private screening of *Fury*. There was a huge silence; no one wanted to say anything. Then the producer began to question the screenwriter (not the director, of course, because for them the director is nothing). Then he turned towards me and accused me of having changed the scene. I asked him how I could do such a thing since I didn't speak a word of English. Mr. Mankiewicz asked for a copy of the screenplay and, after reading it, said, "Dammit, you are right. But it was different on the screen." And perhaps it was different for him. (This story is retold in *Contempt*.)

From 1938 to '39, I did research for the story of a lost mine. We called it *Americana,* and it covered a period of 100 years of history of the country around this abandoned mine. We didn't make it, but that interested Darryl F. Zanuck, who was also as fascinated as I about Westerns, and proposed to me *The Return of Frank James,* my first Western.

You know, baby, I have never made a film which made a compromise. That's one of life's important things, and which we have a tendency to forget. A producer—during the war—called me into his office, at a moment when I wasn't working, and gave me a point of departure for a film. It was extremely favourable towards war: I refused to make it. Another time, I was in a "Hollywood" ennui. It was 1934, I had just arrived and didn't speak, nor write, nor read a single word of English. I received a letter, a pamphlet from some American Democratic Society which asked me to sign I don't know what. I saw there were other signatories, I saw Thomas Mann and some others. I said, "Perfect, Thomas Mann and democracy, I feel strong about democracy, that's perfect." I signed. I discovered later that it was a cover for a Communist organisation. I couldn't find any work in Hollywood for a year and a half. Then I made *Fury*.

In 1953, to give another example of what a filmmaker must deal with, I only had $125 in the bank to live for a month. I had to do something. Harry Cohn, the head of Columbia, hired me and one day at the studio, someone called me: "Harry Cohn"—who was the worst of all—"wants you to have lunch with him." Okay. I put on a tie and since the one thing which really bothered him was my monocle, I wore my glasses. Cohn came in, we were both sitting at the table, he looks at me and says, "Hey, Prussian, where's your monocle?" So I said, "Harry"—it was Harry from henceforth—"when I was too poor to buy glasses, I had to wear a monocle, but now that you pay me so much money, I can buy two. That's when I made *The Big Heat* for Columbia, as well as *Human Desire.* You know, angel, I've always asked myself why it was called "Human Desire"—what other type of desire is there? "How fancy can you get?" Believe me, baby, I think the same about *Human Desire* as you do. Jean Renoir's *La Bête Humaine,* on which it was based, is a much better film. One can't compare the two. Before making it, I saw Renoir's film to be sure that my point of view would be different. I made it because I had a contract. If I had refused, they could have said to me, "Okay, but if we have another film for you, you won't make it or the money." That could have lasted one or two years. So, I accepted.

Another film I wanted to make at that time had water as its subject. A producer named I. G. Goldsmith found me a project on the problems of irrigation between California and Arizona. As I've always been interested by this type of project, I said yes. But there have been so many conflicts between the two states that California didn't want the project considered unless both sides of the conflict were shown, which finished the project for me.

In 1943, there was *The Golem,* an original screenplay by Henrik Galeen and Paul Falkenberg. That was the modern version of the old Jewish legend which took place in Prague during the war. In 1946, *The Body Snatcher,* based on a story by Stevenson on the looting of tombs—but the title was bought by another company. In 1950, aside from *Winchester '73,* I worked briefly on *All the King's Men* by Robert Penn Warren, but it was the film Rossen did which was made: the film on Huey Long. In 1956, *Dark Spring,* for my own company, Fritz Lang Productions, made for United Artists, was written for Susan Strasberg by Michel Latté, and the same year *The Diary of Anne Frank.* In 1963, Rolf Hochuth's play *The Deputy.* I saw it in New York, but I wondered how one could make a film out of that play. It was too long, had too much talking, and had very little action. In any case, I had access to the German version, which was two times as long. I would like to find more varied material to make a film. Speaking of which, in Germany, they wanted to do a play based on *M,* and they wanted me to direct it . . .

I didn't want to make more films, but the next year, Jeanne Moreau sent me a note at the Cannes Festival, saying that she would be happy to act in a film of mine if by chance I decided to come out of retirement. I told her that I didn't make films any more. But I worked on a screenplay . . . that was called *Death of a Career Girl*—I don't know what to call it in French, there isn't an expression for "career girl." It is a critique of that type of woman who is looking for a career but forgets life, and finally dies, or worse, when the heart is already dead before the body. It is taken from an original story of mine. Do you think a woman can live life without a man? (Everyone gives his or her opinion.) Don't give me that, baby, you can't say that to me! No generalities, clichés, slogans or evasive responses. Let's be rude, which is to say, honest. Honesty above all: that is the first human virtue. Don't lie to me, baby. Doesn't matter what the others say or think. The question is: What do you think? You are part of the young generation. Don't you want to embarrass me? I adore you, yes, you, though Lord knows I don't know why!

(Lang then reads some extracts of his screenplay): "She finds herself in an expensively furnished room, walls covered with paintings by Picasso, Chagall. On an easel is a wood engraving of the Redeemer carrying his cross . . . She is in a room full of soldiers. Can we ask soldiers to forget they are soldiers? Can we wish them to remember they are men?

She gives herself to the captain. In his arms, she puts her gold cross between her teeth to stop herself from screaming. . . ."

"I am sure this will be a good screenplay," someone says.

"Why," asks Lang?

"Well, because all your films are good."

"Why?"

"It will be a great honour to read it."

"And a pleasure too, sir."

"I hope so. And don't call me sir. I am not a sir. And why do you all call me Mister Lang? The first initial is F and the rest is ritz (It is 2:30am).

Part Two

Between the first part of this "Viennese Night"—strange confession, a soliloquy in the words of Fritz Lang, charming and moving, on important and unimportant things—which appeared in issue no. 169, and the second, was an interval of 10 months. The filmmaker was hesitant to let us publish this second part of what was for him nothing more than a conversation of an evening like many others, spent with friends, carefree and relaxed, where the talk wasn't official and where, to the contrary, everything ran towards the most liberal amblings of an intimate meditation. Precisely because of this liberty, this semi-abandonment, this proximity to which no interview could ever pretend to reach, in our eyes, is worth the entire price of these dreamy words: Fritz Lang understood, once he read the transcription, that the spontaneity should not be altered. So we thank him here, as well as our friend Herman Weinberg and his daughter Gretchen.

(It is very late. Despite that, Fritz Lang continues his monologue. . . .)

FL: It is true that I acted in certain films at the beginning of my career. I was a "dramaturge," in charge of writing stories at Decla, and the little bit of money I made acting helped me to live a little better. In a Joe May film, *Hilde Warren und der Tod [Hilde Warren and Death],* for which I wrote the script in 1917 in a hospital where I was convalescing from war wounds, I played four roles: an old priest, Death, a young courier and another role which I don't remember. . . . (he stops and looks at the ceiling). Destiny is strange. . . . Fifty years later, I am once again acting, in *Le Mépris,* a Jean-Luc Godard film with Bardot, and which they call *Contempt* in this country. I'm playing my proper role, a movie director, and I myself wrote a good part of my lines. . . .

They discovered by chance a print of *Hilde Warren* in Germany and they asked me to come to a screening of the film. . . . At that time, I did two or three scripts. The first was, I believe, *The Wedding in the Eccentric Club,* which Joe May made in a rush to do the direction and the screenplay himself.

You asked me, Willy, of certain types of technical problems we ran up against. I'm coming to them. But, you see, it was easier to make films in Europe and to make them out of nothing. For example, we weren't obliged by producers (assuming we had one!) to hire a big star: that is an American invention. The success of the films we made was almost always due to the story or to the director, and rarely to the actors. I met new people in all sorts of places. I responded to all the letters sent to me, and I met all those who wish to meet me. Brigitte Helm, a blonde with an interesting face, was no more than 16 years old when her mother brought her to the studio. She wanted to become an actress and play in Schiller's *Mary Stuart,* the play about the poor queen who is locked up by the underhanded Elizabeth, then killed. I believed I had guessed the role she wanted to play (the sympathetic one, of course), but she surprised me by saying "Elizabeth!" I then thought I was dealing with a real talent. Another time, during a two-day press conference in Vienna, another mother brought her daughter to me. The daughter was also very beautiful and very blonde. She had an interesting face. I told her to come and see me in Berlin if she had the serious intention of becoming an actress. Later she came to the studio at Neubabelsberg, and I gave her the role of the diabolical, bad spy with the childlike face in *Spies*. Her name was Lie Dyers. It was also at that time that I saw Gerda Maurus who did very well in a small Viennese role. I was very impressed by the fact that she exploited all the facets of her character, even a hole in her stockings! I gave her one of the principal roles in *Spies,* and later a small role in *Woman in the Moon*. I've always like working with young and unknown actors. They're like fields that haven't yet been cultivated, they're fresh talents. Even if they are of course more technically difficult to work with than seasoned actors, the result, in the long run, is better. Older actors will say to you, "I had a great success in such and such a film, playing the role in such and such a way," and I am forced to respond, "Yes, but that was another film and another role." It is sometimes impossible to break this kind of prejudice. These actors are the same in all their films, which are made uniquely around their unchangeable personality. You could take the essential elements of one of their films and put them in another without anyone noticing the difference. With young actors, it isn't necessary to be bothered about the subject of dangerous "ideas," because they're in a hurry to carve out new paths. (Lang adjusts his eye-patch and quietly continues.)

To make a film for one person, whether producer, director, actor or critic, makes no sense. The cinema has always has been and should continue to be a mass art. Nonetheless, while I don't always think of the public when I make a film, it is probably instinctive that I adapt to certain of their reactions. I have always had a passion for the public. The public changes; I change. Today's youth don't think or live as they did thirty years ago, thank God! And no director can make a film as he did back then. World War I caused a large number of changes in the structure of the world; in Europe, an entire generation lost hope. Young people were engaged in a cultural struggle, declared open rebellion against the previous order, against formalism, passing brutally from the naive 19th century to the age of questionable battles with deadly outcomes; but today, to adopt a similar attitude would be to tilt against windmills.

But today as yesterday, cinema is a vice. I adore it. I've often said that I am all for the Art of this century. It is a vice that I adore, a bad habit (I have only bad habits). Without films, I couldn't live. I love this art form which has sadly become, in most countries, an industry. And in creating an industry, they have almost destroyed an art form. I have always given great attention to the content of films because it seems to me to be more important than form. It is a question of rendering the idea that I had, the phrases that I want to speak to the public. But perhaps the path for doing so isn't unique: it depends on the conception which each of us has of directing. Godard adores improvising, while I like to know exactly what I am going to do when I arrive on the set. I change practically nothing of what I have in my head. But for the actors, I think they should have as much freedom as possible. Personally, I don't restrain them as much as certain filmmakers.

To direct an actor, I must above all make him understand the spirit of his role, the foundations of his character, even if that in fact doesn't enter directly into the events of the film. Sometimes that makes me angry. . . . I sweat bullets to do it, but in the end, I am very happy when I am directing. It isn't a second life for me: it is my life. A good director doesn't, as many do, have to show (I want to say this in jest) to an actor exactly how he should interpret his role. If he has to do that, then the work of an actor is nothing more than copying me. Imagine that: twenty little Fritz Langs running around on the screen! God save us! I simply want to help the actors discover by themselves the role they are interpreting. I try to explain to them what constitutes the personality of their character. I never insist on something that the actor cannot sense: one cannot force this. My only desire is to wake up what he carries in himself, to help extract from his unconscious and to create a character that he didn't know he had deep within him. There are good directors and bad . . . if we can also call someone a director who is a bad director. He would say to an actor, "You have read the scene, you know the role, now go to the door, play the scene and when you have finished, go through the other door." That man is not a director, but a cop who is directing traffic.

(3:35am. Still drinking. Herman Weinberg opens his briefcase and brings out some photos that he spreads around the middle of the table where Lang rests his hands.)

Did you know that I have a plan in hand for each of my films! (He looks at the first picture.) Ah, that's Brigitte Helm in *Metropolis*. God, she was beautiful! *Metropolis*, you know, was born from my first sight of the skyscrapers of New York in October 1924, and then I took myself to Hollywood where UFA sent me to study American production methods. It was terribly hot that season. . . . In any case, while visiting New York, I thought that it was the crossroads of multiple and confused human forces, blinded and knocking into one another, in an irresistible desire for exploitation, and living in perpetual anxiety. I spent an entire day walking the streets. The buildings seemed to be a vertical sail, scintillating and very light, a luxurious backdrop, suspended in the dark sky to dazzle, distract and hypnotize. At night, the city did not simply give the impression of living: it lived as illusions live. I knew I should make a film of all these impressions. When I returned to Berlin, in the middle of a crisis, Thea von Harbou began to write the script. We imagined, she and I, an idle class, living in a large city thanks to the subterranean work of thousands of men on the point of revolting, lead by a daughter of the people. To put down this rebellion, the head of the city demanded that its experts create a robot in the image of the daughter in question. But the robot Maria turned on her people and caused the workers to destroy the "machine" which was the heart of the city, which controlled it and gave it life. (He sighs softly and we watch.) I've often said I didn't like *Metropolis* because I can't accept the leitmotif of the message in the film. It is absurd to say that the heart is the intermediary between the hands and the brain, that is to say, the employer and the employee. The problem is social and not moral. Naturally, during the making of the film, I liked it, if not I wouldn't have continued to work. . . . But later, I began to understand what didn't work. . . . I thought, for example, that one of the faults was the way in which I showed the work of man and machine together. You remember the clocks and the man who worked in harmony with them? He should become, so to speak, part of the machine. Well, that seemed to be too symbolic, too simplistic in the evocation of what we call the evils of mechanization. As well, a few years ago, I had to revise my judgement again, at the spectacle of our astronauts walking around the earth. It was the experts, they were prisoners of their space capsule, nothing else—or almost, a part of the machine that carried them. . . .

(He looks at other pictures of *Metropolis:* the children of the workers fleeing the invading waves, the robot-woman, the revolt of the workers in the machine room. . . .) Well, there is the Shuftan Process, it was Eugen Shuftan who did it. . . . You asked me, Willy, which technical problems we had, well, this scene was filmed thanks to mirrors. (Lang shows a picture of the room with the machine and another of the immense stadium for the children of the ruling class.) Shuftan scratched the surface on certain parts of the mirror; he placed it across from the camera lens so that one part of the set, constructed by a human ladder, appeared in the mirror, which reflected a miniature set representing the machines at work. These miniatures enlarged the real set, which would have been too expensive and too complicated to construct for such a short scene. This combination of reality and artifice was photographed (instead of making them in the lab as we would do now), and that was obviously due to the genius of Schuftan.

(He takes another picture, showing a city with modern buildings with an "avant-garde" conception of cars and planes.)

We constructed a miniature set of the street, 7 or 8 meters long, in an old studio with glass walls, and we moved the little cars by hand, centimeter by centimeter, framing each movement, and filmed this image by image. We put the planes in and filmed them in the same way. That scene, which lasted only one or two minutes on the screen, took six days to film! The difficulties that we met, finally, had nothing to do with filming, but with the lab work. The cameraman told the technicians to develop the film normally. But the head of the lab, knowing the time that we had taken to film that short scene, decided to develop the enlargement himself. No one judged it necessary to say to him that, for reasons of perspective, the cameraman had filmed the background a little unfocused in order to give the impression of great distance. The head of the lab began then to develop the negative by defining the background and not the foreground! The dimensional scale was, obviously, destroyed. I tried to keep calm. "These things happen, children, I said. Let's do it over!" And we did. (The first thing I discovered in making films is that we don't make them alone. Your team helps you. And I had a remarkable team.) As for the "videophone" scene, it was done by projecting a part of the film behind a telephone, across a translucent screen, one or two feet behind. That was the first back-projection, the first transparency. . . . We hadn't realized the importance of what we had done, otherwise we would have made a fortune for a process which is universally employed today. At the time, we knew only that there was a problem and we had to solve it. My cameraman, Gunther Rittau, decided not to use trick photography, he used his intelligence to arrive at the solution: he placed the camera in sync with a projector that projected the shadow of a man on the "videophone." That was done with linked rods with mobile joints going from the camera to the projector which were, because of the film set, far enough from each other. Then, when the scene began, the two machines functioned at the same time perfectly together. The flooding of the workers' city was real, filmed in normal scale. Hoses at street level projected the water like real geysers.

Another camera was occupied with the robot Maria. The concentric rings of light which surrounded her and which moved from top to bottom was, in fact, a little golden ball, rapidly turning in a circle, and filmed on black velvet. We superimposed these shots in the laboratory on the shot of the sitting robot that we had already filmed. . . .

The city lit up at night was an animated drawing. The way in which we filmed the explosion of the machine (you remember?) had been one of the first uses of the subjective camera, and gave the public the impression that the two actors actually felt the shock. The camera was attached to a swinging pulley on a vertical board and advanced toward the machine that was on the set, then was retracted to give the impression of an explosion.

Sergei Eisenstein was in the studio at that time and we had a controversy over the mobile and fixed cameras, but we didn't discuss it for long because of filming. I expected him to come back to it later, but he had left Berlin and I never saw him again. I was told that he did a study of my work on the first *Mabuse* (which, I'm told, he edited in Russia).

Opinions were very diverse over the subject of *Metropolis*. H. G. Wells thought that it was the most stupid film he had ever seen, but Sir Arthur Conan Doyle said, "I loved it beyond my wildest dreams."

Look at this photo: This is Paul Richter in *Die Nibelungen*, when he got the javelin in the back. Those are real flowers on the border of the fountain; we planted the seeds in autumn, and in the spring the "set" was ready. . . . Do you know how the rainbow was done at the beginning of *Nibelungen?* With a superimposition of the mountain, done in the studio, and an arch drawn in chalk on a black card. When the sword splits the feather, it was in effect two feathers that fell, and filmed in reverse.

Since we're talking about camera effects, there are some that could only be done thanks to make-up. For example, in *The Last Will of Doctor Mabuse*, when Dr. Baum meets the ghost of Mabuse at night, he sees on the head of the ghost the living brain he had dissected the same morning, in order to find what anomaly had made Mabuse into a great criminal. Here's how that was done: we had a special crane on which were glass tubes in the form of a brain. The tubes were filled with mercury, the type of liquid that would move when Mabuse moved. Between the glass tubes, the makeup artist had placed locks of real white hair, like Mabuse had when alive, which gave the public the impression of seeing his brain through his skin. To increase the horror, half of an eggshell was placed on each eye and the cornea was painted in a deformed way . . . (Lang smiles and his face is veiled.) But that was the happiest time of my life and nothing in the world could have made me want to miss it. . . . It was like a great college: we spent long hours, after work, in the cafeteria, discussing the film, my collaborators and me. . . . It was like we revisited our college days together.

(Lang takes the photo of a man in the street, sinking and shaking his head.) Lorre. I discovered him for *M*, you know. . . . He died in Hollywood last month. . . . I liked him very much . . . we had been friends for 35 years. (Lang raises his eyes and grimaces.)

After the large frescoes of *Die Nibelungen, Metropolis* and *Woman in the Moon*, I was more interested in human beings for the motives of their acts. Contrary to what many people think, *M* wasn't taken from the life of the infamous killer of Dusseldorf, Peter Kürten. It happened that he had just begun his series of murders at the time Thea von Harbou and I were writing the screenplay. The script was completed before he was caught. In fact, the first idea for the subject of *M* came to me when reading an article in the newspaper. I always read newspapers for a point of departure of a story. At that time, I was working with "Scotland Yard" in Berlin (at Alexanderplatz), and I had access to certain confidential files. These were reports on certain unnamed killers like Grossman in Berlin, the terrible Ogre of Hanover (who had killed so many young people) and other criminals of the same ilk. For the judgment in *M*, I received the unwanted help of an organization of wrongdoers, among whom I had made friends at the beginning of my research for the film. In fact, I used 12 or 14 of these outlaws, who were frightened at the idea of appearing in front of my camera because they had already been photographed by the police. Others would have been happy to help me, but they weren't known by the police. I was completing filming these scenes with real criminals when I was informed that the police were on the way. I asked my friends if they couldn't stay for the two final scenes. They agreed, and I filmed rapidly. When the police arrived, the scenes were in the can, and my "actors" had all disappeared into the scenery. . . .

(Lang takes another picture.)

Marlene . . . in *Rancho Notorious*. The original title was "Chuck-a-Luck," which is the name of a ranch in the film, of a game of chance, and finally the title of a song of which we hear fragments throughout the film. The idea of using a song for technical as well as dramatic reasons to advance the action interested me, and proved to be the first time a song had been used in such a way in a Western. (*High Noon* did it later.) With five or six verses of the song, I quickly made the point and I also avoided certain things that would have been bothersome for the public and without importance for the film.

What I wanted to show in *Rancho Notorious* was a young woman who owned a ranch, a sort of retreat for outlaws, opposed to a celebrated killer who had become too old to draw quickly. Enter into the game a young man who is quick on the draw. The eternal theme of the Western. Mr. Howard Hughes, who owned RKO, the company for which I made the film, changed the title to *Rancho Notorious* because, he said, no one will understand what "Chuck-a-Luck" means. But in Europe do we understand any better "Rancho Notorious"?

(Lang stops and lights a cigar.)

Unfortunately, we directors have little control over this type of thing. You know, there is no copyright for a director in the film industry; I've been told, more or less, that was the case in France. But there is one thing we have in the US, of which I approve, and which is unknown in Europe, and that is the "Preview." If those who are called producers were humans and real friends of the director, instead of being jealous, they would realize that there is only one way to judge the merits of a film, and that is of course to see if the public likes it . . . to use a preview. Once, in one of my films, there was a scene with Ida Lupino and Dana Andrews which the producer didn't like, but which I found very funny and very good. For a week, I argued with him about the quality of that scene, but he wasn't convinced and he remained obstinate that he wanted to cut it. I said, "Why not let the preview decide?" He organized one to prove I was wrong. But the public liked the scene, they laughed and applauded. The producer was furious and very spiteful. He said to my editor, Gene Fowler, "I'll continue to organize previews for this film until I find an audience that doesn't like the scene, then I will cut it."

What I think of producers, I said in the Godard film. After everything I said on the subject, I believe I will never have another proposal to make a film. . . . I have a phrase in *Contempt* in which I believe deeply: "Death isn't a solution."

Listen, Herman, suppose I am in love with a woman. She betrays me. I kill her. What's left for me? I've lost my love because she is obviously dead. If, instead of killing her, I had killed her lover, she would hate me and I would have still lost her love. No, children, death is not a solution.

If I had been associated with a producer, I could never have made *M*. What producer would have wanted a film without a love story, or where the hero is a child killer? As *M* was my first talking film, I had some experiences with sound that were obviously not possible in silent films. Do you remember the blind beggar who went to the beggars' market to rent a hand organ? When he plays a piece, some of the notes ring in his ear; he brusquely puts his hands on his ears to avoid hearing these discordant sounds, and at the same moment, the music stops in the film. There are other moments where I used sound: the footsteps in the strange silence of a street at night, or the heavy breathing of a child killer. . . . But, just as sound can lend intensity to a scene, the deliberate suppression of an action can augment the dramatic content. Let me explain. . . . When the child is killed, her little ball rolls away and finally stops in a hedge. The audience identified with the little girl, and beyond that, by association, they know that with the stopped movement of the ball, the life of the little girl is stopped as well. I could not of course show the horrible sexual violence done to that child, but in not showing it, I obtained more reaction from the audience than if I had shown the act in detail. I forced the spectator to use his own imagination. As well, a simple procedure can increase the intensity of a scene by showing what the actor is supposed to be thinking. Do you remember the mobile "gadget" in the toy store window? An arrow moved up and down towards a bull's eye. For the murderer, that was a sexual signal about which the audience was fully aware.

(Lang takes a picture showing the face of man in a Nazi uniform.)

Hans von Twardowsky . . . Heydrich in *Hangmen Also Die*. There was something very disagreeable with that film. It had very little success in 1944: people told me that it reminded them too much of the realities of war. But, 19 years later, in Paris, the film was well liked by the critics. Even today, it seems to me that *Hangmen Also Die* shows the fight of the entire population of Prague against Fascist troops. The final title, which says "Not the end," was in fact prophetic because the same thing is happening right now, except that the invaders are coming from the other side!

I have always been interested by battles, by all forms of battle, against the police, government corruption, that of children against their parents who don't understand them. . . .

Ah, Tracy in *Fury*. . . . (Lang looks closely at a picture of Spencer Tracy with a small dog.) When I made this film on lynching, I could not hope to stop this odious practice; I could only put my finger on the question—otherwise

I would have gone into politics. It's always thus: I can only show certain things and say, "I believe this is reality. Look." That's all I can do; I am not a miracle worker. I don't consider myself an artist. . . . "Artist" is only a word. I have made many films . . . I am a filmmaker, a director, nothing more, nothing less.

(He looks at the color picture of a young Marilyn Monroe in *Clash By Night*).

Such a beautiful young child, so misguided. I liked her very much, but in the film, Stanwyck was the real star, and she never complained about the number of retakes Monroe required.

(He leans over the pictures.) So many pictures. Henry Fonda and Sylvia Sydney in *You Only Live Once*, Walter Pidgeon and Joan Bennett in *Man Hunt*, Randy Scott in *Western Union*, Edward G. Robinson in *Scarlet Street*, Dana Andrews and Ida Lupino in *While the City Sleeps*, Debra Paget in the two Indian films. . . .

(Lang adjusts the eye patch and begins to meticulously stack the pile in front of him.)

I have often said that a director, working with actors, should be a sort of psychoanalyst. Not for the actors themselves, of course, but for their characters. They exist in the first place on paper; the director has to make them live for the actor, then for the audience. Once in Hollywood, a writer said to me, "I know exactly what you were thinking when you did such and such a scene in *M*," and I responded, "Tell me." He spent a long time explaining his theory, and he was completely wrong. That's what I thought at the time, but years later, during a press conference in Paris, while I was re-telling that story, I stopped because I suddenly realized that there could be a profound truth in such things . . . that what we call the "touch" of a director comes from his subconscious—and he himself is unconscious of this during filming. Sometimes, as well, I think that a good critic is a sort of psychoanalyst himself, and that he could probably tell me why I did such and such a scene in a certain way. . . . But it is a double-edged sword. I knew a writer whom I liked very much, he was psychoanalyzed, and two years later, he was incapable of writing. I believe our creative work is the result of certain frustration, no perhaps "frustration" isn't the exact word—neurosis would be better. But when these frustrations or neuroses disappear, what happens then?

For me, a film is a child that I bring into the world. When I have given it life, if I can say this, I abandon it. . . . When I finish a film, I don't want to see it again. I can't do anything more for it. It has its own life and is no more a part of mine. Often I am asked which of my films I prefer. Does a mother choose one child over another? A mother gives birth only to one child at a time, a director gives birth to a film at least three times: the first time, when he works on the screenplay, the second in making the film, the third in editing it. I believe, nonetheless, that the films which I prefer are *M, The Woman in the Window, Scarlet Street,* and *While the City Sleeps.*

It is difficult to say, when I think about it, what is the essential theme of my films. . . . It is possibly the struggle of the individual against fate—the eternal problem of the ancient Greeks, the battle against the Gods, Prometheus's fight against Destiny. It's the same thing today: we fight against laws, we fight against rules that seem neither good nor just. We are always fighting. I believe this combat is more important than the result. . . . The "happy ending," does it really exist?

Well, children, it is already daylight. Let's stop this stupid conversation about me. . . .

(Herman Weinberg lifts his glass and recites some dialogue from *Contempt:* "He who knows and doesn't know what he knows is sleeping. Wake him up. He who knows and knows what he knows is a master. Follow him . . .")

Interview with Fritz Lang

ALEXANDER WALKER/1967

ALEXANDER WALKER HAS BEEN film critic of the London Evening Standard since 1960 and three times named "Critic of the Year" in the annual British Press Awards. He has written over twenty books on aspects of Anglo-American cinema, the latest being *Stanley Kubrick, Director* (Norton, 1999).

LANG: The director, in my opinion, is the one who keeps everything together. Primarily, the basic element for the film in my opinion is the script, and the director has to be the servant to the script—he shouldn't make too many detours. In the last years, the part of the producer has taken over certain things that I think a director should do. I think a producer could be a very good friend of a director if he keeps away from him things which hamper him in his tasks, but usually, as it is now in most studios, the producer tells him what he must do. In this case I call the director a "traffic cop."

WALKER: *Is it correct that you took the story of* M *from the newspapers about the story of the Dusseldorf murders?*
LANG: So many things have been written about *M*, it has become so to speak *the* motion picture. I made it 37 years ago, and it plays constantly in Switzerland, France and even the States. If a film survives so long then there may be a right to call it a piece of art.

The story came out of the fact that I originally wanted to make a story

---

From BBC Radio (1967). Published with permission of the BBC and Alexander Walker.

about a very, very nasty crime. I was married in these days and my wife, Thea von Harbou, was the writer. We talked about the most hideous crime and decided it would be writing anonymous letters and then one day I had an idea and I came home and said, "How would it be if I made a picture about a child murderer?" and so we switched. At the same time in Dusseldorf a series of murders of young and old people happened, but as much as I remember the script was ready and finished before they caught that murderer.

I had Peter Lorre in mind when I was writing the script. He was an upcoming actor, and he had played in two or three things in the theater in Berlin, but never before on the screen. I did not give him a screen test, I was just absolutely convinced that he was right for the part. It was very hard to know how to direct him; I think a good director is not the one who puts his personality on top of the personality of the actor; I think a good director is one who gets the best out of his actor.

So we talked it over very, very carefully with him and then we did it. It was my first sound film anyway, so we were experimenting a lot.

WALKER: *How did you come to leave Germany at the height of your career and seek refuge outside the country?*

LANG: I had made two *Mabuse* films and the studio had asked me if I could make another one because they made so much money. So I made one which was called *The Last Will of Dr. Mabuse* (1932).

I have to admit that up to two or three years before the Nazis came I was very apolitical; I was not very much interested and then I became very much interested. I think the London *Times* wrote about the fact that I used this film as a political weapon against the Nazis—I put Nazi slogans into the mouth of the criminal.

I remember very clearly one day, I was in the office and some SA men came in and talked very haughtily that they would confiscate the picture. I said if you think they could confiscate a picture of Fritz Lang in Germany then do it, and they did. I was ordered to go and see Goebbels, and they were not very sympathetic to me, but I had to go, maybe to get the picture freed, so I went.

I will never forget it. Goebbels was a very clever man, he was indescribably charming when I entered the room. He never spoke at the beginning of the picture. He told me a lot of things, among other things that the Führer had seen *Metropolis* and another film that I had made, *Die Nibelungen,* and the Fuhrer had said, "This man is the man who will give us *the* Nazi film." I was perspiring very much at this moment, I could see a clock through the window and the hands were moving, and at the moment I heard that I was expected to make the Nazi movie I was wet all over and my only thought was "How do I get out of here?" I had my money in the bank and I was immediately thinking "How do I get it out?" But Goebbels talked and talked and finally it was too late for me to get my money out! I left and told him that I was very honored and whatever you can say. I then went home and decided the same evening that I would leave Berlin that I love very much.

WALKER: *The theme of man and his destiny and of man trapped in an inimical kind of fate runs right through your work.*
LANG: I am quite sure that this is correct. It would be very interesting if a psychoanalyst could tell me why I am so interested in these things. I think from the beginning, one of my first films, the fight of man against his destiny or how he faces his destiny has interested me very much. I remember that I once said that it is not so much that he reaches a goal, or that he conquers this goal—what is important is his fight against it.

WALKER: *It must be very difficult to make films about destiny and God in that sense today, when people don't believe in heaven or hell in the vast majority. Do you substitute violence or pain?*
LANG: Naturally I don't believe in God as the man with a white beard or such a thing, but I believe in something which you can call God—some kind of an eternal law or eternal mathematical conception of the universe. When they said in the States that God is dead, I considered it wrong. I said to them, "God has only changed his address, he is not really dead." That seems for me to be the crux: naturally we cannot believe in certain things that have been told us over the centuries.

When you talk about violence, this has become in my opinion a definite point in the script, it has a dramatogical [sic] reason to be there. After the Second World War, the close structure of family started to crumble. It started naturally already with the first one. There is really very, very little in family life today. I don't think people believe anymore in symbols of their country—for example, I remember the flag burning in the States. I definitely don't

think they believe in the devil with the horns and the forked tail and therefore they do not believe in punishment after they are dead. So, my question
was: What are people feeling? And the answer is physical pain. Physical pain
comes from violence and I think today that is the only fact that people really
fear and it has become a definite part of life and naturally also of scripts.

Interview with Fritz Lang

AXEL MADSEN/1967

AT 76, HE IS A MAN FOR ALL SEASONS. To a growing number of cinephiles, Fritz Lang, who stumbled into films in 1916 and became the towering name of Germany's haunting but brief Golden Era, is a many-splendored figure of cinema history and, perhaps more important, of its rewrites.

This Viennese, who still sports the junker's insolent monocle and knows more four-letter words than the Berlin cab-driving fraternity, has spent nearly half his life in America, but his vision has its origin in the atmosphere of a fallen Germany. He has never forgiven the Hitler folly, but German's haven't forgotten his exile and, like Marlene Dietrich, he is badly loved beyond the Rhine. To compensate and to justify, he has become Francophile, pilgrim of festivals and citizen of Beverly Hills. To a thinning circle of friends, he is a man of many moods, thoughts and beliefs, someone living intensely because these are the autumn years with their regrets of things left undone, but also someone at peace with the relativity of accomplishments.

Lang doesn't think highly of Man, but has indulgence for his arts. To him, the 20th Century is Dachau and Hiroshima more than it is Einstein, acceleration of knowledge and humanitarianism through abundance. Mankind's history is written thicker in blood than in poetry, and notions of brotherhood and the approaching century will not necessarily mark man's mutation to braver worlds or final solutions to needs and inequity.

From *Sight and Sound*, 36.3 (Summer 1967), British Film Institute: 108–12. Reprinted with permission of *Sight and Sound*.

* * *

While whirling down the Summit Ridge Drive on a starry night after an evening heavy with Langian philosophy and Lily Latté's *mousse au chocolat,* I
have wondered if his essentially apocalyptic view of man's future, which
seems to be out of place in the Californian never-never land, is eminently
personal or the inevitable conclusion of a generation which twice saw the
world go up in flames. Glittering their insolent denial below are the million
and one lights of the Los Angeles basin, the toolshop where man's most
daring dreams are invented, blueprinted, mocked up, prototyped and turned
into streaks into the blue yonder. The awesome Californian scientific community has written off the dire prophecies of Huxley, Orwell and their generation as obsolete fantasies of another era. But high above the lights in
Benedict Canyon, where the Beverly Hills slope into the Santa Monica
Mountains, sits Lang, a Goethian figure of splendid isolation, a man of other
worlds and other times who has but forbearance for the self-confidence of
the future planners below. Seeing me to the car after a long evening, he stops
in the scented, semi-tropical night to look at a full moon. "It's a night for
evil spirits and prayers of unloved maidens," he smiles softly.

But Lang is also here-and-now appetites and heated argument for argument's sake. Tell him you think *Metropolis* is great and he will machine-gun
you with staccato whys. Tell him you think that the episode of *The Avengers*
he has insisted on seeing looks like a remake of a *Die Spinnen* (*The Spiders*)
episode, and he will ham up an answer to the effect that you are a perfect
idiot only because you thought of it first. Lang hates adulation but blooms
in bouncy conversation, good cigars and filial irreverence. Tell him you think
a new era is dawning in American cinema and he will shut you up with a
blunt "Name one great American film in the last twenty years." You may
stammer a couple of titles, but he will reiterate his question until you give
up and are forced to admit that there aren't any.

Georges Sadoul has written silly things about him, he says, but if historians misrepresent him, it is his own fault. An untiring talker, Lang reacts as
much as he acts and his answers are colored by the context, the tone and
repartee of a conversation. Ask him cold his opinion of *Le Mépris* (*Contempt*)
and he will come up with a neat and lofty defense of Jean-Luc Godard's
integrity; but put the same question to him some time later in a flow of
pleasant after-dinner chatter and he will make a plea for creators' right to
failures. He will add sarcastic afterthoughts about the vicissitudes of film-

making, conjure up examples from his vast storehouse of anecdotes, and gracefully floor you with cynical portraits of persons you thought would be sacred cows even to him. Lang's best audience and living encyclopedia when stories have to be authenticated or fleshed out with detail is Miss Latté, a former Berlin writer, with whom he has shared his life for the last thirty years. "Mickey," he will call out in her direction, "isn't it true Harry Cohn nearly didn't want me to direct *The Big Heat* because I showed up with glasses and he found me less authoritarian than when wearing my monocle?" Lily will confirm the story and sometimes add a punch line he has forgotten.

Lang has the emigré passion for intrigue, but he has no taboos, only subjects he doesn't care to dwell upon. One is his brief association with Bertolt Brecht in World War II Hollywood. Brecht was a haughty latecomer in the cautious German-speaking colony, arriving from his Scandinavian exile in 1941, and it was only because of an impassioned plea from Leon Feuchtwanger that the refugee playwright got the bread-and-butter writing job on *Hangmen Also Die,* the blatant propaganda picture both Lang and Brecht soon repudiated. Brecht had only contempt for cinema in general and for the *Hangmen* assignment in particular, but Lang manages to excuse his erstwhile screenwriter.

"Brecht got a raw deal here. There were endless fights with producers and so on," is about all Lang will say. If pressed, he will add that their acquaintance was casual, that Brecht's Santa Monica house was a weird place full of emigrés forever playing chess, that the Feuchtwangers, critic Eric Bentley, the composers' nucleus of the German colony, and, towards the end of the war, Charles Laughton, were his friends and that he himself is no Brecht fan. "I mean Francois Villon did all that five hundred years ago, n'est-ce pas?"

Money is another realm Lang doesn't care about. Lang is not unmindful of the need for commercial pictures and has made his share. A majority of his American pictures have been box-office failures and he has developed a thick hide and clever phrases against pecuniary considerations. His enemies, and they are numerous, say his wife's jewellery financed his 1933 exodus; others have it that he left behind a fortune accumulated as Germany's top director. None of his last pictures were successes, but he lives in frugal comfort.

Germany is a vast subject. Lang made his last three films—*Der Tiger von Eschnapur, Das Indische Grabmal (The Indian Tomb), Die Tausend Augen des Dr.*

Mabuse (The Thousand Eyes of Dr. Mabuse)—in Germany. His return in 1957 was welcome and the German press only soured on him after the costly *Tiger* and *Indian Tomb* duo—advance-billed as surefire launching pads for a resurrected German cinema—turned out to be box-office failures.

The city of Berlin has honored Lang and the West German government decorated him in 1963 (France made him "officier des arts et lettres" two years later), but another instance of German officialdom has teased old wounds. Lang was a jury member at the 1966 Rio de Janeiro festival and because he sneaked to the men's room during the screening of Michael Pfleghar's *Serenade für zwei Spione (Serenade for Two Spies)*, a storm was kicked up with embassy queries for an explanation of his "snubbing" of the official West German entry. "Hitchcock claims a film's length should be related to the endurance of the human bladder," he sighs after telling me the story.

Lang has not yet seen any examples of "Bubi's Kino" (vs. "Papi's Kino"; Bavarian slang for boy's cinema versus *"cinéma de papa"*). Alexander Kluge was an assistant on *The Indian Tomb*. Lang knows about *Der junge Törless (Young Törless)* and is happy that Volker Schlöndorff has been able to sign a six-film contract with Universal. He gleefully rubs his hands when told that Hansjurgen Pohland's filmisation of Gunter Grass' *Katz und Maus (Cat and Mouse)* has become a political issue in Bonn because of its irreverent treatment of yesteryear's master symbols, but shakes his head in disbelief at the Berlin entrepreneur Artur Brauner's folly of remaking *Die Nibelungen*.

"These young Germans are frightfully insolent, but so were we. However, they lack self-discipline. Eckelkamp told me one of these boys came to him with a project, saying he would die if he wasn't able to make it. Nah-yah, Eckelkamp thought of the French wave and decided to produce it. After five weeks shooting and a million marks, the young man came to Eckelkamp and said he was sorry but he had lost his feel for it and wouldn't be able to finish the film."

Lang is instinctively with "Bubi's Kino" and has no ready-made explanation for Germany's failure to spawn a second Golden Era as fertile and explosive as Berlin's festival of the arts after World War I. He feels one reason could be a lack of producers with vision. "There are no Erich Pommers these days. Some say Pommer destroyed UFA; he said UFA destroyed him. I really don't know, but he was a bitter man to the end," Lang sighs. "Producers want to be sure their films make it, but nothing is sure. Even death; I sometimes wonder."

If the *Serenade für zwei Spione* affair sticks uncomfortably in Lang's throat, he admits anti-German anthologies such as Siegfried Kracauer's *From Caligari to Hitler* are unreadable today; and he finds there is something sick in US television's perpetual harping on World War II violence with series such as *Rat Patrol, Combat, Jericho* and *Hogan's Heroes.* "But how can you imagine a country with 800 years of blood-drenched history becoming a model democracy overnight?" he asked me once with an expression that hesitated between anger and irony. More seriously, he admitted that the legendary heaviness and yearnings for netherworlds of the Teutonic soul are overworked cliches, and that no nation has any monopoly on cruelty. "What this country needs is perhaps an atomic war to learn to be human," he added as a dark afterthought.

"The History of German Cinema is yet to be written and it won't be Enno Patalas and the *Filmkritik* clique that will do it. But Sadoul has also written silly things about German cinema and me. What? Taking the sentence, 'We are all descendants of Cain' out of one of my early films, he concludes that the all-obsessive theme of my life is guilt. I'm interested in other things also—in what happens to my characters. That's why I don't think Antonioni is very healthy for the younger generation, because his pictures say that there is nothing to hope for."

But if Antonioni feels negativism *is* the message today?

"No. Film is too vast a medium for self-indulgence. It's a dangerous tool and you must be responsible when you use it."

You're limiting cinema, then?

"And why not? I still think that the struggle is the important thing in life, even more important than goals. Brutality is permissible—dramatically. People no longer believe in hell and brimstone, or even in retribution, but they fear physical pain; so brutality is a necessary ingredient in dramatic development and denouement, as I've said before. But to tell people there is nothing—no."

Lang was also disappointed with Luc Moullet's book on him (Paris: Seghers, 1963) and wonders why an art as new as film is already cluttered with so many historical inaccuracies.

The son of Paula (née Schlesinger) and Anton Lang, a prominent Vienna architect, Fritz is a graduate art student, painter and caricaturist making his first steps in Munich and Paris bohemia when the shot rings out from Sarajevo. Arrested by French authorities as an "enemy alien," he manages to

escape and to reach Vienna, where he is drafted into the Imperial Austrian
Army. He serves on the Western front, becomes a lieutenant and nearly loses
his right eye when a shell explodes 50 feet from him. Evacuated to Germany,
he sees a Max Reinhardt show for injured servicemen, plays in a Red Cross
revue and feels the performing arts are to be his life. During a lengthy conva-
lescence, he starts to write playlets and simple scenarios and in 1916, Joe May
cranks out a two-reeler from a Lang scenario. At the end of the war, Lang
mingles with Berlin's demobilised artists. He soon gravitates toward cinema,
newly discovered by Dadaism and expressionism, meets Pommer, producer
at Decla (Deutsche Eclair) and works as a reader of scripts. He marries Thea
von Harbou, already a well-known writer of thrillers. Together they collabo-
rate on scripts. Pommer encourages Lang's directing ambitions, and in 1919
Lang makes his first picture (after his own scenario)—*Halbblut (Half breed)*,
an exotic latter-day Madame Butterfly allegory.

Von Harbou, whom Lang divorced in 1934, has had a profound influence
on the Golden Era, not only as the writer of her husband's big silent movies
but also as screenwriter for Murnau, Ewald Dupont and others. She never
leaves the country and continues her career under the Nazi regime and
through the post-war era, writing for Veit Harlan, Josef von Baky, Gerhard
Lamprecht and others.

With Pommer producing and his wife writing, Lang makes three *Die Spinnen* serials, starring a fearless character named Kay Hoog, who is a cross
between Judex and a Teutonic Dorian Gray forever fighting a secret, world-
wide crime syndicate called The Spiders with headquarters in a Central
American jungle. (Phillipe de Broca pays tongue-in-cheek homage to The
Spiders by ending *That Man from Rio* in a similar way-out decor with the
same two-dimensional characters.) Lang specialises in exotica and makes a
half-dozen small pictures laid in faraway lands, and follows up with *Der müde
Tod,* a tale of romantic necrophilia in which Death allows two lovers to live
their destiny over again three times; and, in 1922, the small hit *Dr. Mabuse,
der Spieler.*

UFA absorbs Deutsche Eclair and gets Pommer and Lang in the bargain.
Die Nibelungen, which makes Lang world-famous, is a UFA double-feature
taking seven months to shoot during 1923–24. It is a national monument to
·Germania and expressionistic architecture in which an Aryan Siegfried,
loved by a long-tressed Kriemhild, rides through colossal, half-medieval,

half-cubist sets to express primitive guilt, wrath and vengeance and foretell Wagnerian doom.

In 1925, Lang comes to America, stays eight weeks in Hollywood and on his return says he was "unbelievably impressed." While on the boat waiting for the quarantine officers, he glimpses the Manhattan skyline and begins to plan a vast fable of the future.

The making of *Metropolis,* with its gigantic sets and casts of thousands, nearly ruins UFA, but the film impresses the German public and is widely discussed abroad. Picking up the Mabuse theme again, Lang makes *Spione,* a story of a master criminal turning into a kind of Dr. Strangelove. The film is a hit, but *Frau im Mond,* a science fiction yarn featuring a quite credible rocket trip to the moon, doesn't impress. In 1931, Lang makes his first talkie, *M,* his most famous and, to himself, best film. Like so many Germans of the period, he is a profound romanticist, fascinated by cruelty, fear and horror. He personally knows and studies a number of murderers, including the notorious child slayer of Dusseldorf. *M,* based on this almost clinical interest, arouses comment all over the world.

German exhibitors beg Lang for another Mabuse picture. He is himself looking for some way in which to show his distaste for Hitler and his Brownshirts and makes *Das Testament des Dr. Mabuse* (*The Last Will of Dr. Mabuse*), the story of a mad scientist. Lang places Nazi philosophies in the mouth of the madman and the film is banned. The new regime is ready, however, to make allowances for Germany's best known film-maker, and Propaganda Minister Goebbels offers a leading post in the soon-to-be-reorganised industry to Lang just before he leaves the country. In Paris, he adapts fellow Austro-Hungarian Franz Molnar's *Liliom* with moderate success. David O. Selznick, then vice-president of Metro-Goldwyn-Mayer, is visiting Paris and signs up the director.

Lang spends a long year in Culver City watching and learning English, and makes his American debut with *Fury,* an indictment of lynch law and mob rule with a front office-imposed ending, which is universally praised when released in 1936. After *Fury,* Lang leaves M-G-M and begins to freelance. *You Only Live Once* is a bitter tragedy of a young couple dogged by the police, and *You and Me* again stresses the responsibility of society to prisoners and ex-convicts. All this time Lang is studying American ways, and makes long trips through Nevada, Arizona and Navajo territories, leading to his pair of Westerns for Darryl Zanuck—*The Return of Frank James* with Henry Fonda in the title role, and *Western Union. Time* magazine says of the latter that it has "the same swift pace and scenic beauty that distinguished John Ford's *Stagecoach.*"

Between Pearl Harbor and VJ Day, Lang makes *Man Hunt,* the story of a renowned English big-game hunter (Walter Pidgeon) who goes out to kill his biggest game; *Hangmen Also Die,* inspired by the slaying in a Prague street of Hitler's Czechoslovakia Kommandant Reinhard Heydrich; *Ministry of Fear,* a Graham Greene adaptation starring Ray Milland; *The Woman in the Window* with Edward G. Robinson and Joan Bennett, and *Scarlet Street.* After two 1946 *policiers, Cloak and Dagger* and *Secret Beyond the Door,* Lang directs in 1949 *House by the River* and the next year the war movie *American Guerrilla in the Philippines.* His next is his third and best Western, *Rancho Notorious* (screenplay by Daniel Taradash), followed by an adaptation of Clifford Odets' *Clash by Night,* the Anne Baxter-Richard Conte thriller *The Blue Gardenia,* and the very successful *The Big Heat* with Glenn Ford and Gloria Grahame. His last four American films are *Human Desire,* an adaptation of Zola's *La Bête Humaine,* the Nibelungen-accented *Moonfleet* and the cheaply made, tightly constructed thrillers *While the City Sleeps* and *Beyond a Reasonable Doubt.*

The majority of the last dozen pictures are box-office failures, and in 1957 Lang returns to Germany at Brauner's invitation to recoup. For CCC Films in Berlin he makes two costly Eastern epics—remakes of his ex-wife's *Tiger of Eschnapur* novel (von Harbou had died in 1954) and of Joe May's 1921 serial *The Indian Tomb;* but these attempts at resurrecting the past are commercial disasters. "The world of these films had died with their public," wrote *Filmkritik,* "and the missing dialogue with the sound screen . . . paralyses all bravura." In 1960, Lang makes his 43rd and, to date, last film—*The Thousand Eyes of Dr. Mabuse,* a moderate box-office success. In 1963, he plays himself in Godard's haunting big-budget fiasco *Le Mépris (Contempt),* writing most of his own lines himself.

Lang shies away from questions about future plans, usually saying that he is superstitious about announcing projects but managing to imply that something is pending. Recently, he wondered aloud to me if he shouldn't imitate his neighbor Jean Renoir and tell whatever he has to say on paper rather than try to mount a production. "The medium really doesn't matter as long as you can express yourself," he sighed.

* * *

Who is Mabuse? If the question is put to Lang, he will squash all notions of transcendency, philosophy or of a Germanic "Ubermensch" figure. "The 1922 *Dr. Mabuse* was a routine adaptation of a Norbert Jacques' thriller," he says. "It grew out of its time. Germany was a place where every type of excess was encountered and the film reflected the inflationary hysteria, the anarchistic streak, the despair and vices of the time. The public loved it, as they did *Spies*. Now, *The Last Will of Dr. Mabuse* eleven years later was of course a veiled commentary on Nazism. The original of *The Thousand Eyes of Dr. Mabuse* was a newspaper article describing an experimental US Army bullet that leaves no marks, and I wanted to make a brutal and realistic picture.

"In the original film, I had left Mabuse in a madhouse and I hesitated to bring him out again when Seymour Nebenzal thought we could make a pile of money in 1932. I saw the possibilities of snide commentaries with this story of a director of a lunatic asylum hypnotized by his patient. It was rather sophisticated, but Goebbels banned it on March 29, 1933 even before any trade screenings were held. Goebbels apologised and told me that he and Hitler had seen *M* together in a small-town movie house and they wanted me to make films for them."

Jean Domarchi has formulated nebulous theories to the effect that Lang's American movies are superior to his Berlin output. Lang refuses to cleave his work nationally but acknowledges that the 1920s were his most creative and independent years. He rather likes his three Westerns and tells how an Arizona old-timer wrote him that *Western Union* was the most authentic Western he had seen. Lang was to have made a fourth Western in 1950, *Winchester '73*, but after his option on Stuart N. Lake's novel expired, Universal assigned Anthony Mann to direct it.

Lang has no love for the US film industry and says he would never again make a Hollywood picture. Retrospectively, however, he admires the iron fists of "czars" like Cohn and Mayer. "Hollywood exists only to make money. I haven't seen an American picture in years that I would like to see again and that's some sort of guideline for me. I hate over-dialogued cinema and that's where America is right now. I have seen a lot of TV recently, for reasons . . . anyway, TV is awful, it's like looking at a play with opera glasses."

To Lang, directing is applied psychology and a good director is simply a good analyst. "The power of the screen has always been its intimacy—at least up to CinemaScope, which I hate. The director would command an audience to see only what he regarded as dramatically important. He used the close-up to say something without distractions. But Godard never uses any close-ups, which is contradictory since he and his contemporaries are interested in form. I'm more interested in content, I must confess, but something *does* come out of the form-over-content thinking."

Lang cites the Jack Palance-Brigitte Bardot fatal car accident in *Le Mépris* as a revealing example of the generation gap. "Now, we would have shown the whole thing—the car at high speed, whining tires, impact, all those things—but Godard is more interested in what the accident does to the story, the surviving characters. His interest is in the consequences of things. There is a great difference in work methods also. My generation, when we started in the silent era, had to think in terms of action. We created pictures in motion. Godard, who is very consistent, goes to great pains to continue our work. Our methods are different, of course. I come to a studio in the morning knowing what I want. I don't change.

"Sound is rarely used dramatically these days and yet the world is becoming auditive, Easternising itself. Our civilization is moving away from the visual toward the auditive. The visual is the only sense that gives us detachment, objectivity, rationality. All the other senses are irrational, discontinuous and disconnected, especially sound. We're Easternising ourselves. . . ."

Lang thinks *Metropolis* is pretty bad today ("that sort of Eric Masterman holding back the man-sized hands of the clock is really too much, isn't it?"), but he doubts whether a new *Metropolis* could be made, whether there is really anything new to say. "All right, so man has to live with the machine," he says with an annoyed gesture of helplessness. "Is that a message today? He still has to live with himself first."

Lang can make an eloquent plea for youth and on more than one occasion has gone out of his way to help young Europeans coming to Hollywood. I have seen him spend an hour painstakingly composing and rewriting a letter of recommendation for a young German trying to break the union barrier, gallantly offering to say the youth was his assistant on his latest picture if it would help.

Lang thinks the Californian university youth with its generosity and golden insouciance is beautiful, as are its revolts, but he has a father's apprehension for its future. "They shouldn't fight their parents' battles although it's hard for us to admit," he smiles. "Let's not diminish their birthright."

Fritz Lang in Venice

MICHEL CIMENT, GOFFREDO FOFI, LOUIS SEGUIN, AND ROGER TAILLEUR/1967

THIS INTERVIEW TOOK PLACE during the Venice Film Festival (September 1967) in the presence of Madame Lotte Eisner.

FRITZ LANG: I am here for a round table on Expressionism. You know why this is called a "round table"?: because there is no table and nothing is round.

Q: *And Expressionism?*

LANG: I am not an Expressionist. Note well that I am not saying that because I'm President of this colloquium. Rather, I believe that a director should make films, not talk. In fact, I don't know what Expressionism is. If you say to Mme Eisner that one could not really speak with me on this subject, and you then ask her for an opinion, she will respond with, "I can only tell you that it is the opposite of something else. One can never really say what it is." Moreover, it is not for a filmmaker to explain such things. Paul Wegener said today, and I repeat this often: I am not an Expressionist, and I don't want to make Expressionist films. A filmmaker should make films without considering their genre, otherwise the film will be bad.

Q: *Certain German filmmakers of your era, Wiene, for example, were Expressionist. . . .*

From *Positif,* 94 (April 1968): 9–15. Reprinted with permission. Translated by Glenwood Irons.

LANG: True. Professor Mitry has stated a truth: one can't say that Carl Mayer created Expressionism. In fact, he created "Caligarism." In one sense, it was Schoenberg who, in music, started Expressionism. Someone said to me yesterday, and I didn't stumble—I have a "poker face"—that in the first *Mabuse* I showed "time" by using an interior eye. It's possible, I don't know.

Q: Mabuse *wasn't Expressionist. In films, Expressionism is no doubt the use of décor such as that in* Caligari, *or else shadows, grotesque gestures, and exaggeration, in one sense to photograph things which are exceptional, which are not. . . .*
LANG: Like reality.

Q: *A distortion, a manipulation of reality.*
LANG: If you want to show a man who is strange and you simply illustrate that through deformities, that isn't Expressionism. It is the subject which dictates the style. When I am drunk, I see double. That isn't Expressionism.

Q: *That is realism.*
LANG: I don't know. When I show something that is in our spirit, that is deformed by our spirit, that isn't natural, one can't say that is Expressionism. Outside of *Caligari,* where do you find deformation in German silent films? Max Reinhardt, for example, wasn't Expressionist, or else, if he is, we can say that everyone is.

Q: *You collected contemporary paintings during the 20's, Egon Schiele in particular. Did you know him?*
LANG: Yes. But I don't have those paintings any longer. When I came back to Berlin, they had disappeared. When I left Berlin, I left the paintings with my wife, as we say in German, "in good hands." But when I returned to Berlin, my wife had died, and the paintings had gone. Once, in Montreal, I saw a very nice canvas by Schiele, but nothing like the ones I had. I had a collection of drawings, paintings, and watercolors by other painters. In particular, I had a Lasker, *Saint Francis of Assisi with the Birds* and a *Noah's Arc.*

Q: *Before going to Berlin, did you feel you had a rapport with Viennese culture?*
LANG: Since 1908 I had no contact with Vienna. I was in Brussels, then Paris. I haven't really lived in Austria since then, but I had known Schiele since my youth.

Q : *Did you know Brecht before going to America?*

L A N G : Yes, but I don't remember how we met. You know, Mme Eisner was the first person to say to Brecht that he was the most important German poet of his time. I believe Brecht influenced everyone. In the US, I made my first flop, my first failure—*You and Me*. I had wanted to make a "didactic" film [*"lehrfilm"*]. I worked with Kurt Weill, who eventually left the project because of other commitments. Then I was left with a screenplay written for music.

Q : *In your films, there is an interesting use of dialectic, as in Brecht.*

L A N G : I don't know. When I made *M*, I didn't know that, and I believe *Fury* is the continuation of *M*. Brecht was the poet, not me.

Q : *Do you sense a difference between your German films and your American films, particularly from the point of view of style?*

L A N G : I don't know if there is a difference in style. But I believe there are very large differences in general. You would say to me, for example, that in *You Only Live Once* Fonda cuts his wrists with a piece of metal, and that in this scene, the jail-cell's bars were photographed in such a way that they could qualify as Expressionist, that the shadows and light had an almost unreal appearance. Obviously, you haven't seen that jail cell at San Quentin because it is reproduced exactly in the film, even with the exact lighting. In one sense, there is a documentary quality to that scene, a fidelity with reality.

Q : *What did you learn in America?*

L A N G : That Americans don't like symbols in their films. In *Fury*, I showed women who gossiped, then I showed geese that honked. That was a surprise for an American audience. The producers told me, "We don't want that." And they were right. They added, "We aren't so stupid that you need to show us geese to make us realize that they honk." This was a leftover from the silent era and I no longer use such symbols. You don't find that problem in *Mabuse*. But I remember that, in *Der müde Tod (The Weary Death)* we see a tree with little flowers, and it becomes a skeleton. That too wasn't necessary.

Q : *But* Mabuse *resembles your American films.*

L A N G : Yes, but it isn't a fantasy. It is a documentary on the post-war period.

Q : *Your American films tend toward abstraction.*

L A N G : The direction is actually much simpler. In the beginning, I was interested in things which were very "pretty," and then, little by little, I got rid of them.

Q: *Did your choice of actors correspond with your interests in simplicity, with your search for neutrality of expression?*
LANG: I don't think so. A director chooses actors who can explain his ideas. Sometimes I had to take others because of an obligation: George Raft, for example, who is a "character" rather than an actor. I have always liked working with unknown actors whenever possible. I have always tried to avoid stars.

Q: *Before choosing actors, there is the choice of screenplay.*
LANG: I always work with the screenwriter. When I am asked, "Would you do so?", I always reserve the right to make my own changes to the screenplay.

Q: *Are you ever given a synopsis of two or three pages, to make a film?*
LANG: Sometimes. In *Fury*, for example, there were two or three pages which implied the possibility of a film about lynching. I took the project on. I also wanted to buy the Graham Greene novel, *Ministry of Fear,* but I didn't have the means to compete with Paramount, who had an interest in the book. I regret that very much, because soon after, my agent proposed making the film for Paramount, but in the contract I didn't mention the possibility of changing the screenplay. In Hollywood, I was forced to make the film without changing a word, and I don't believe it was a good film. It was far removed from my original intentions. In any case, I've rarely had exactly what I wanted. When you make films for Big Business, you rarely do exactly what you want.

Q: *There are, in many of your films since* Die Spinnen (The Spiders), *a taste for soap opera, espionage, reversal of fortune.*
LANG: I believe that a director should live in the real world. We begin things, then we add our experiences. That happens in each film. So, at the end of a career, one can clearly see a pattern. I took many ideas for screenplays from newspapers. Two years before *Fury*, there was a lynching in San José. I put some elements from that story in my film. One thing which I learned later, and which I regret not having filmed, is that people went by

bus from San Francisco to San José (half an hour by car) to see the lynching. That would have given a completely different point of view on lynching, on the idea of "spontaneous" fury, wouldn't it?

Q : You Only Live Once *was also very much inspired at the time.*
L A N G : A man can't find work. That's a common problem. But in *You and Me* the owner of a large store gave work to criminals released on parole. Sometimes ideas develop. . . .

Q : *Another idea which "developed" was Mabuse: television, films within films, and then* Liliom, *where the life of a man is "registered" in heaven.*
L A N G : I don't know whether that was my idea or the writer's, but it wasn't in the play by Molnar. As for *Mabuse,* it would be impossible to make in the United States: the idea of the superior race, of a race of masters, simply doesn't exist. In Germany, even when you are dead, you must obey, "your corpse must obey." I don't believe there is another people who are as ready to die without knowing why. Mabuse is a super criminal, but the criminals in America are not super men. In *Fury,* I wanted my hero to be a lawyer so that he could explain things. The screenwriter and I were met and were told that "Heroes in America are average people, men of the people because we don't want the public to think they are heroes." That was a big lesson for me: in a democracy, one can't create a superman.

Q : *We like* House by the River *very much in France.*
L A N G : At the time, there were witch hunts. I was never a member of the Party, but my sentiments were for the Left. And of course, everyone said I was a Communist. I didn't know why, but I didn't have a contract at that time. My agent was simply told there wasn't any work for me. My lawyer was told that I wasn't accused of being a Communist, but that I might become one. So I made that film because I hadn't any work for a year and a half. What interested me, since one always tries in a film to give the most of one's self, was that nocturnal atmosphere, of water, of a drowned woman. I don't know whether you are aware, but even a director needs money to live. Francs, for example.

Q : *An interview is a bit of a witch hunt, a police interrogation. "Where were you?" "What did you do?"*

LANG: Yes, but I have an answer for everything. I have a book in which I write everything I do, day by day.

Q: *That's like in* Liliom. *When we arrive in Heaven, there is a great registry.*
LANG: I must say something here: I will never go to Heaven.
   (Laughter.)
LANG: You find that funny?

Q: *Does guilt preoccupy you in your films?*
LANG: Let's just call it the battle against destiny. I believe that it is necessary to fight destiny. It is the battle which is important, not the goal.

wants attention   distortion

Q: *Isn't the idea of having committed a crime in* The Blue Gardenia *or* The Woman in The Window *the same thing as destiny?*
LANG: There is obviously something there which interests you more than me. My passion is: what does one do when accused of a crime? You, you are interested by the man who is thought to have committed the crime. So it is up to you to respond to your question. In *The Woman in the Window,* killing is by chance, without will. The English title—*Once Off Guard*—suggests "Un moment sans vigilance." And during this moment, something happens. This title wasn't used because of the potential confusion with "Once off God." In any case, it is only in dreams where men commit three crimes.

Q: Scarlet Street *has the same idea at the outset.*
LANG: It was called *Scarlet Street* because *The Bitch (La Chienne)* doesn't give the same idea in English.

Q: *Renoir made* Woman on the Beach *(Bitch).*
LANG: Now it is you who will go to Hell.

Q: *There is a sequel:* The Son of a Bitch.
LANG: Yes, the second episode.

Q: *There are many violent scenes in your films. What is your point of view on violence?*
LANG: After the war, there was no longer a sense of family. We no longer loved the flag or honored our country. We didn't believe in God, the Devil,

or Hell. What could we be afraid of? Not even punishment. There was only one thing: physical pain. And when we are afraid of violence, then it *Violence.* becomes an element of drama. We can't avoid violence because it is everywhere. It should be present in films. But everything depends on the way it is shown. I detest violence when it is shown as a spectacle or when it is used to make us laugh. And that is how it is used more and more on the screen. There is the same problem with love as it is incessantly shown in films. Now everyone knows that women have more up top and men have more on the bottom. It's just common knowledge. The Canadian film *High,* by Larry Kent, which I saw in Montreal, and which was ultimately banned, used nudity correctly. A man and a woman on drugs killed a lover of the woman. As the crime was committed, the woman began to laugh. She took the body to a meadow, all the while laughing. She fell into the grass with the man, completely nude, and made love in front of the camera. I believe that such a dramatic summit is possible for people who have committed murder. I wouldn't do it, but I accept it. However, there were orgy scenes at the beginning which were simply pornography. It was this to which the censor objected. But I am against all censorship, no matter what the reason. You remember in *M* how I showed the murder of a child? We simply see the ball bouncing. I could have shown the murder, but it is a question of tact and of taste. Even if I had shown the murder, I would have touched only a small public because each of us would commit such a murder in a different way. Since I didn't show the murder itself, I forced everyone to imagine it in the worst way.

Q: *Does the Western have the same documentary point of view as your other films?*
LANG: I have tried to understand the US, and I believe that Westerns are the real historical American films. I like good Westerns, for example by Ford, which really show history. But nothing in *Western Union* was historically accurate. The man who brought the telegraph to San Francisco was married with seven children. In the film, he is a bachelor. And the construction of the telegraph line wasn't terribly difficult. The only difficulty was when buffalos rubbed up against the poles to get rid of ticks and knocked some poles over. Since there were no real problems, I made a love story for the hero and threw in the Indians. I needed a lot more people and took a lot longer to make the film than it took to build the telegraph line (6–8 months as

opposed to 4 months). When the film was shown, I received a letter from someone near the Grand Canyon who said, "Mister Lang, we're Old Timers who know the exact history of the West, and we have never seen a film which shows the West as exactly as you have shown it." I was flattered, but in fact this inexact representation of the West presented it as people would like it to have been. They believe in it. Why? Because I included little authentic details which made viewers believe the entire thing. All of that is due to wishful thinking. Just as Frank James wasn't a hero. And if you saw a picture of Jessie James, you would see an idiot. To make a film about Jessie James in the spirit of *M* would be interesting. But with a handsome actor like Tyrone Power, a Western in the spirit of *M* would be impossible.

Q: *Some of your projects have never come to fruition. Are there certain screenplays which you liked less than others?*

LANG: Of course. There are screenplays which I chose not to do—for example, *Moonfleet*. I don't know why I was banished from MGM for 20 years after *Fury*. I agreed to do what they wanted in that film. There are things I would like to have done in that film. *Human Desire* was also not a subject I wanted to explore after Renoir. But after McCarthyism, I didn't have the chance to direct. There was a man who wasn't well liked, but whom I liked a lot, Harry Cohn, the boss at Columbia. He suggested a screenplay to me, but I refused it. I said it was a war film. He said I didn't have any money, which was true—I had only $50–100 in the bank. Directors are somewhat like prostitutes and in some ways worse than prostitutes. But there are some things which I simply won't do, and those are things which go against my conscience. When I have needed money and been given a screenplay, I have tried my best. During a trip to Hollywood in the '20's, a big man in Hollywood said to me, "We don't want to make good films. We want to make successful films, with no risk attached." Which explains why I haven't made a film in America since '57 or '58.

Q: *What interested you in the Indian films which followed your departure from America?*

LANG: That's a long story. In 1920, Mrs. Harbou, who wasn't yet my wife, wrote a book which was bought by director Joe May, who wanted me to direct the movie. We had done a screenplay which was too long, so we made it into two parts, which in fact was the German style at the time. We did one scene on one page, another on another, just so we could change the order easily. Then I discovered that Joe May didn't want me to be the director because no one would give him the funds for someone as young as I was. I was hurt. One day in 1958, the 30 or 31st of December, I was sitting with a woman whom I liked very much, and I received a telegram from Germany proposing that I remake the film. For me, the circle was finally closed. I made the film for very little money, about $200,000 for the two parts. After that, I thought they would let me make the film I really wanted to make. You know the rest. . . .

Q: *What are your future projects?*
LANG: When one is young, one revolts against parents, against society. That is natural. But I believe that in today's world, one has many more reasons to revolt. I don't believe that what we have left to the young is particularly beautiful, or agreeable. It is a rather poor inheritance. I spoke with students in California, and one said to me, "We don't want to change the world, we want to escape the world you have left us." That interests me since I am entirely in agreement. The aggression and sexual freedom that we see in America today is a reaction against all that. Parents should understand their children, not the other way around. I want to make a film on youth because it is necessary.

Q: *Do you still read many newspapers?*
LANG: Naturally. I have an entire collection. But to speak again of youth, some take LSD to shock us, but many take it to know themselves. That is truly possible. We laugh when one of them gives us a flower, but when you really look at the people who do that, you don't find it so funny. It is a real counterpoint to violence, and it is always necessary in America. At one time, people killed for reasons like money and love. Now we have young people who have killed three women for no apparent reason. Even psychoanalysis has no explanation, and brain damage is certainly no reason. This development in violence is very significant.

Q: *You want films to be witnesses to their time. Is that for you what the cinema should be?*
LANG: Yes. An example: I believe that *M* is a kind of documentary. A remake has been tried. It was Losey, at a time when I wasn't in the United States, but

I was in the Philippines. If not, it wouldn't have happened. It took place in New York, and that didn't work. *M* is a witness to the 30's. I very much appreciate Renoir for that. For his story. Look at *La Marseillaise,* which I saw at the Montreal Film Festival, and which I liked very much. He also made a film which I haven't seen, *Le Crime de Monsieur Lange.* I assure you, I'm not lying.

Q: *No, but you weren't guilty.*

Interview with Fritz Lang

CHARLES   HIGHAM   AND   JOEL
GREENBERG/1969

THE CHAUFFEURED LIMOUSINE—supplied by courtesy of Universal Pictures—sweeps past some of the world's most opulent private homes, lush and handsome in the Californian afternoon sun, depositing us finally at Fritz Lang's house atop Summit Ridge Drive, beside a canyon so redolent of the Australian bush that—apart from the built-up surroundings—we might almost be in New South Wales. At the door to greet us is Lily Latté, the director's devoted secretary, who has been with him for more than thirty years. Possessor of an agreeable sardonic sense of humour, she promptly conducts us to the living-room where Lang, a barrel-chested septuagenarian dressed in a casual open-necked sports shirt and slacks, makes us run through our proposed list of questions prior to the actual taping, which occurs to the accompaniment of full-throated outdoor birdsong. His presence is awesome: here is someone who has seen and experienced it all, Berlin's Golden Age in the twenties and Hollywood's in the thirties and forties; and their passing has not left him embittered—as it well might—but serene and detached, contemplating their folly and grandeur with a super-sophistication that manifests itself in a simplicity and directness quite devoid of affectation or pretense. "The last of the dinosaurs" is how he half-mockingly describes himself, and the image is apt: for giants such as Fritz Lang have long vanished from the motion picture scene, and we shall probably never see his like again.

FRITZ LANG: By birth I am Austrian, not German. But I liked pre-Hitler Germany very much and I liked the German language, so I was very hurt that such a thing as Nazism could happen. When, in 1933, the then Minister of Propaganda, Joseph Goebbels, offered me the leadership of the German film industry, I left the country that same evening and did not return until 1958, on my way back from India.

From that moment I never spoke German again. I spent nine months in Paris and made a film there for French Fox from Ferenc Molnar's play *Liliom*, starring Charles Boyer.

Then David O. Selznick brought me over to the United States on an MGM contract. He was on a talent-hunting European trip, and in those days it was the fashion for Hollywood producers or studio-heads visiting Europe to come back with some—I say it in all humility—famous man. That's how Selznick found me.

I'm quite sure now that I made many initial mistakes here and I know what they were. I spent a whole year at MGM without being given a picture, and when the year was up they said, "Goodbye, Mr. Lang."

That wasn't unique. There was a very famous story about a writer—I forget his name—under contract to the studio head, Irving Thalberg. The writer was eager to work, but Thalberg never summoned him. Every time he tried to see Thalberg the latter was always too busy and said he'd call. However, the writer still drew his weekly cheque. This went on for months, until the writer finally said, "To hell with this, to hell with the cheque," and, locking the door of his office, he went to Europe for three months without telling anyone. At the end of that time, his conscience made him come back, and under his door he found all his weekly cheques for the previous three months: when Thalberg did get around to calling him a couple of days later, no one knew he had ever been away!

During some of the time that no pictures were offering, I lived with the Navajo Indians on their reservation, meeting traders and sharing their existence. That was an extremely interesting experience. I did it because I'd always been interested in the Red Indians and wanted to know as much about this country as possible. At the same time I acquired my lousy English by reading American newspapers and, most of all, by reading funny papers.

Eventually I approached Louis B. Mayer's right-hand man, Eddie Mannix, saying, "Look, Eddie, you can't do this to me. I came here willing to work and with a considerable European reputation. If I'm not given anything to

do, my reputation will suffer." Eddie Mannix realized I had a genuine griev-
ance, and that's how I came to do my first American film, *Fury*.

Fury was a film based upon a three-page or four-page long story by the
writer, Norman Krasna. He and I spent the time and worked as long as we
wanted to on the script, and when it was finished I had ample time to pre-
pare the picture. Later, conditions were not quite so favourable; schedules
gradually became tighter, much more so than they had been at UFA in Germany. For example, I shot a silent film called *Spione (Spies)* in about a hundred days, while here I've never had more than forty-two or forty-five days
in which to shoot a film.

I found the whole procedure of shooting a picture quite different from
Europe. In Europe, for instance, I didn't have to halt filming after five hours
so that extras or the crew could eat. I'd dismiss, say, *half* the crew, and the
cameraman and I would continue working in the studio with a sandwich or
something; then, when the half-crew came back from their meal, we'd send
out the other half. Naturally, I made lots of mistakes here in the beginning,
and learned how to do things the hard way.

Louis B. Mayer interfered only once on *Fury*, and for a very peculiar reason. In the picture I had a scene showing a group of Negroes—an old man, a
very beautiful buxom girl, and a young Negro with two children—sitting in
a dilapidated Ford car in the South listening on the radio to a transcription
of a lynching trial. As the state attorney spoke about the high incidence of
lynchings in the U.S. each year, I had the old Negro just nod his head silently
without a word. Mayer had this scene, and others like it, removed because at
that time I think even he was convinced that Negroes should be shown only
as bootblacks, or carhops, or menials of some description. Otherwise I was
allowed complete freedom.

The only other time I struck the Negro problem in one of my films was in
a picture I don't particularly like: *House by the River*, with Louis Hayward. It
opens on a very hot summer day. Hayward's wife is out of town, and on the
staircase of his house he encounters a coloured maid, just coming out of the
bath. He tries to kiss her and she fights him. During their fight—which is
quite friendly, not sexy or anything, almost joking—he looks out of a big
french window and sees a female neighbor, a woman who likes to chat and
gossip. He's so afraid that she might talk about his attempt to kiss the girl—
who's yelling "Leave me alone!" etc.—that he puts his hand over her mouth.

She struggles and he struggles and finally he strangles her. The Hays Office would not permit me to make this a colored girl; she had to be white.

After I finished *Fury,* nobody at MGM believed that it was any good. A reporter, who has since died, asked them one day: "What kind of a picture are you previewing today?" "Oh," they said, "a lousy picture. Don't watch it, it is by that German son of a bitch, Lang." But he knew of my European reputation and insisted on seeing it. And, contrary to the expectations of the people at MGM, the picture turned out a tremendous success. I received national prizes for it, but wasn't given another job at MGM for nearly twenty years.

My next assignment after *Fury* was *You Only Live Once* with the independent producer, Walter Wanger. The script, based on a story by Gene Towne and remotely suggested by the exploits of Bonnie Parker and Clyde Barrow, was almost finished, but I worked on it as I'd been used to doing in Europe. I think a director should always work on a script. I knew I would have Henry Fonda, who'd recently made a very successful motion-picture debut, as the leading man, and for his co-star I brought over Sylvia Sidney, whom I'd used in *Fury.* The other parts were filled by General Casting.

I think there is one thread running through all my pictures: the fight against Destiny, or Fate, or whatever you want to call it; this has maybe something to do with my so-called philosophy of life. In *You Only Live Once,* it is the fight of a three-time loser against something which is stronger than he is.

In those days, there were still certain strange taboos in the movie industry. For example, I wanted to have a kind of ironic touch when Fonda and Sidney flee from the law and she goes and buys him some cigarettes, which ultimately provide the means for his betrayal. I wanted her to buy Lucky Strike cigarettes to stress the irony of the bad luck they bring him. But that was forbidden because it constituted advertising.[1]

I can't explain why I used the sound of bull-frogs' croaking over one of the love scenes in *You Only Live Once,* any more than I can explain the use of rain against the window in a similar scene in *Fury.* There are certain things you cannot explain. Very often people ask me, "How did you do it?" or, "Why did you do it?" Well, those things make a director. It is a little more

---

1. The situation has since altered radically the other way. (original note by Higman and Greenberg)

than instinct, it is something you cannot analyse but which you know will "hit."

You Only Live Once was a success. But Walter Wanger had prominently displayed in his office a portrait of Mussolini. Now if I am anything I am an anti-Fascist, and I didn't like the whole setup. Meanwhile, in New York, I'd become friends with Katharine ("Kit") Cornell, then the first lady of the American stage. Despite my friends' warnings not to write anything for her because she would never consent to make a picture—and she never did—I still went ahead and wrote a long, unfilmed scenario for her; I was very green and inexperienced in American ways. It was a panoramic story, stretching from the First World War almost till 1936; I've forgotten the details.

Simultaneously, I met a man who had a lot of influence at Paramount. Afterwards he went into politics and became, I think, U.S. ambassador to Spain. He, Kit and I were very close and at his suggestion I went to Paramount to produce and direct just one film, *You and Me*.

I don't think *You and Me* is a good picture. It was—I think deservedly—my first real flop. I made it probably a little under the influence of my friend Bertolt Brecht, who had created a style in the theatre which he called *Lehrstücke,* meaning a play that teaches you something. And I wanted to make a didactic picture teaching the audience that crime doesn't pay—which is a lie, because crime pays very well. The message was spelled out at the end by Sylvia Sidney on a blackboard to a classroom of crooks.

Kurt Weill had nothing to do just then. You may think whatever you like of him—some people said he could only write in one key—but he was good. He and I worked together, and he composed introductory music for certain sequences. For one scene, in which a bunch of crooks sit together around a table on Christmas Eve and indulge a sentimental nostalgia for prison— which is, of course, stupid—I wanted to have not music but only sound effects: people hitting the table, or one glass against another, etc.

But then Weill left me in the lurch by going to New York where he had an offer to work with the Spewacks. The music score for *You and Me* was finished by Boris Morros, a Russian who was then the head of Paramount's music department, and as a result it was no longer truly Kurt Weill.

For a while, after finishing *You and Me* I was out of work. Then a producer at Twentieth Century-Fox, the late Kenneth Macgowan, offered me a picture called *The Return of Frank James,* a sequel to the Tyrone Power vehicle, *Jesse*

James. That was the first of my three Westerns, the other two being *Western Union* and *Rancho Notorious,* and I thoroughly enjoyed doing it.

I found some new locations for it which no one had ever used before; they were north from here, near the Sierra Nevada. The same thing happened on *Western Union,* for which I found in Utah a very isolated spot—since used often by movie companies—where there were *real* red and blue mountains. *Frank James* was my first colour picture, which made it an additionally enjoyable experience, and Fox's technical facilities were really wonderful.

That was the greatest difference between Europe and America: Hollywood's mechanical superiority. In Europe, for example, we didn't know what a crane was. We had quite different lights. I remember that on *M* I wanted to have a camera follow someone down a staircase, but we had no way of doing it. So we took a chassis—four wheels with ball-bearings—and in front of it we put a very long two-by-four, and at the end of the two-by-four we put the camera, and that was our crane.

Most of *Frank James* was imaginary, not historical, except for certain minor things like a contemporary song about the James brothers and how Jesse was killed. My contribution extended also to the script, although in a minor capacity; for *Western Union* I wrote much more. That was based on a Zane Grey novel which Darrel F. Zanuck had bought, but we practically ignored the book.

The film, in fact, was almost entirely imaginary and fictitious, not based on actual episodes at all—although it purported to deal with the laying of telegraph-wires from Omaha to Salt Lake City in the 1860s. We depicted the engineer, for instance, as a married man with children, whereas he was really a bachelor.

The only true incident we used was when the linesmen went down into nearby valleys looking for timber for their wire-posts after some buffaloes, plagued by itchy ticks, had rubbed themselves against the existing posts and dislodged them.

I shot *Western Union* in two months—longer than it took them to lay the actual line—and after its release I received a letter from the Old Timers' Club of Flagstaff, Arizona, saying: "We have never before seen the old West more accurately depicted in a motion picture than in your *Western Union.* How is this possible for a foreign-born director?"

While I was naturally tickled pink by this letter, it was based on a misconception, on these old peoples' idealization of the West as reflected in the film. The real West was certainly quite different, as I knew from stories which had been told me and from certain things I'd seen.

Zanuck had liked *The Return of Frank James* so much that, when John Ford turned down a script, it was offered to me through the producer of *Frank James*, Kenneth Macgowan. I read it, had some more work done on it, and then made it as *Man Hunt;* it was based by the screenwriter Dudley Nichols on Geoffrey Household's novel *Rogue Male.* That was my first picture with Joan Bennett.

I made it deliberately "Germanic" in style, which was rather funny because this was just before America entered World War II, and Zanuck had told me, "Fritz, don't show too many swastikas; we don't like them in this country." But you cannot make an anti-Nazi picture—and for me it was primarily an anti-Nazi picture—without showing swastikas. So I shot it the way I wanted it, only to have many things changed by the studio. The scene showing Hitler at Berchtesgaden was done with an actor, and a mask over the camera lens to simulate a telescope.

I then became interested in doing *Confirm or Deny* because the original script incorporated reports we'd heard about Hitler's attempt to cross the Channel to England. But the final script eliminated all that and consequently it didn't interest me much any more.

I also wanted it to contain echoes of my last German picture, *The Last Will of Dr. Mabuse,* which I'd used as a political weapon against the Nazis. In *The Last Will of Dr. Mabuse,* I'd put all the Nazi slogans and catchcries into the mouth of an insane criminal. The Nazis said for example: "We must destroy the average citizen's self-created belief in the authorities, and when everything has broken down we will build on the ruins of the old order our Thousand-Year Reich." So I had my insane criminal propose a "Thousand-Year Era of Crime" as a mockery of this doctrine.

In *Confirm or Deny* I wanted to do something similar but I couldn't convince Zanuck or anybody, and I thought the whole thing as the studio envisaged it was very phony. Fortunately, after I'd been shooting the picture for about four or five days I had a gall-bladder attack. Now, contrary to European practice, you cannot change an actor in Hollywood because he's already on film, it costs a lot of money to replace him and reshoot his scenes. But you can easily change the director. If a director is sick for maybe two days and he's in very good standing with the company, they might get another director as a temporary replacement to shoot certain scenes in order to save time and money.

My case was different, however. I was delighted that I was unable to shoot, and told a very good friend, who acted as a go-between between all the shooting companies and Zanuck, that my doctors had put me out of action for three or four days or a week. So when he came one day shortly after and told me that Zanuck had taken me off the picture, I couldn't have been more pleased.

My next project was to have been a musical with Rita Hayworth. I would like to have done it very much because—apart from *You and Me*—I'd never done a musical and had many new ideas about the genre which I thought extremely interesting. But Zanuck, who liked my work very much, said, "Fritz, I have something much better for you." And he assigned me to *Moontide,* starring Jean Gabin.

Gabin hated the picture, probably with justification. I didn't like it either, but when you're under contract you often have to do things you don't like. Audiences usually have a very false notion of a director: even a director has to live, he cannot afford to be put on a lay-off.

Anyway, I started to shoot *Moontide* and was very unhappy about the whole thing. Originally it had been planned to make the film on location on the quay at San Pedro. But the war interfered: it became a strategic area, the whole vicinity was mined, and it was impossible to do the film there. So Zanuck decided to do it entirely in the studio, although it was set mostly on the high seas. They accordingly built an artificial indoor quay on the Fox lot and stuck blue backdrops all around it, and I was even less happy with the project than before.

Gabin's dissatisfaction grew, too. He was very good in other types of parts, but he couldn't persuade the producer to change the script, because the producer was a tyro and insisted on shooting the script Zanuck had handed him. Then something personal occurred between Gabin and me and he told Zanuck he could no longer work with me. I was very happy indeed when Zanuck then took me off the picture.

I'd no sooner read about the assassination of Reinhard Heydrich, the Nazi *Gauleiter* of Czechoslovakia in World War II, than I immediately thought it would make a great picture. At that time the German playwright, Bertolt Brecht, was living in America. I liked him very much—he was never a Communist Party member, incidentally—and was very glad to have been instrumental in bringing him over here by putting up certain guarantees and complying with other formalities, the details of which I've forgotten.

I used to meet him quite frequently, and when I put up to him the idea of working on a picture about the assassination of Heydrich, he readily agreed. It was such an obvious motion-picture theme that we had a story outline written within a day, and shortly afterwards I concluded a deal with an independent outfit to make the film.

However, we had a problem with Brecht, who didn't speak English at all and wanted to write his contribution in German, because he was, after all, a professional German writer. He'd always written in German wherever he was—in Denmark, France or the U.S.—and always looked forward to the time when he could go back to Germany. I, on the other hand, *never* wanted to go back; besides, I had meantime become an American citizen.

I felt his attitude was perfectly justifiable and so we found a bilingual collaborator for him. But to my distress he quarrelled with this man, who claimed sole screenwriting credit for himself. The whole matter came up for arbitration before the Screen Writers Guild, and at the hearing—attending by both Brecht and his rival—the composer Hanns Eisler and I appeared as witnesses for Brecht.

Despite our testimony, they withheld screenplay credit from him, and for a very peculiar reason. "Mr. Brecht" they said, "is going back to Europe eventually and thus doesn't need a screen credit, whereas the other writer does need credit."

In the circumstances the most I could do for Brecht was to give him joint credit with myself for the story idea and its construction. I think it was all rather unfair to him, because the picture contained certain scenes which no one but Brecht could have written.

For example, there was a scene in which the Czech professor, played by Walter Brennan, instructed his daughter in the ways of clandestine anti-Nazi resistance, drawing on examples illustrated by letters of the alphabet; and when he came to the letter "G" he declared: "And this stands for Gestapo!" Another scene involved the professor, visited in a Gestapo prison by his daughter, dictating a last letter to his son for her to memorize. Both these scenes were so typical of Brecht, as indeed was the whole film, its entire construction.

I was extremely pleased with the performance of Hans von Twardowski as Heydrich. I'd known him in Germany—he'd acted in a picture of mine called

Spies—and he was unemployed here at the time. I was less happy about the casting of the girl [Anna Lee] but I couldn't help that, despite the fact that I fought as hard as I could over it with the independent producer who wanted her in the picture.

Alexander Granach I loved; he was my choice; and Brennan's unorthodox casting—he usually played cowboy types and deputies and that kind of thing—was my doing, too. In my opinion, he was extremely good as the Czech professor.

I shot the film in, I think, the former Chaplin studio, where I built one or two street corners in an attempt to reproduce Prague. By some lucky accident, I managed to get hold of actual shots of the city—I remember particularly a clock with mechanical figures walking around it as it struck the hour, a death's-head skeleton, and others—and, by cutting these into the picture, I gave it great authenticity.

Although I don't know Graham Greene personally, he is one of my favorite writers, and I wanted very much to make a film from his "entertainment" novel, *Ministry of Fear*. Accordingly, I instructed my agent to try to buy it for me, but he declared it was impossible because Paramount, who were also interested in the book, were outbidding us.

Then I went to New York, and one day received a cable from my agent containing an offer to make *Ministry of Fear* for Paramount. I jumped at it, but made a big mistake by not specifying in my contract that I wanted to be able to work on the script; I took it for granted, after all the years I'd been accustomed to working on scripts, that my agent would have seen to it that the contract contained some such clause.

When I came back here, I found someone in charge of the film who'd never made a picture before and who'd been a trombone player in a band or something. On top of that, I was handed a script which had practically none of the quality of the Graham Greene book.

When I wanted to have changes made in it, the writer resented it deeply. Then, when I wanted to step out of the project, my agent told me I was contractually obliged to complete it. So I finished the picture to the best of my ability.

While I don't care for *Ministry of Fear* as a whole, there are still some things in it that I like: the seance, for instance, in which Hillary Brooke was very good, and the performances of Marjorie Reynolds and Dan Duryea. He was excellent, I thought, in the scissor-stabbing scene, which was my own invention and not in the book. I liked, too, the performance of the English actor Percy Waram as the police inspector.

The script for my next film, *The Woman in the Window,* was written by Nunnally Johnson and based on a story by J. H. Wallis called *Once Off Guard.* They changed the title because they thought the word "guard" sounded too much like "God."

I had known Nunnally since the days we both worked at Twentieth Century-Fox in the early nineteen-forties. We didn't get along too well then because he had notions of becoming a director himself, and wrote articles attacking other directors, which he was later forced to retract.

However, I liked the script for *The Woman in the Window* very much. There was only one thing wrong with it: all the male parts in it were written for old men, not only Edward G. Robinson's and the man who kept Joan Bennett, but also the part ultimately played by Dan Duryea. I'd liked Duryea's handling of the scene with the scissors in *Ministry of Fear* so much that I was able to persuade the studio to let me bring him in; that was the only way I could introduce someone relatively youthful into the male cast.

Various things appealed to me in the story, but I took the liberty of changing the ending with such a corny old trick that it seemed almost new: I had the whole thing turn out to be a dream. I did it by having the main characters in the story revealed as employees of the club—the hat-check man, the porter, etc.—in which Robinson falls asleep. Having won the fight about Duryea, I had little difficulty in convincing the studio about this also.

"Look," I argued, "the whole story is not so heavy and serious that you can afford to have three deaths. Your audience will say, 'So what?' Robinson kills one man in self-defence with a pair of scissors, Duryea is killed"—I think—"by the police, and Robinson commits suicide. If the picture ends there it will be an anti-climax."

In the opening scene we'd had Eddie Robinson contemplating a portrait of a girl in a shop-window near his club. Then a girl strongly resembling the one in the portrait accosts him; he goes home intending to sleep with her, and the story unfolds from there.

At the end of the picture, after we've revealed that everything is a dream, and Robinson has seen Duryea as the club's hat-check boy and the murdered man as the porter, he contemplates the portrait again; and suddenly another girl, mirrored in the window-pane, materializes and asks him, "You wanna come with me?" Robinson takes one look at her and runs away exclaiming, "No!"

Thus I was able to end the film with a laugh. That, coupled with the feeling of relief engendered in the audience by the revelation that it was all a dream, was a major reason, I think, for the success of *The Woman in the Window*. Both these things were strokes of luck for which I was not one hundred per cent responsible.

Some reviewers attacked the "dream" ending, but that didn't worry me. I don't care about reviews, and I think my reasons are valid ones. Motion pictures are and have been the content of my life, everything. You conceive a picture, you write it yourself or help to write it; that is the initial creative process. Then comes the actual direction, in which my crew and I work for months, very seriously, doing the best we can; that is the second stage of creation. Finally comes the cutting process, in which I always have the main say; that's the third time you create something.

At last you give the finished picture to the audience and along comes a reviewer who has to meet a morning edition deadline. In addition, perhaps his wife is betraying him or maybe he has hemorrhoids or something. In any case he cannot write an honest review and, good or bad, favourable or unfavourable, I cannot accept it. That's why I don't give a damn about reviews.

After I'd done *The Woman in the Window*, David Selznick wanted me to make a picture for him to star Ingrid Bergman and to be written by Dore Schary, later head of production at MGM. I signed a contract with David, to make this picture, and we started to write it. But—as I found out later—Ingrid Bergman was fed up at that time and didn't want to make any more films here, especially not with David Selznick. So the whole thing came to nothing.

When that happened, Selznick wanted to pay me out for less than the amount specified in my contract. I protested, but my lawyer—a wonderful guy—urged me to make a generous gesture in the hope of winning Selznick around. "What kind of a gesture?" I asked. "Tell Selznick," he advised, "that you don't want anything at all."

I told Selznick that, whereupon he said, "Thank you very much," and I didn't get a penny compensation for the entire four weeks I'd worked for him.

Meanwhile I had created my own company, Diana Productions, in partnership with Joan Bennett and others. I owned fifty-one per cent, she owned twenty-five per cent, and the rest was split up among various people. Walter Wanger was not one of them; he was retained under contract at $40,000 per picture.

In those days I worked a lot with the writer Dudley Nichols, whom I liked very much. (He's dead now—I'm the last of the dinosaurs.) I'd heard that Paramount, on the recommendation of Ernst Lubitsch, had bought the rights to the old Jean Renoir picture *La Chienne,* which I remembered having seen in 1932, and that no one knew what to do with the property.

I discussed it with Nichols, and we bought it very cheaply from Paramount. My idea was to transpose the story from Paris into a kind of similar American *milieu,* retaining the basic situation of the novel by Georges de la Fouchardière. I wanted to set it in Greenwich Village in New York, and that's exactly what Dudley Nichols and I did, retitling it *Scarlet Street.*

Neither of us looked at the Renoir film again; not a single scene was copied, and in that sense it was really one hundred per cent Dudley Nichols's creation.

We devised a very unorthodox downbeat ending for the film, allowing Edward G. Robinson to evade legal punishment for murder. Now, a director is something very peculiar. He has a nose for something, he smells something; I cannot explain it otherwise. He's not bound by laws such as "upbeat endings are mandatory." If you believe in what you are doing, the audience will never let you down. I found that out long ago in Germany, when the audience sat on its hands in response to flashy display sequences I'd inserted just for effect. But that will never happen if you do something honestly, something in which you strongly believe.

And I did believe strongly in the ending for *Scarlet Street,* which occasioned my second fight with the Hays Office. My first one was over the ending of *Hangmen Also Die,* when Hays had said to me, "You want me to approve a film in which every Czech is—by implication—shown as a liar?"

"What would you do," I retorted, "if you were living under Nazi occupation?"

I had to give in finally on *Hangmen also Die,* and now I clashed with him for the second time on *Scarlet Street.* Arguing with Hays's chief aide, Joseph Breen, I said: "Look, we're both Catholics. By being permitted to live, the Robinson character in *Scarlet Street* goes through hell. That's a much greater punishment than being imprisoned for homicide. After all, it was not a premeditated murder, it was a crime of passion. What if he does spend the rest of his life in jail—so what? The greater punishment is surely to have him go legally free, his soul burdened by the knowledge of his deed, his mind constantly echoing with the words of the woman he loved proclaiming *her* love for the man he'd wrongly sent to death in his place. . . ." And I won my point.

In a certain sense this man, played by Robinson, was doomed from the start. It was yet another struggle against destiny, against Fate. The man, Christopher Cross, a humble clerk, tries to escape from himself and becomes a painter, like Henri Rousseau (*Le Douanier*) in Paris. The paintings in the film were done by a dear late friend of mine, a man called Decker. I discussed the effect I wanted with him: it was to be a kind of primitive style, a little *bourgeois,* but still with the qualities of the French painter Rousseau.

Decker was a very peculiar man. "I can paint like any other painter," he would complain, "but I still haven't found my own style." He was unquestionably an alcoholic, and the last time I saw him was with my secretary Miss Latté when he was in the Cedars of Lebanon Hospital suffering from cirrhosis of the liver. They'd given him about thirty-six blood transfusions, which didn't help at all. It was maybe twelve hours before he died. We talked, and I thought he could be saved, but he was past saving.

Then something very strange happened at the last memorial rites in his studio. In it was a framed painting of perhaps his best friend, John Barrymore. If I remember rightly, it showed Barrymore on his death-bed, and it always stood on a big easel. The room was very crowded and everybody present can testify to the truth of what I'm about to relate.

The last speaker had alluded to the dead man's friends, saying finally: "And now he has gone where he will rejoin his dear friend, John Barrymore." And at that moment—*crash!*—the picture of Barrymore fell from the easel onto the floor. I'll never forget it.

I received a lot of money from Warner Brothers for making *Cloak and Dagger* the following year, but that's not why I made it. I made it for one reason only, and that reason was nullified by studio cutting.

The picture ends now with Gary Cooper saving the professor, played by Vladimir Sokoloff, and boarding an airplane back to the U.S. But the original script was different. In it the professor is a sick man unable to walk; they have to help him escape, and he dies of a heart attack. The American and English secret service people, anxious to discover German plans, find a snapshot of the professor and his daughter in the dead man's pocket, and in the background they notice a certain peculiarly-formed mountain in Bavaria. The next thing we see is hundreds and hundreds of parachutists dropping down on what was called during the war Hitler's "Last Redoubt" in the Bavarian Alps, and among them is the American physicist, played by Gary Cooper.

Cooper's part was based on the late J. Robert Oppenheimer, whom I had met and who had given me a certain insight into the experiments at Los Alamos and the first atom bomb.

Anyhow, Cooper and his fellow-parachutists come across camouflaged highways and big barbed-wire barriers, but not a single shot is fired, every pillbox is empty. Trained soldiers among them test the wire and find it is not charged with electricity. They keep going and finally come to a tremendous cave in a mountain. Walking in, they discover on the first floor traces on the ground of enormous machines that have recently been removed.

One of the generals in the party then remarks that they are probably too late, that those formerly in charge of the establishment are doubtless now in South America or somewhere like that. At that moment a sergeant enters announcing that on the second lower level they'd found—and this was historically correct—the bodies of sixty thousand dead slave workers. And that was the reason I made the picture.

Gary Cooper walks out of the cave knowing Germany is beaten, and outside is a paratrooper sitting in high grass and chewing on a stalk.

"Nice weather, isn't it, professor?" he asks. And Gary Cooper says, "Yes," adding: "This is the Year One of the atomic age, and God help us Americans if we think we can keep the secret of the atomic bomb for ourselves." End of film.

All that was cut out by Warner Brothers. Don't ask me why. The producer was Harry Warner's son-in-law and he offered no explanation. I couldn't do anything about it.

Secret Beyond the Door was a very unfortunate adventure, made for my own company, Diana Productions, immediately after *Cloak and Dagger*. If one thing goes wrong with a project, then everything goes wrong; and this one went wrong from the beginning.

I don't know whose fault it all was; probably much of it was mine. The cameraman was very bad, Joan Bennett wanted to divorce her husband—lots of things like that went wrong. The basic idea—the bodies in the various rooms—was good, but our solution, which involved talking someone into a radical change of outlook, was too glib, too slick. It would be very nice if a mentally disturbed patient could talk with a psychiatrist for two hours and then be cured; but such things cannot be done so quickly. And that was a great mistake in this picture; besides, I never really wanted to do it anyway.

During the war Darryl F. Zanuck had wanted to make a film set in the Caribbean, but the picture never eventuated. Now, five years after the end of the war, he decided to do it in the Pacific instead. He was on excellent terms with the Filipino representative in the Senate or House of Representatives—I forget which—and so I headed a unit sent out to the Philippines to make *I Shall Return* (called in some parts of the world *American Guerrilla in the Philippines*).

The producer [Lamar Trotti] was also the scriptwriter and he'd based his script on an obsolete book. Many of the things mentioned in the book no longer existed because of the war, and so we had to make considerable changes on location. We shot much of the film in Bataan with the help of the U.S. Navy: I remember the sunken battleships still reposing at the bottom of Manila harbour. It was an awkward time to be making a film because there were big clashes going on involving the Communist Hukbalahap forces.

I was very lucky in one respect, however. I was shooting some dancing scenes in the big park of a Filipino estate and needed just one or two more shots when the first downpour of the rainy season started, wetting everything. Just as everybody left off eating and drinking and laughing the sun suddenly broke through. I hastily had everything dried and got my missing shots. After that, the rain didn't bother me.

I had long wanted to make a film with Marlene Dietrich, who was a friend of mine, so when Howard Welsch, a producer at RKO, told me I could have her if I could supply a suitable script, I collaborated with an extremely good new writer, Daniel Taradash—the same man who later wrote twenty-four *From Here to Eternity* scripts for Harry Cohn—on a Western story which we called *Chuck-a-Luck*.

The original Chuck-a-Luck is a very famous game, a kind of vertical roulette played with a round turning wheel. I myself have seen it played in a Mexican border town. The story revolved around a cowboy trying to find the outlaw killer of his fiancée at a ranch called Chuck-a-Luck, and this was, I think, the first Western to use a ballad theme throughout to point up the narrative. Lewis Milestone had done it in a war picture [*A Walk in the Sun*], but mine was the first such Western. The song was a very good one, with the same title as the film: "Chuck-a-Luck."

When the picture was finished something happened about which I can smile today, although then I was furious. Howard Hughes had just bought RKO. None of us had met him. It was Christmas Eve, and in Hollywood on 24th December you officially work from 9 a.m. till 12 noon, but nobody really works. You may have certain things to shoot, and you shoot them, but after that you proceed to celebrate from one office to another, while everybody gets drunk.

So in the afternoon I went to the office of the man who ran the studio for Howard Hughes—he was also head of the Hughes Tool Company or some such thing. "Mr. Hughes liked your picture very much," he told me, "only he changed the title to *Rancho Notorious* because he thought no one would understand the meaning of *Chuck-a-Luck* in Europe."

"Is that so?" I said. "Well, I suppose they'll have no difficulty understanding *Rancho Notorious!*"

It was a stupid thing to do because the words "Chuck-a-Luck" are constantly repeated in the song, and the ranch at which the cowboy locates the killer of his fiancée was also called Chuck-a-Luck.

Howard Hughes's behavior was altogether most peculiar. When the news came around that he'd bought RKO, all the big-shot producers who usually turned up for work at eleven o'clock or later were there at 9 A.M. awaiting the new boss, who never appeared. This went on for about a fortnight until they said, "Oh, the hell with it," and lapsed back into their old ways.

Then after several weeks Howard Hughes finally appeared. I'll never forget it. He had a large entourage and never spoke to *anyone.* He went through the whole studio, looked at every stage, every shop, and after two hours and twenty minutes all he said was, "Paint it." Then he walked out and was never seen again. I was told that he looked at the rushes of one of my subsequent RKO films, *Clash by Night,* every evening: they would mysteriously vanish from the cutting room and turn up again the following morning and no one was sure whether he had really seen them or not.

The collaboration with Marlene Dietrich on *Rancho Notorious* turned out less happily than I'd hoped. I had the foolish idea—foolish because it led to a lot of unpleasant fights with her—of wanting to give Marlene a new screen image. In the script I'd described the character she played as "an elderly dance-hall girl," and she came on looking younger in each scene.

She has learned, I think, very much from von Sternberg, who was a cameraman before he became a director. They had a long love affair about which I
don't feel entitled to speak. You can buy von Sternberg's book, *Fun in a Chinese Laundry,* and find the lot there. She claims to have learned much from
him. On *Rancho Notorious* she would suggest certain things saying von Sternberg had done it that way; but this was my picture, not his, and so I did it
my way.

I'm very happy with the way my next film, *Clash by Night,* turned out. I
was very fond of the project, and of the late Clifford Odets, author of the
original stage play. It had been set on the East Coast in the early 1930s, but
the producer, Jerry Wald, and the screenwriter, Norman Krasna, updated it
and changed the locale to Monterey, California.

I had some wonderful actors: Bob Ryan, Paul Douglas, Barbara Stanwyck,
and, of course, Marilyn Monroe. Poor Marilyn was a scared girl, scared of
everything. God knows why she was so frightened. I'm quite convinced that
she never wanted to die. She'd taken those damned sleeping-pills, and I was
told that they found the telephone-receiver dangling from its hook, which
probably meant that she wanted to call somebody for help but was too weak
from the pills.

But working with Barbara Stanwyck was one of the greatest pleasures of
my career. She's fantastic, unbelievable, and I liked her tremendously. When
Marilyn missed her lines—which she did constantly—Barbara never said a
word. I remember a particularly difficult scene between the two of them in
which Barbara was hanging out some laundry and Marilyn had to say one or
two lines. Although Marilyn missed her cue three or four times, all Barbara
said was, "Let's try it again."

It was all rather distressing for Barbara and for us because we were all
doing our best, and reporters would visit the set saying, "Who wants to talk
to that old Stanwyck dame? Who's that girl over there"—indicating Marilyn—"with the big tits?" That sort of thing made everyone very unhappy.
Paul Douglas, in fact, hated Marilyn.

After finishing *Clash by Night* I suddenly stopped getting jobs. Howard
Hughes's representative promised me heaven on earth but I got nothing.
Wherever my agent went they said, "Yes, yes, we know Fritz Lang is a great
director, but we just don't have anything that fits his special style."

Finally I discovered that I was on a black list, alleged to have been a Communist, which I never was; this was the height of the McCarthyist Red-bait-

ing period here. My New York lawyer reported that some people in the American Legion had not actually accused me of subversive activities, had *not* said, "Hollywood, watch out, here is a Communist"; what they said was, "We have found Mr. Lang's name on the stationery of certain pro-Communist organizations."

That could have been easily explained. One day, for example, while shooting *Scarlet Street,* I got a letter from a very famous actress asking for contributions to such-and-such an organization. I instructed my secretary to send them a hundred dollars and thought no more about it, until I suddenly found myself described as a sponsor on the letterhead of an organization later characterized as pro-Communist.

Thus my accusers, while not actually describing me as a Communist, nevertheless wanted producers to have me checked. Now you know producers: why should they check? They don't run a detective agency. It was much easier for them to say: "No more pictures for Lang—to hell with the son of a bitch."

As a result I was unemployed—in the "doghouse," as they say here—for a year and a half, until finally Harry Cohn obtained a job for me at Warner Brothers. The film was *The Blue Gardenia,* which I made in twenty days for a producer who was married to Billy Rose's sister in New York. It wasn't much, but I was very happy with Anne Baxter's performance in it. She's a very good actress.

Then I made two films at Harry Cohn's own studio, Columbia. I liked the first one, *The Big Heat,* very much. It was fun to do, shot mostly in the studio and on the Columbia ranch. Based on a story by the excellent crime-writer, William P. McGivern, it appealed to me because it combined yet another struggle against the forces of fate with a certain social criticism.

Those scenes in which Lee Marvin and Gloria Grahame have boiling coffee thrown in their faces were based on an impossibility: you cannot disfigure someone with boiling coffee, it would just heal. Alexander Scourby was very good as the crime boss, and there's a whole story about Gloria Grahame and the picture which I'd rather not discuss.

She starred also in the second picture I made under the Harry Cohn contract. It was called *Human Desire,* and was based on a very famous novel, Zola's *La Bête Humaine.* It was a great success in France, I don't know why. It certainly doesn't deserve it.

There is, as you know, vanity in every man. I did a very good job at MGM with *Fury* in 1936, but subsequently never landed another assignment there. So when, nearly twenty years after *Fury*, they offered to let me direct *Moonfleet*, I naturally said, "Yes."

In *Moonfleet* we tried to create a period film entirely in the studio; we shot everything there, even the exteriors. That was the first time I worked with CinemaScope, and I made a remark about it which has since become famous—or infamous, if you prefer. CinemaScope, I said, is a format for a funeral, or for snakes, but not for human beings: you have a closeup and on either side there's just superfluous space.

The producer, John Houseman, was very nice to begin with, approachable and friendly. Then things began to deteriorate: Stewart Granger, whom MGM had under contract, never knew his lines. We had a child actor, a little boy, who tried hard but just wasn't good enough. As a result, we fell further and further behind schedule.

I don't know what ending *you* saw, but my original ending had Granger deliberately deceiving the child in the little hut on the ocean shore, saying farewell, and then boarding the barge and sailing away. The boy stands by the window saying, "You will come back," but by then Granger is dead; we fade out as the boy stands there and waits. That was *my* ending.

Afterwards the studio substituted an ending in which Granger survives and returns to the old mansion, which is now his: does anyone care about that kind of thing?

Producers' cuts not only drastically reduced Viceca Lindfors's part but rendered certain sequences almost unintelligible. The overturning of the coach, for instance; Granger hears the news of this diamond, disguises himself as an officer and goes to the well where the diamond is hidden; this was much more elaborate in the version I originally shot. They get the gem and flee, and then he comes back and saves the boy.

Then Granger makes a deal with the rich man played by George Sanders, and with Sanders's mistress [Joan Greenwood]. Everybody tries to cheat each other and Granger, overcome by qualms of conscience for having wronged the kid, leaves the coach. A shooting affray follows, and as Sanders tries to stab him, Granger shoots; Sanders dies, the horses bolt, and the coach is destroyed.

Following *Moonfleet*, I made a successful picture for an independent producer, *While the City Sleeps*, a film I personally like very much. In one scene, Dana Andrews, as a crime reporter, is sitting alone, almost drunk—let's say he's tipsy—in a bar at night, when in comes Ida Lupino, a sob sister on the same paper, with instructions from her lover (George Sanders) to seduce Andrews because he wants to have Andrews on his side in an office power struggle.

She orders something fancy to drink—Pernod or something—and then takes a color slide from her handbag and begins studying it. When Andrews asks her what she's looking at, she replies, "Oh, nothing, nothing." But you can sense that she's looking at a picture of herself naked; it was played wonderfully.

Andrews wants to see it, she won't let him, there's a bit of a struggle and the slide-viewer falls behind the bar. A bespectacled barkeeper pounces on it, takes one look at it, and registers disappointment: it's a closeup of a naked baby on a fur coat.

I thought the scene was very funny. My producer thought it stank and didn't want to have it in the picture. Now, in all my contracts I have a clause stipulating that a producer, or production company, can only cut a picture after it has been previewed. After five days, I finally persuaded the producer to allow the scene to remain in the film.

Then came the first preview. Naturally I'm sitting there sweating blood and tears, wondering how the audience will react to my pet scene. To my great joy, they started to laugh and roar and applaud. The producer goes straight to my cutter and exclaims: "That son of a bitch Lang was right again! I'm going to preview this picture so often that I'll eventually find an audience that *doesn't* applaud the scene, and when I do, I'll cut it out." And that's the sort of thing you have to fight constantly in Hollywood.

No sooner had I finished *While the City Sleeps* than the same producer [Bert E. Friedlob] offered me another picture. I agreed to do it provided I could make certain script changes. The producer promised that I could make whatever changes I liked, but owing to my agent's negligence, I had nothing to that effect in writing.

Once having signed a contract to do the film I found that I didn't in fact have the right to change anything. So I made the picture—*Beyond a Reasonable Doubt*—under duress. I hated it, but it was a great success. I don't know why.

I will tell you why I was opposed to *Beyond a Reasonable Doubt.* The story revolved around a scheme by a newspaper tycoon and his prospective son-in-law (played by Dana Andrews) to prove that circumstantial evidence is not enough to condemn someone to death.

Having already made a picture against capital punishment in *M,* I saw this as an opportunity to make another. But in the end it turns out that Andrews really has committed murder and is seeking his future father-in-law's help to escape trial. I cannot, I said, make an audience love Dana Andrews for one hour and thirty-eight minutes and then in the last two minutes reveal that he's really a son of a bitch and that the whole thing is just a joke. But thanks to my agent's mistake I was contractually bound to shoot the producer's original script.

He died soon afterwards of cancer, so he was probably already in pain, and it was a very disagreeable experience altogether. For example, he said: "Let's start with a scene showing a man being taken to the electric chair."

I knew San Quentin, had visited the death-chamber there, and had visited Sing Sing during the making of *Scarlet Street.* "Fine," I said. "Showing the reality of capital punishment is a very effective argument against it."

"Please make it as realistic as possible," the producer added.

My argument against capital punishment is that the law forces some other man to commit murder. If he throws a switch or administers poison pills, he is responsible for the death of somebody else; so the State, trying to punish a murderer, makes another man commit murder. That is my main reason.

I accordingly shot the scene in question the way I myself had seen it: how they drag the man in, how he struggles and doesn't want to go, etc. It was very realistic. Now, every Hollywood set harbors a front-office spy, and the one on this particular set, who didn't know that I had talked the scene over very carefully with the producer, ran up to the front office crying that I was shooting something monstrous, horrible.

Front office calls the producer and what does the producer do? He denies everything, comes down to the set, and shouts at me: "How dare you shoot such stuff?" You have to have a scapegoat and the scapegoat is usually the director.

No wonder I was unhappy with the finished picture; and yet the producer still approached me with further offers, saying, "Let bygones be bygones." But by then—this was 1957 or 1958—I was really fed up with Hollywood. I'd seen too many people die here of heart attacks.

"I don't want to make any more films here," I told the man; "I don't want to die of a heart attack."

Then something very strange happened: I was sitting in Washington—
where I had gone to spend the Christmas-New Year period—with a woman I
loved very much when I suddenly received a telegram from my secretary
announcing that a German producer, Artur Brauner, wanted me to direct a
remake of *The Indian Tomb,* a very successful German silent picture of the
early 1920s.

The Indian Tomb was based on a book written by my former wife, Thea
von Harbou, in 1920. It had been bought by a German producer named Joe
May, and I was originally supposed to direct it. Mrs. von Harbou and I—we
were married later—collaborated on the script, which followed the then current fashion of envisioning a two-part film, each part of feature length and
designed to be shown on successive evenings.

We gave the finished script to Joe May to read; with him were his wife,
the silent star Mia May, who still lives here in Los Angeles (he's dead), and
his daughter. In silent film scripts each scene occupied a single page, the
advantage being that you could interchange them, you didn't write the thing
consecutively; you could interpolate new and/or better ideas as you went
along.

Anyhow, the May family read each page in turn and were wildly enthusiastic. "Fantastic!" they chorused. "The greatest script we've ever read!" Mrs.
von Harbou and I naturally went home elated.

Three days later she brought me sad news. "Fritz," she said, "you cannot
make the picture." When I asked why, she told me that Joe May—despite his
name he wasn't English; he was a Viennese called Otto Mandl, and that was
just his professional name—had declared he was unable to obtain for a
young director, such as I then was, the amount of money necessary to make
a big film like *The Indian Tomb.*

The fact was that he wanted it for himself. The result, a two-part film
starring Conrad Veidt, was very successful indeed.

So when, nearly forty years later, I received Brauner's offer to make a new
version of something I'd begun in the 20s, it was like the closing of a mystic
circle, an illustration of the maxim that "everything comes to him who
waits."

I got Brauner's telegram—which instructed me to be at a certain place in
Europe on 2nd January 1958—on 30th December 1957. Despite the fact that
my passport was in the bank in Los Angeles and it pained me to leave the

girl I loved in Washington, I cabled back that I would be there as soon as I could.

I left Washington for Los Angeles on New Year's Day, wound up my affairs, took out my passport on 2nd January, left on the 3rd, and on the 4th reported at the designated place, a little town in Northern Austria.

On reading the two horrible scripts they gave me, I called up my agency's European representative and announced: "This is ridiculous; I'd better go back. I can't do these two stinkers."

She urged me to calm down and cool off, and eventually they agreed to let me rewrite the scripts in whatever way I chose. When that happened, I stayed on and made both pictures, each running 105 minutes, and bringing the pair of them in at a total cost of $1,050,000, including the producer's phony overhead.

I certainly didn't expect my version of *The Indian Tomb* to be a great artistic achievement, but I wanted to prove to the producers here in Hollywood that a picture which would cost here some eight or nine million dollars could be made cheaply in Europe and still show a large profit. That way I hoped ultimately to persuade them to let me do whatever I wanted.

That turned out to be a fallacious idea. Although the film made a lot of money in Europe, it failed here because the American distributors reduced the two feature-length parts to a composite ninety minutes and added a badly dubbed English-language soundtrack. When I saw it, I was nearly sick.

After that I did another Dr. Mabuse picture [*The Thousand Eyes of Dr. Mabuse*] for the same producer and, although it was a great success, I would rather not have made it. It's impossible to work properly in postwar Germany, just impossible.

Besides, I'm not liked there today. They don't want to hear about the "Golden Twenties." Maybe it's because they can't make any good pictures themselves. There are many reasons for this, into which I don't want to go now—it's none of my business, anyway. I'm told that lately there've been one or two good ones, but one of them was made by a Swiss, and the other by a young man who's spent his whole life in France.

I am, however, greatly liked in Paris. Godard constantly maintains he has learned a lot from my films. When I appeared (as myself) in his movie version of Alberto Moravia's novel, *A Ghost at Noon* [*LeMépris/Contempt*], I found that he improvised all the time. I will never forget a four-page letter to the producer which he'd interpolated in the script in place of a scene in which Brigitte Bardot is supposed to take a bath.

"Dear Mr. Producer," it said in effect, "I cannot tell you how this scene will play, what the characters will say, or even what chairs they'll be sitting in . . . ." I could hardly believe my eyes, accustomed as I was to the American method of strict adherence to a given shooting-script.

Another instance of Godard's penchant for improvisation occurred in a scene in which a very good actor, Michel Piccoli, and I are walking down a mountain path leading to the ocean. He played Bardot's cuckolded husband in the picture, and we were supposed to be discussing Ulysses and *The Odyssey*.

Both Godard and myself felt the scene lacked something, but couldn't decide what it was. Then, as the actor and I talked of Ulysses' homecoming and how he kills all the men in his wife's house, I had an idea. "You know," I remarked, "murder is no solution." And Godard loved it. That was the way we worked.

His aesthetic is that of the *nouvelle vague*. They want to shoot everything just as it is. Let us say, for example, they wish to shoot a scene of people sitting at Chez Fouquet, one of Paris's most famous outdoor cafés. They include all the miscellaneous sounds of traffic, of people going by, of random conversations, etc.

Is it art? I spoke earlier about my use of sound. If I sit alone in a café facing the street, I notice the traffic, the girls going by, and the noises they both make. If, however, I'm sitting with a girl I love, I'm no longer conscious of these things; I see and hear only her.

I remember a scene in a *nouvelle vague* picture—I forget which one— showing two people in bed, accompanied by so much noise that I thought they were in the sleeping compartment of a train. Actually, they were in a small room and the noises all came from outside. I personally think this sort of thing is wrong.

So you must admit that I'm correct if, when shooting a similar scene, I leave out extraneous noises or dub them down. My way of shooting is through disciplined selection. I'm therefore absolutely opposed in principle to what the *nouvelle vague* does. I think it is the death of art, which is primarily selection.

But today's youth—and I will always defend youth—have different ideas about art. The older and younger generations have never understood each other. Perhaps the younger people today are creating genuine new forms; I really don't know.

Take Antonioni. I never liked his pictures—until *Blow-up*—because they all seemed negative; they all seemed to be saying, "You can't help it, life is like that." I think such sentiments are very dangerous to put before today's young people who are struggling to find themselves, who are faced with a world which they haven't created but have inherited from older generations and which is not a very pleasant place for them to be in.

I liked *Blow-up* very much indeed because I thought I detected in it—for the first time in Antonioni's films—something which is almost positive.

Fritz Lang: Reaching Out to the Young

GÉRARD LANGLOIS / 1969

FRITZ LANG IS ONE OF THE greatest living cinematographic geniuses. His films still draw crowds in spite of the multiplicity of audio-visual options available in today's modern world. Film buffs tremble at the mere mention of his name. (Let's remember the huge audience *The Demon Screen* drew.)

This is the filmmaker whose work has generated the greatest critical response and had the analysts designing new methods: to talk about Lang is to talk as well about "the sign" (his famous hand, for example).

This is the film-maker who reconciled the proponents of form and of content and for whom the word "style" is justified. This is the filmmaker who proved best able to establish communication between generations by giving his films an air of premonition. His role in Godard's *Le Mépris [Contempt]* could not be more symbolic.

This is the filmmaker who best understood Freud, Brecht and, having given expressionism moral values which added to the aesthetic qualities that time was to dissolve, lead us best to understand and see America by ennobling the Western, adventure film and thriller, while all the while adding his famous themes on justice.

Even if he has not made a film (as a director) in almost ten years, rest assured that he remains in touch and that his unique focus on the world remains fixed, lucid, curious and benevolent.

We spoke about this and many other subjects as well during a short meet-

From *Les Lettres Francaise* (16 April 1969): 16–17. Translated by Jane Koustas.

ing and prelude to a re-release of one of his best thrillers ["policiers"] *The Woman in the Window*. I realized to what extent this portly man has remained young in spirit, optimistic in thought, lucid in judgment, determined in intention and warm in human relationships. Lang's hand is a great source of warmth.

G L : *"If we were to put* The Woman in the Window *back in its political and cinematic context, what feelings motivated you at the time?"*
F L : "It was after the war. Life in America was the same as always. Nothing unusual. Feelings, however, were different. I think it is fair to say that I always enjoyed making films. For me, making a film is a labor of love. I had already worked once with Joan Bennett and once as well with Dan Duryea. I wanted very much to reunite them. The idea of the film, that one always has to be on the lookout for oneself, came from an American book. *Once Off Guard.*

Fritz Lang interrupts and asks the press agent to show me a letter from the screenwriter, Nunnally Johnson:

"My association with Fritz Lang would not have been more agreeable. The script was ready the moment it was offered to him. When he read it, I remember only one conflict of opinion."

Fritz Lang interjects, "It wasn't the only one! The word conflict is inaccurate. It was more like a difference of opinion in respect to the handling of the story within the story. I did not want the inner story to be a dream."

Fritz Lang adds, "He wanted to tell the story in a linear fashion. As for me, I thought that the three deaths (the murder, Robinson's suicide and the death of the singer) just because a man tried to save himself from love were not justified. The audience wouldn't accept that solution either. That is why I wanted to tell it as a dream but not like an ordinary dream since in it there are people that he knew in a different way, in different roles."

G L : *"I never really liked dreams in film."*
F L : "Me either."

[The letter resumes] "It was clear that Fritz was right and not I. The film gave him a chance to the make one of his most ingenious shots, perhaps the most ingenious one I know. The one in which Robinson must be brought out of his dream and back to reality. Robinson, after taking some poison, falls asleep. Just at that moment, the phone rings. If he has the strength to answer, the audience will know that the mystery was solved and that in all likelihood, he is strong enough to take an antidote. That's where the dream must end. As the phone continues to ring and Robinson starts dying, Fritz brings in the camera to take a close-up. One assumes that Robinson is dead. Then suddenly a hand enter the picture, taps him on the shoulder and wakes him up. Then Fritz pulls the camera back without cutting. Robinson is once again in his armchair at the club and the maître d tells him that it is time to get up."

FL: "It was the hardest to film. I had 20 seconds to change the décor, the little items around and to get him into a different suit. This shot, which involved a complete costume and set change, was made without cutting. It was done so perfectly that they had to explain the technical side to me. Robinson was wearing a suit that could be taken off. During the few seconds that the close-up lasts, an assistant crawled under the camera, took off the garment and slid it under the clothes Robinson had been wearing when he fell asleep in his chair in the club. During these same seconds, the effects people switched the scenery. Etc., etc., etc."

GL: *(It was that sort of ingenuity that made Fritz Lang the great filmmaker we know.) "Wasn't it to emphasize foreshadowing that you used the dream in this way?"*

FL: "No. It was only because I thought that the audience would not accept seeing three deaths resulting from a few seconds of inattentiveness. Furthermore, I think that there is a great deal of tension at the end of the film and that the audience experiences a certain relief when it sees Robinson leave the club. When the hooker asks him for a light and he refuses and runs away, the audience has a good laugh and this is very healthy."

GL: *"Yes, but is a false sense of relief."*
FL: "Yes."

GL: *"I noticed that at the beginning of the film, before the dream, you make large sweeps with the crane. Are these symbolic?"*
FL: "I think that it is bad when you notice the camera movement because it means that the technique has taken over. I don't know if there is anything in it. I move my camera when my characters move. Can you give me an example of symbolic movement?

A V O I C E :   *"In* Hiroshima, mon amour, *Resnais uses tracking shots in the corridors."*

F L :   "Let's say, for example, in *Hiroshima, mon amour* the boy and the girl were sitting in a café discussing something very personal. The camera pulls away and you see shots of the horrors of war. There you are right, that is a totally symbolic camera movement.

I don't think I used it in any of my films. I always tried to give my films a documentary flavor and symbolic camera movement."

G L :   *"I read that when* Le Mépris *finished shooting you said that you would never do any films other than in a natural setting. Do you think that studio work is outdated?"*

F L :   "Not at all. Take *Le Mépris.* They tried to shoot one scene in a projection room. It would have been better in a studio. I remember that Godard had not been able to do what he wanted with the camera.

I think that the set should provide information on the character's personality. At the beginning, when I began to work in Hollywood, I had heated discussions with the set designers over this."

(Fritz Lang takes a piece of paper after telling something to the stuffed monkey on a piece of furniture and begins to sketch out a set that an architect had suggested to him. There a window, further away a door, between them empty space. In a corner, at the other end of the room, near the window, a desk where two people are seated. Lang explained to me that the distance the woman has to cover to exit the room is too long and that the film would become boring. So, he crosses it all out and moves the desk near the door.)

F L :   "Not only do you save on film, but you keep the film's style.

"In Hollywood we had streets in the studio exactly as they were in reality. There was no reason to shoot elsewhere. One day, I went to a shoot in a natural setting by a New Wave filmmaker. I heard noise while he was shooting. I asked him what it was and he told me that it was nothing, just the noise of the city. But I couldn't hear the actors' lines! That doesn't happen when I make a film!

G L :   *"Objects always have a precise meaning in your films. When you put together a scene, do you start with the objects or do you put them in later?"*

F L :   "That depends on the situation. I don't think that there is a rule. When someone asks me if there are rules, I say that there are none. Because there is always something different. You have to try to place yourself in a scene. Once, I made a film with Joan Bennett, *Scarlet Street*. There was a scene with a conversation in a kitchen. I thought it was too long. In the middle of the conversation, Joan took a cigarette and threw it in the sink. There was a chance to cut. Just when she tosses the cigarette, I filmed the sink in which it falls. Then I added an insert shot of a sink of dirty dishes. That adds another element to her character."

GL: *"How do you explain your retirement? Do you think that you have come full circle?"*
FL: "Firstly, I think that it is time for the young to make films about the problems of our time. It is idiotic to talk about liberty or sexual equality when there are so many other problems to address. For example, the understanding between generations as suggested by a young man that I like a great deal who would not believe in the validity of a solution given by a man on the other side of the generation gap. You know, I haven't retired yet. I have given many lectures in universities."

GL: *"But your themes are still modern."*
FL: "That is not altogether true. If you want to talk about corruption in the US, it still exists. Capital punishment remains as much of a burning issue as when I made *M*. When I made *Fury*, I talked about lynching and I think that the assassination of Martin Luther King is the same thing as a lynching. In that respect, you are right. But there are many others that only the young can address."

GL: *"And to make a film outside the US?"*
FL: "If you wanted a film on French youth, I would have to stay here at least six months. In America, I already understand the problem. I am in the center of the movement. At Berkeley we could talk to students about the reforms needed. A professor in his forties told them, 'Listen, my friends, when I was your age, me and my generation wanted to change the world.' A young man got up and said, "Excuse me, Sir. We do not want to change the world. We want to save the world from what you have created."

GL: *"May I ask why you do not like some of your films?"*
FL: "I decided to make a film adaptation of Graham Greene's novel, *Ministry*

of Fear. My agent drew up a contract. I went to New York to discuss it with the producer, who was a former sax player. I read the script that was supposed to be based on the novel and I realized that, except for the beginning, it was completely different. I refused to make the film, but I had signed a contract. So I did my best with what I had but I never believed in the film."

GL: *"And* Moonfleet, *which is still a great film?"*
FL: "That's funny. Yesterday someone said the same thing to me. It was my first film in Cinemascope and I always say that Cinemascope is a format 'for snakes or funerals but not for human beings.' I was wrong, of course, but I said it. They re-edited it behind my back. They shot an additional scene without telling me. That is the sort of thing I really don't like."

Interview with Fritz Lang

BERNARD ROSENBERG AND HARRY SILVERSTEIN / 1970

FRITZ LANG: My father was an architect; my mother a housewife. We lived in Vienna, where I was born eighty years ago. I ran away from home. Every human being should do that. Unlike most people of my generation, I really like contemporary American youth. I was asked in New York this year to make a picture about young people. If I had, the theme would have been: It's not you people, but your parents, who need an education. That gives you a little idea of my point of view.

I went to the Realschule and to the equivalent of an American university, the technical high school. I found it terribly boring. I wanted to become an artist. I went to Belgium. I longed to learn as much as possible of the world, so first I stopped in Nuremberg and Munich, and then went on to Frankfurt. In these days, around 1908, such towns had a lot of what was called good art in their museums. I was always interested in people, too. Finally, I landed in Brussels, where I ran out of money. So I started to sketch postcards and sold them. There I fell in love with a woman. Her mother was from Indochina; her father was an officer in the French army. Later on, when I recuperated from that affair, I went to Paris, and on through the Orient. After a year of traveling, I returned to Paris, where I started to paint.

Once, while I was painting in the street, a man offered me paints, brushes, and canvases if I would paint for him. I was very happy to do that. He gave me old paintings for canvases. I didn't know that I was forging the canvases

From *The Real Tinsel* by Bernard Rosenberg and Harry Silverstein (New York: Macmillan, 1970).

that I painted over. It turned out that he sent them to New York. And at the same time, he would write a letter to the New York Customs' officials to this effect: "Watch for some fake paintings. Remove the surface paint and you will find . . . ," I don't know, a Renoir or something. Under my painting, there really was a forgery of a Renoir or of some other famous painter. The customs' officials certified it as an original, for which full duty had to be paid. Then the conspirators could sell it at a high price to an affluent art collector. I discovered all this by accident.

I remained in Paris until 1914, living in Montmartre and working in Montparnasse. When the war broke out, all my friends left in time—but I stayed on. I finally took the last train out of Paris; we were stopped at the Belgian border and arrested. Some of us broke out of jail. We passed over the German frontier. In Germany, I didn't have a penny, but I could travel by train wherever I pleased. And so, I came back to Vienna just before the first hostilities.

I served one year "voluntarily" in the army. In Austria, no one with such an education as I had was forced to serve three full years. You entered the military for one year, and at the end of that time you became an officer. I was twenty-three years old, and I had passed all the examinations three times. But I was unable to serve because of a hernia, which I later corrected, so I was free. Instead of enjoying myself, I suddenly suffered a rash of patriotism and felt it my duty to go. Four years later, after I had been wounded three times, I had had it up to here. First I was in Russia, then Rumania, and finally Italy.

I was the leader of a very well-known scout patrol. I belonged to an artillery battery. The Austrian army first went forwards in Russia and Galicia and then moved backwards. It was in Rumania when we should have gone on the offensive, under German supervision. Their intelligence service was faultless—only no one told them that the Russians had just removed and shipped all this artillery to the North. Now they used the artillery against us, and the whole offensive in Rumania was killed. We were sent to Italy. I was wounded and returned to Vienna.

I was working there with the cadre, a lieutenant by then. I had a sweetheart and no money. Including sickness and hospital compensation, I got exactly 120 kronen, which would equal maybe $30 a month. One day, I was sitting in a café in Vienna worrying about where to lay my hands on a little money when a man approached me. I wore a monocle and a few fancy decorations.

"Please forgive me, Mr. Lieutenant, but would you be willing to appear in a Red Cross play?" said the man.

"Who are you?" I said haughtily.

"My name is Peter Ostermeyer."

"That can't be helped," I told him, haughty as haughty could be.

"I'm the director," he added.

And I, who had never been on the stage, but had already become interested in motion pictures in Paris, inquired, "What are you paying?"

"Seven hundred and fifty kronen."

Now, I had about 120 kronen, so my heart fell. But sometimes I have a bright moment, and I had one this time when I said, "That's not very much."

"We couldn't pay more than one thousand," he replied.

"O.K."

I was supposed to play a *Prussian* officer, but I couldn't. With the best will and the best coach they were able to give me, nobody with my Viennese accent could portray a *Prussian* officer. Then something which only happens in fairy tales took place: since I had a contract, he had to give me not the subsidiary role I couldn't play but the main part, that of a wounded Viennese lieutenant who is captured by the French.

In Paris, I had become interested in motion pictures for a particular reason. I wanted to be a painter, and it thrilled me to see *pictures in motion!* I spent many long hours viewing motion pictures. While performing in these plays, I was introduced to a man who eventually became very important in my life. He was Erich Pommer, who died only a short while ago. Erich Pommer was responsible for the golden years of the German film—1919 to 1933— the Weimar period which lasted until Hitler's time. Pommer, at first, didn't want to know anything about me. He had seen me with the monocle and thought I was an arrogant son-of-a bitch. Finally when we talked (he wrote this somewhere), he got interested in me and offered me a job as a *dramaturg* (in his company in Berlin)—which is a man who checks manuscripts that writers offer to a motion picture company. I was something like a script editor. For this job, you must have the ability to judge, to suggest to the front office that such-and-such a script should be done.

In the meantime, I was still officially in the Austrian army. I went to a friend of mine at the cadre who had the authority to ask for a furlough for me because Pommer had told me, "Look, we will go to the German High

Command to have them free you from your duties as an officer." That seemed to be a good idea. I left Austria two months before the revolution in Germany which ended the war. Erich Pommer was working not in Berlin but in Rumania. After five or six weeks in Berlin, I got a letter from my friend in Vienna telling me, "You must come back. Your furlough is over!" I asked, "What about the German High Command?" It turned out that the Berlin film company hadn't approached the high command and I was practically a deserter. But being technically employed, I didn't have to go back. I was writing scripts which everyone liked very much, but I wanted to be a director.

After four or five months, they gave me a chance to direct my first film, which I had to shoot in four days! From 1919 on, I was a director. The first was a feature-length picture. It took Monday, Tuesday, Wednesday, Thursday, Friday. Hold on, five days.

Many years—ten or eleven—later, I had contract problems with UFA, the biggest German film company. I was disgusted and decided to make no more motion pictures. At that stage, and most perversely, I wanted to become a chemist. I don't know why. It was one of those stupid ideas. (When quite young, I had seriously, foolishly, wanted to become a detective.) Anyhow, someone else asked me to make a picture for him. I refused because I didn't want to work with him. On the one hand, I had a law suit with UFA. On the other hand, this man came and came and came every weekend until finally I succumbed: "All right, but under one condition. I can make whatever I please, and you have nothing to say." I was married at the time. I asked my wife, "What is the most despicable crime that you can imagine?" We started to talk about the idea, and suddenly I thought, "A murderer who kills a child because of sexual deviation."

The picture that resulted was *M.* Now, I'll show you the difference between this picture, *M,* and my first American film, *Fury. Fury* was an anti-lynching picture. The victim, accused of having raped and killed a child, was an innocent white man. He really hadn't done it. But at least I could say something about lynching. If you want to make a real lynching picture, though, it should be about a *colored* man who rapes a white woman, which *proves* that lynching is wrong, but in America, I was forced to use a *white* man who really was *not* a rapist. In *M,* the lead part was a child-killer, and I said in the end: "Whatever you do to him is unimportant because it doesn't bring dead children back to life. What is important is we have to watch the little ones much better." That is the difference.

I stayed in Germany till the rise of Hitler. In my final German picture, called *The Last Will of Dr. Mabuse,* I put Nazi slogans into the mouth of an insane arch-criminal. He says, "I have to shake the confidence of the bourgeoise in just those authorities he himself has appointed. When the average citizen finds out that the authorities don't work, they will revolt and topple the whole structure into this chaos we will create. . . ." Where Hitler referred to "our realm of a thousand years," Dr. Mabuse promised to create a "realm of crime." I finished this picture, and presently two men in uniform materialized. I told them, "When you think you can confiscate the picture of Mr. Lang, do so." They did.

One day, I got an order to visit Mr. Goebbels. I didn't feel very happy. I wore the official uniform for visiting a minister, cutaway striped trousers, stiff collar. I walked into the Ministry of Propaganda. There was a desk on the left with two men in uniform. One of them asked, "What do you want?"

"I want to see Mr. Goebbels."

"You mean the Minister of Propaganda?"

I showed him the order.

"Go down that corridor and on the next crossing you go right and you will find his office."

The corridors were very wide, with big stone floors. You walk and you hear every step. It was not very agreeable, believe me. I came to two guards in uniform, with pistols, on the right and left. "What are you doing here?" they asked. I told them, and after an eternity, I wound up in a round room and there was a door. I got to the door. Just as I was about to knock, it opened, and a man asked, "What do you want?

"My name is Lang."

"Oh yes," very polite, "certainly. Please will you wait, the Minister is. . . ."

I waited ten or fifteen minutes; then the man came out.

"Mr. Lang, please."

It was a long, long room and on one end, very far down, was a desk. Goebbels approached; he limped, as you know. He was a charming man when he wanted to be. He said nothing about the picture, never mentioned it until the end. He said that the *Führer* had seen two pictures of mine, *Metropolis* and *Die Nibelungen,* and afterwards declared of me, "This man will make us *the* Nazi picture." I was wet all over my body.

"I'm tickled pink, Herr Minister," I said.

What else could I say? To myself I said, "Get out of here as fast as you can." It must have been half-past twelve, and I knew the banks closed at two o'clock. Outside was a post with a big clock on top of it. When you looked out the window onto a little square, you could see the time. Goebbels continued, "We would like you to head up the German film industry. We know your pictures."

"Wonderful, wonderful."

I kept looking at that damn clock and finally it was two o'clock and I knew I couldn't get my money out of the bank. At the end, he came to *Dr. Mabuse:* "I'm terribly sorry, but we have to change the last reel."

"What would you propose?"

I was now expecting him to say that the slogans would have to go. Oh no!

"In the end, Dr. Mabuse goes insane. That is wrong. He has to be killed by the people, by the fury of the people."

"That is wonderful."

At last, I could go. I was sweating, simply soaking all over my body. I went straight home, and the same evening, I left Germany, with almost no money, with nothing. Fortunately, I had a passport with visas for London and Paris where I had business connections. I had big collections of Chinese and South Seas art objects. I always had 5,000 marks, which is a little more than $1,000, in the house. That was all I could take with me.

I made a picture in Paris called *Liliom.* Erich Pommer, who was Jewish, left sooner than I, advising me to stay and see what could be done. One was very stupid in those days. He worked for the French Fox for whom I made *Liliom.* I did not know the author, Ferenc Molnar. The only correct copy of this film is at the Cinématheque in Montreal.

In those days, it was fashionable in Hollywood, when a producer or an agent came over to Europe on a spree, to bring a famous person back to Hollywood. Mr. David Selznick and his brother, Myron, who was an agent, chose me as a trophy for MGM. I had no idea of what to expect—or I might not have come at all. My colleagues and I knew only that American pictures had developed terrific technique. I had never heard of *producers* in Germany. For instance, with Erich Pommer, I made *Die Nibelungen,* a German epic. In one scene, over a hill came 400 Asiatic Huns. Pommer calls me (we were very good friends), and he says, "This scene costs a lot of money. We have to shoot it next week. Think about whether it's necessary." I thought it over, and went back to him, "Erich, I want to tell you something. I don't think that we should compete with American mass scenes. I believe we can drop it."

"Fritz, I thought it over too. I believe we *should* do it."

I was not warmly received when I arrived in Hollywood. My reputation did not really precede me. In Germany, credits went like this: "*M*, a film by Fritz Lang," followed by the other credits which were listed alphabetically: writers, architects, also the crew. It was really a collective enterprise. Here a producer is responsible to the top. I do not like producers. In the beginning, I spoke very little English and what I did speak was lousy. Later on, well, I am one of the very few people who liked Harry Cohn, the head of Columbia. With him you could talk. He used very dirty language, but you could talk to him. I didn't want a long-term contract. I preferred an arrangement either working on a picture of mine or collaborating on an idea with a writer. I'd make one picture at a time. That way I supposed there would be less trouble.

I have always been a loner. I have had too much to do just thinking about the art of motion pictures. You have a vision if you are creative. You have an idea which is very vague. If you try to grasp it, it goes away. You can, *maybe,* when you are with a very good friend, talk about this vision over coffee, over a martini, and then in a long conversation that goes on for weeks. How can you convince a producer in one short meeting? And not just one producer, you have to convince five or six people. It's very hard.

For one year, while under contract to MGM, I wasn't assigned to any pictures. After a year, they wanted to kick me out, very politely! "Mr. Lang, we will let you go." I went to a man who is dead now. Mannix was his name, the right hand of L. B. Mayer.

"Eddie, I am the most famous director in Europe. I came here and I never had a chance to do anything."

Mannix was once a bouncer, and maybe as a man who came up the hard way, he was responsive to my plight.

"All right. What do you want to do?"

I had found a four-page story by Norman Krasna—I wanted to do that. Then I located a writer, Bartlett Cormack, who is also now dead. We wrote the story together, even though I knew very little English.

My best ideas come from newspaper clippings. This happened with *Fury*. I missed only one thing in that lynching picture. You know what it was? A real lynching had happened in San Jose, and in San Francisco, a conductor stood in front of three buses and yelled, "If you want to see a lynching in San Jose, come with us." They waited in San Jose until buses arrived to lynch the guy. Unfortunately, I didn't have this vignette in my picture. Since Stephen Foster was something new for me, I made one scene of a colored girl hanging laundry on a line. She is singing, "I want to go to a happy home where all the darkies are free," and a colored man answers her with another song while he is washing a car. I made a scene in which the district attorney speaks to the jury! "There have been so-and-so many lynchings a year." Then I showed a dilapidated car in the South. Inside was an old white-haired Negro; outside, a very buxom colored girl and a boy and two children. From the car radio came the accusing voice of the district attorney. The only reaction of the listeners is that the old man nods knowingly. That scene was taken out of the picture after my first cut because L. B. Mayer was against showing colored people in films. *Fury* was a great success, and for years publicity called me "Fritz (Fury) Lang."

After that, I did no more work at MGM. Only twenty years later, when everything was forgotten and L. B. Mayer wasn't there anymore, I made another picture for them. I took it only so that I could say I was back. The next film in America I made for Walter Wanger, *You Only Live Once.* Then I got a job as producer at Paramount, where I made one lousy picture—*You and Me.*

I'll tell you a typical story about a producer. I was once in New York at Keen's English Chop House, just sitting there. A woman and a man came along and sat at another table. He showed her some photographs (slides). They laughed, and I thought they were looking at dirty pictures. But in reality, these were photographs of their food, the meat they were about to eat. That incident gave me an idea for a scene I used in a picture called *While the City Sleeps,* with Dana Andrews and Ida Lupino. I had a scene in which the lover of Ida Lupino, played by George Sanders, who was working for a kind of Hearst paper, says to Ida Lupino, "You have to help me to get him [Dana Andrews] on my side. You can do whatever you want." He adds, "Whatever you do, I know you will do for me." She understands that she should sleep with him if necessary. She tries to find Dana at a reporters' hangout. She finds him alone, sitting at the bar, half drunk. He greets her, and she says, "Hello, how are you?"

"Can I offer you a drink?"

She orders a fancy concoction with two drops of Pernod. They start to talk. Finally, she opens her handbag and takes a slide out. She looks at it and smiles, and he's dying to know what's there. She played the scene so well that you positively knew it was a picture of Ida Lupino naked. He keeps exclaiming, "Let me see it, let me see it." She refused and there is a little bantering. He grabs, and it falls behind the bar. The barkeeper, a character I showed as a learned man with glasses, absolutely different from the usual type, jumps over to the picture and looks at it. We see for the first time that it is a naked baby on a rug. I thought that was very funny.

Mr. Producer didn't like it. My contract specified that I had the right to show it at the preview in my way. The producer violently objected, "No, that is not funny. Cut the scene out." I had to fight five days for something that was written in my contract. I won my fight. It comes to the preview and my scene is in the picture. I tell you very honestly, I was sweating blood and water because now everything depends on the audience. When the scene is finished and they see the little baby on the rug, the audience applauds and roars. Gene Fowler, Jr., was my friend and cutter on this picture. He stands outside; the producer comes along: he is furious. Gene says, "Lang was right." The producer yields nothing. "Yes, he was right now. But I will preview this picture until I find an audience that doesn't applaud, and then I will cut it out." It never was cut, but that's unmitigated vanity. They cut themselves in their own flesh.

Let me tell you another case. I made a picture originally called *Chuck-a-Luck*. It was all based on that word, "chuck-a-luck." Howard Hughes, who was then owner of RKO, without asking me (because he is God personally), changed it to *Rancho Notorious*. It's a Western. Somebody tries to find a murderer who has killed his fiancée. All that's known about the culprit is that one word "chuck-a-luck." There was a song in the picture about chuck-a-luck. Now the name of the picture has to be *Rancho Notorious*. What is chuck-a-luck? I asked a man from the Howard Hughes' Tool Company, who was running RKO. "Why did he do it?"

"He thought in Europe they wouldn't understand what 'chuck-a-luck' means."

I couldn't suppress an ironic comment. "It is a good thing they know what 'rancho notorious' means."

As a young man, I roamed around the world. I really had an education in life, as a director should have. I wrote too, but I am not a writer. I dabbled in many things, in religion and in everything else that interested me. Nothing is more important for a creative artist than that he be curious. In this respect, the artist is like a creative scientist, only he should take care not to become specialized.

I'll tell you another story, this one about Jerry Wald. He wanted to make a picture about the unemployed, based on Odets's *Clash by Night.* Wald wished to place it in Monterey among fishing people. He asked me if I knew anything about fishing. What could I say? "Jerry, a director doesn't have to know. If I do the film, I *will* know." That is the crux of the matter. Superficial knowledge isn't enough.

I made an American Western after living very long with the Navajos. On a busman's holiday, I was the first to photograph Navajo sand paintings. I made many friends among the traders, too. Later I made a Western called *Western Union,* which was a perfect example of several things. Zanuck bought a Zane Grey story, but our picture had nothing in common with the book. To Zanuck, "Western Union" signified the colors yellow and blue. He wanted something yellow for the telegraph company and blue for God knows what. So the covered wagons were yellow and blue! Zane Grey's hero was married and had seven children, but naturally, he had to be a bachelor for the picture. The only adventure which actually took place during the building of the line from Sioux City to San Francisco involved buffalo rubbing off ticks against telegraph posts, which thereupon collapsed. That was all. Naturally, we had *everything* that could possibly happen in the picture!

But Zanuck was a very good producer in those days. When the picture was released, I got a letter from Flagstaff that ran like this:

"Dear Mr. Lang: We have seen *Western Union.* It is the first picture to depict the West that really was. What authenticity!" How is that? From a European director? In fact, my picture was not at all like the old West. But the whole spirit of it was true: what we captured were the old-timers' dreams about their past. And that, too, is a species of reality.

I've said motion pictures are the *art* of our century. Certainly finance is a headache, but I have never found that honest pictures lose money. Practically all of my pictures showed a profit. I had only one flop, and it happened when I tried to copy Brecht in *You and Me.* It was the only really lousy picture I ever made precisely because I wasn't being myself, and it didn't work. However, I made certain pictures which I detested, and made them just because I needed the money. There was a time, during the McCarthy affair in Hollywood, when I couldn't find work. Everybody believed I was a Communist.

After a year and a half, Harry Cohn gave me a job and the whole thing blew over.

I like audiences. Producers don't. They used to say that audiences had the mentality of a ten-year-old child. Ridiculous! On the lowest level, my picture *M* is a cops-and-robbers story. On a higher level, it's a police procedure. On a still higher level, it is a documentary of the times. And on a very high level, it is an indictment of capital punishment. Here you have all the possibilities in one picture. You have to satisfy yourself, and you should not underestimate yourself. You make the picture for yourself. You are interested in life, in what's going on. The producer is just interested in making money. I did an anti-Nazi picture called *Hangmen Also Die*. And the publicity department was upset. They panicked because it had no love interest. What could they publicize? By being interested only in money, they wind up by never being able to make it.

Hollywood is peculiar in so many ways. I had a good friend, Ruth Chatterton, who was really a star. We saw each other every day. I had a rented house in Santa Monica, and she had a wonderful house just south of Sunset Strip, with a British butler and so on. She was a literate woman. When she didn't want to make films anymore, she wrote one or two best-sellers. Out of the blue, she says, "Fritz, I'm leaving."

"Ruthie, where are you going?"

"Oh, I have to go."

She gave up her house, her library, her dogs, and disappeared. I didn't hear from her for six years. For a long time we had seen each other every day. Then, poof! No more Ruthie. I was crossing Madison Avenue at two or three o'clock one afternoon when I heard somebody yell, "Fritz." And there's Ruth Chatterton. She had married and now acted as if nothing had happened. She came back to California and wrote a novel, but not one person invited her out for Christmas. They use you as they would cardboard in the studio. In Germany or in Europe, when you are under contract, you have the *right to work*. They can't just pay you and say that's that. You can break any contract if you don't get work. I didn't want to be used like a piece of cardboard. You are filed somewhere. When they need you, they take you. When they don't need you, you get your money.

In a certain way, this complex extends to the social community as well. It's only interested in you as long as you are in the limelight. Income alone makes you acceptable as a poker player. If you earn $500 a week, you cannot play poker with someone who makes $5,000 a week because he will bluff you out of everything.

Only people in the same income bracket can be found together. In Europe, I could name you many, many actors and actresses who get old and are still beloved. Here? Nothing. I am told that Mary Pickford in her heyday was once manhandled at a station where her train stopped. They treated her without any respect or love, pawing around and tearing her blouse. It is the same thing with actresses in New York! They can play two years in a successful play, and then have no job for the next two years. Take any newspaper and look at the advertisements. You will find producers mentioned. Naturally, they're most important. Directors, too, but you will seldom find the writer's name. Hollywood created the star system. First you had one star, and then one wasn't attractive enough so you had two, then four, and so on. Stars, stars, stars, stars.

From the standpoint of the industry, the star system was not a mistake. From the standpoint of motion pictures, it was and is. This system didn't exist in Europe when I began. In Europe one asked: What is the play about? What is the picture about? Above all: *What do you have to say?* It was the story that sold *M*.

The writer was very important in Europe, but here he is transformed into a mechanic. In any major studio, there are ten writers working on a single script. You never know which was the first. This has not changed. How can you expect anything to come of it? How can an idea be developed by ten different people who are competitors, who don't know each other? When I was under contract at MGM in 1934, one man got a script which I found was extremely good. We had the following exchange:

"I have to rewrite almost every line of it."

"But why? The script is fine."

"Yes, the script is fine, but how can I prove to them that I earned my money? I have to rewrite, even though it will not be as good as the original. They gave it back to me, and I have to do something."

It is a vicious circle.

I always fought very hard in Hollywood, and as a result, some things I made there are as good as what I did in Germany. Now and then I won a battle and beat the system. That could come to pass because I was a free agent. Nobody under contract really fights. An executive of a big company once put it to me: "Mr. Lang, we are not interested in making good pictures.

We are interested in making successful pictures with as little risk as possible."
Theoretically, a producer could be of great help to the director. He could
move big stones from the director's way. What he should never do is write a
scene or otherwise interfere with the director. Every picture has a certain
rhythm which only one man can give it. That man is the director. He has to
be like the captain of a ship.

I'll tell something about Thalberg that relates to me. One day he said to
his writers, "Now, you bastards, I will show you a *picture*." He showed them
M, the story of a child-murderer with *no love interest*. When it was finished,
he asked them, "Well, what did you think of it?" They all said that it was a
wonderful picture. He recommended that they study it and learn. But one of
the writers got bold and ventured a question, "Mr. Thalberg, what would
you have said if I had brought you the script of this picture?" Thalberg
answered, "I probably would have said, 'Go to hell.'" There you have it.

One producer I know gave his directors exactly twenty to twenty-one days
to make a picture. On the first picture *he* directed he took eighty-seven days.
I knew producers who, when they started to make the schedule for a picture,
ordered so many shots per day. If a unit manager claims the schedule's
impossible, he's told to shut up: "Give the director so many shots. Otherwise
he will get too uppity. This way, he'll try to work fast, fast, fast." There is no
respect, no *esprit de corps* or comradely feeling. I read a defense of producers,
written or spoken by a producer, according to which he alone should choose
the material. Most men of this ilk use best-sellers, period.

I recently saw Jack Palance on TV in *Dr. Jekyll and Mr. Hyde*. I had once
seen the film version with Freddie March and Miriam Hopkins, Rouben
Mamoulian's piece. Also I know it with Spencer Tracy and Ingrid Bergman.
Now I saw Palance. I became interested. It had been so long since I'd read
the book that I reread it. I still have my copy. Not one picture version had
anything to do with Robert Louis Stevenson's novel. Stevenson's Mr. Hyde
is younger than Dr. Jekyll. Everybody who sees him has an indescribable
feeling of repulsion because he is *evil*. That's all. But nowhere does it say that
he looks like a monster. And all those stories with girls—you'll find none of
them in the book. The producers never read Stevenson. They only saw one
picture which feeds on itself.

I took myself out of the Hollywood film-making process ten years ago.
Next year I may do something in Paris, but I don't ever want to do anything
in Hollywood again.

The Sunset of a Poet

PETER VON BAGH / 1972

PETER VON BAGH MET THE old master director Fritz Lang at the festival in Berlin last year and succeeded in landing an interview with critic-loathing Lang. "Get out of here and never come back!" was Lang's last line. Before this, the following was said.

Fritz Lang turned 80 on December 5th, 1970, but as a person he hasn't lost any of his awareness and vigour. "The world's greatest director"—this is how you remember him—for many years providing movie-goers with exciting experiences, the ultimate experience being in 1963 at the Jyväskylä Festival with almost 15 films. These were almost simultaneously scrapped a few months later and have since then been invisible—however, he hasn't staged anything at all in 10 years, not since *The Thousand Eyes of Dr. Mabuse*. The reason has been explained in passing: his eyesight is failing and far-developed plans have had to be given up.

At the Berlin Festival in 1971, people were gossiping that Lang was in town and soon the rumor was confirmed officially—it said that the city of Berlin wanted to honor the man who was one of the most famous creators of the glamour and reputation of the city during the 1920s and '30s: the key to the new city hall had been handed to Lang. From afar I caught wind of a cocktail-party and thought that perhaps I could get a glimpse of the great one if I waited outside.

But I made another plan with the English critic Mike Wallington early one

From *Chaplin*, 112 (1972): 22–25. Originally published in Finnish in *Filmihullu*, 4 (1971). Reprinted with permission of *Chaplin* and Peter von Bagh. Translated by Bodil Little.

morning at the hotel: if possible we would approach Lang directly and immediately. We soon became aware that Lang was still in town, but that he hated
critics, particularly German ones. Contacting Lang via telephone didn't seem
right, so we went directly to Hotel Kempinski. We lucked out: Lang was
roaming around in the lounge.

The rumors seemed to have been well-founded, because Lang asked us
immediately why in the world we had the nerve to assume that he had time
for us. He asked us to wait for a while, made a trip to the dining room and
back and explained that he was waiting for a good friend and asked us to sit
down.

This friend was—of all the people in the world—new film's most brilliant
lout, Reinhard Koldehoff (sometimes also called René Koldhoffer), who has
a small part in the last Mabuse film, was one of the main characters in Visconti's *The Damned* as the fascist industrialist, and had the role as a colonial-
ist in Glauber Rocha's significant *Der Leone Have Sept Cabecas (The Lion has
Seven Heads)*, in which he sings:

> I hate Negroes. I hate Jews.
> I hate commies. I hate hippies.
> But I love sex and gold. . . .
> Old Lenin was a mad one
> in 1917 he put fire into great Russia
> and dirty mujiks invaded the pretty palace of my Czar
> and the milky water of my dear Volga became red, red, red.
> And Adolf Hitler was a mad one too
> trying to rule over the whole world
> has killed millions of David's sons
> and the sun didn't shine for a while
> and the sun didn't shine for a while
> over my blue, blue Danube
> Oh, Tannenbaum, oh Tannenbaum
> There will never be again a day
> for Hitler's sons.

This is actually irrelevant, but it is a hell of a ballad. Anyway, Lang became
sufficiently warmed up by the actor friend's jolly attitude that he granted us
an interview after having drilled us about where we were from and what we
represented: Wallington, *Sight and Sound* (could be that he would rather be

seen in his own periodical, *Cinema*) and myself, *Filmihullu,* which seemed implausible to Lang. Lang asked us to return at 5:30 p.m.—without a camera: "I am too old to have my picture taken"!

With shaky knees, Mike and I went back to think of a strategy: Lang's way to immediately control the situation, with humor, but without mercy to decide the rules of the game, had made a strong impression. We retired to a shabby café to discuss Lang and to plan our series of questions, something which would later turn out to be a fatal mistake.

We took our places at Kempinski in good time in order not to have anything unforeseen happen. The atmosphere at the lobby was like a huge sports event; journalists and photographers were crowding around a few objects. Suddenly our hopes burst and through it walked new film's most beautiful female star, the main character of Bresson's *Une femme douce (A Gentle Creature)* and one of the main characters from Bernardo Bertolucci's *Il Conformista (The Conformist),* Dominique Sanda. After her, the old stallion Vittorio de Sica, precisely as Max Ophüls showed him in the masterpiece, *Madame de. . . .* (Who are those men who go to the club, go hunting, play pool? For what purpose do they exist? They are born, they live and they die constantly surrounded by waiters, but without leaving a trace of themselves. That is no life—that is merely existing. Or even less—a non-existence. And yet these people, with their parties, receptions and meaningless diversions, are looked upon as stars of the human race. My film is in its indirect way incredibly bitter and a thousand times deeper than the anecdote upon which it is based."—Ophüls)

To be specific, this is actually also irrelevant to our interview; it is only an association which quickly disappeared again, as soon as de Sica got into his car and the sliding doors opened with Lang entering the lobby. After a little hesitation he looked in the direction where we were and started approaching us. He didn't recognize us until he was a couple of meters away. The sad truth is that Lang, who has been blind in his left eye for half a century, now moves around in almost total darkness. This is accompanied by rather poor hearing—two facts which obviously inhibit Lang's conscious efforts to control his surroundings as much as possible.

The discussions start with a dispute as Lang doubts Mike Wallington's identity and now questions that he actually represents *Sight and Sound.* He again is astounded that the other person present represents *Filmihullu* and later demands that we both write our names and periodical on a piece of paper. "I am a friendly person, but the moment I feel that you are lying to me, I will throw you out."

Our first question relates to the old *Dr. Mabuse, der Spieler (Dr. Mabuse, the Gambler)*. We have imagined that the first part of it concentrates on rituals, customs and the environment while the other is more action-packed.

Lang does not hear the question and wants to know which Mabuse film we are referring to: there are three (1922, 1933, 1961). Then he crushes our question by saying that we forget that at that time it was normal to make films in two parts, of which the first was shown one evening and the other the next. We are, then, dealing with one 4-hour long film and the plot could not culminate the first evening, as it would detract from the starting point of the other.

We pushed on with the question: is there, in Lang's own opinion of his work—though very separate, and yet—two principal lines: action as well as a clinical analysis of rituals? What is the producer's role: was it perhaps that the producing process forced the producer to concentrate more on the intrigues than what was necessary?

First, Lang claims that both elements are contained in all his films and then adds, "Who is forcing me? I don't understand your thinking. I make all my films for the general audience, and I produce all my films myself," says Lang.

We try to explain the question. At an earlier stage, as far as we knew, Lang did not produce his own films, and also we remembered an interview in which it stated how the films had been changed after Lang had completed them.

"Define the producer," demands Lang.

We try to refer to the fact that Joe Mankiewicz produced Lang's first American film, *Fury*, but we are informed that J. M. at the time tried to leave being a scriptwriter to become a producer and only in name acted as Lang's producer, as a stepping stone for his own activities. Is the producer then a person putting in money, we try, after first having used the expression "it depends on . . ." (to which Lang says: "depends on, depends on . . . define!"). No, says Lang, it is the investor. What do we do with a producer!

But, I try again: isn't it a fact that at least some of your later films, such as *Moonfleet*, were taken away from you, before the final version was completed?

LANG: What makes you think that?

Q: *Because I have read it.*
LANG And you believe everything you read!

Q: *Not necessarily, but that's why I am trying to ask. . . .*
LANG: Let's see! The director has no copyright. Perhaps to a certain degree
in France and to an even higher degree in Czechoslovakia, I have heard. If
anybody makes any changes to my work after I have completed it, I no
longer have a say in the matter. Unfortunately, this is quite possible in
America.

(This is followed by a long dispute about the roles of the producer/inves-
tor. Lang wants to know if under any circumstances we would give anybody
a free rein. When I say yes, Lang claims that I am lying.)
LANG: The director can only hope that the producer is intelligent. If he is
jealous of the director or wants to be the one to decide or arbitrarily wants
to change something, it is obvious. But the producer may be the director's
genuine friend, if he takes care of the, to the director, unnecessary tasks such
as financing, etc. That's all.

(Lang still reminds us that during the era of silent movies there were no
producers. Then the American investors discovered that they needed someone that could keep the director on track. Then the producers were
invented.)

I now ask about the violence. "I hate violence," Lang says quickly.

Q: *There are a lot of violent scenes in your movies: is this due to the fact that you
try to portray life as real as possible?*
LANG: My movies are not violent!

Q: *But they do contain scenes that portray violence, I insist.*
LANG: You claim that you know my movies. Can you name just one scene
of violence?

Q: *When Gloria Grahame in* The Big Heat *gets a cup of coffee in her face.*
LANG: There is no violence in that! All we see is that Lee Marvin does something and then Grahame comes and tells us what. Has it now come to the
fact that it is violence if you throw a little coffee around. . . ?

(In my inner thoughts I still think that this is the case, but I give another example: the last scene in the same movie, the duel between Lee Marvin and Glenn Ford. This, too, Lang denies; if it really were a question of violence, then Ford would have killed Marvin. Afterwards Lang does admit to having used violence in one of his movies. Guess which one.)

LANG: As an example, in my film *M* there is no violence, all this happens behind the scenes, so to speak. I give an example: you remember the scene where the little girl is murdered? All you see is a ball rolling and stopping. Afterwards a balloon getting stuck in the telephone wires. Where is the violence?

(Well, in that scene there is no violence, I try.)

LANG: Yes! The violence exists in your imagination. Let's assume that I had shown a scene between the child and the murderer. Let's forget for a moment that such a scene would be very tactless and extremely disgusting to look at. I could then show an example of what a sexually deranged child molester would do. But by not showing it, I force you as spectators to think about the most frightening thoughts you can imagine. What spectators imagine can vary a great deal, but I force them to help me get the greatest effect out of the scene as possible. In other words, the scene contains no violence.

I now tell of a scene that contains violence. It is to be found in *Cloak and Dagger,* which for me constitutes a description of liberties as a contrast to fascism. I recognize this incidence of violence. I am an enthusiastic opponent to fascism and in this work Gary Cooper is seen killing a fascist before our very eyes. But this is the only scene I remember in my work which contains violence.

Well, let's see. Do you know *Scarlet Street?* One may call it violence when Edward G. Robinson kills Joan Bennett, stabs her with his ice pick. I would personally only call it violence if it happened the way it happens in many later movies, if you saw the victim do something, if the man stabbed her continuously, if blood was flowing. In my movie, Robinson hits the woman lying in bed, because she laughs at him. I hate violence. I am against violence—I always try to depict scenes which have nothing to do with that kind of violence that you see in Westerns and movies of that genre.

Lang claims that the audience, mostly in the US, is completely used to violence, which is everywhere, especially the information media, which is flooded by it. This is enough of an argument not to include violence in movies for the sake of violence; that, on the contrary, one should be aware of such movies, which are totally interchangeable.

We try to continue with the same topic. In *The Big Heat* there is a scene where the police car explodes and the wife of the police officer (Glenn Ford) dies; in this image Lang has compressed a *peripeteia* after which the main character's life no longer is as before, but takes a new catastrophic direction.

"But isn't life just that!" says Lang and protests against the indirect question: we do not see the car explode at all. Lang now accuses us of our interpretations: critics try to read more into his movies than what he had intended.

LANG: Many people have the erroneous impression that everything is a great mystery. This doesn't exist. If there is a deeper meaning in my movies, it is definitely not planned. Once, many years ago in Paris, I said to some critics that it would be interesting if the director at a certain point after completing his work would take psychoanalysis. The director does things, but under no circumstances in such a way that he figures out that one plus one equals two and then three. It is very hard to describe the creative process. I cannot do it. Impulses, personal experience, etc. influence it. Perhaps the psychoanalyst could describe this process.

Q: *Do you think that the best moments in your movies are those that you haven't thought about in advance?*
LANG: I always think out everything beforehand. My very good friend Godard tries to improvise. I never do. Perhaps sometimes when it comes to the placement of the camera, but my script is completely clear. Sometimes you have to change things; for example, when the actor cannot handle his lines, but not even then do I change things in such a way that the original meaning is changed.

Q: *You have worked with many famous photographers: James Wong Howe, Stanley Cortez (Lang: "Cortez is not a good photographer"), Charles Lang, George Barnes. . . . Can you give us your opinion of their work?*
LANG: The photographer is the director's closest colleague. That's all.

Or let me give you another example. I did my first Western. The woman in the movie was sitting and had to get up. The photographer said: I cannot film this, which is idiotic, anybody could film something like that. I had two possibilities. Start a fight, after which the photographer would have shot the scene and done it poorly and thus had his way, you see, it didn't work. OK, I said, we take a close-up. And that was the solution. Do you understand what I mean? On the other hand, if I had discussed this with the photographer and he had said, "Fritz, how about we take two—three scenes of the script in one shot," then my negotiations would have been over. The main thing is that the cooperation is very intimate.

Q : *Do you always adjust the shot yourself?*
L A N G : Yes.

Q : *By looking through the lens?*
L A N G : Yes. Always.

Q : *So that the shot is an architectonic, geometrical entity. . . .*
L A N G : Perhaps so, but I do not like the word "architectonic."
   Suddenly Lang says, "I stopped doing movies in the US for reasons that I do not intend to reveal in this interview. This happened in 1957 and some years later I decided to stop doing movies altogether due to my failing eyesight. Now I have a feeling that people think far too little of sound. You asked if I would use sound as horror elements. I would really like to use music in a frightening, horrifying way. I do not say that you should, but one could. Let's imagine another world.
   "I imagine three astronauts' tragic death. Nobody really knows what actually happened. It may, as they say, have been an accident; they had forgotten to shut something properly. Let's examine another alternative. The astronauts spend 20 days in outer space, weightless. The human body is not used to such a condition. I can imagine that on the moon, at the time of death, something happens which instills the deepest fear; another world, the realm of death. This vision is connected to your question of the use of music."

Q : *Your relations to the experimental arts have always been intimate: Oscar Fischinger, Walter Ruttmann during the 20s. Your answer leads us right into experimental art. . . .*
L A N G : I have never been a director doing several movies a year. I loved film and still love it. I think that the young talents of today, especially the underground directors, emphasize the technical aspects too much. We had noth-

ing but a small, moveable camera. No zoom, none of the so-called technical equipment of today.

I believe that most new movies lack content, lack a message. My film *M* is almost 50 years old, but is still shown every day all over the world. To me, technique is not the main thing, as appears to be the case for the new talents.

Q: *What is the scoop with Fritz Lang and the actors? Where does the "inexpressiveness" typical for Lang come from, evident in* While the City Sleeps *and* Beyond a Reasonable Doubt, *characterized by Dana Andrews. To Lang, is the actor almost a sculpture in which he blows life or personality, functioning on his own terms?*

LANG: Why should I lead the actor in any particular direction?

(We now try to talk about Lang's personal vision; we seem to have experienced such and we naturally believe that the vision influences the actors' work through Lang's entire work.)

LANG: Hold it! You are wrong, 100% wrong! First there is the script. There are certain characters in the script. That's the main thing.

Q: *Yes, the main thing from a practical point of view. . . .*

LANG: No! It is the main thing from the point of view of reality and ideas! In my view, the director should be a friend to the actor. What are the director's obligations? You think that the director is a dictator, that he orders the actor to do such and such. In that way you get nothing out of the actor. Now, you try to forget the question about Dana Andrews—I'll not remind you of it. I must explain to the actor why certain things happen: the director must be like a psychoanalyst. The director points out possible mistakes in the interpretation of the actor, tries to analyse the reasons for the mistake. I have never liked working with so-called stars. You see, the star is not always a first-rate actor by any means: he has created an image of himself and is able to carry it along from movie to movie. I cannot make use of such a star, as I try to create intense human beings, different in each film.

After having grown dead-tired of an actor, many directors tell that actor that he will show him how to play the part. I would also be able to play in front of the actor in this way. However, I wouldn't do it, as I am not interested in watching 25 Fritz Langs on the screen. The duty of the director is to work as sensitively as possible with the actor.

So, what was it you said about Dana Andrews? Do not read in your paper; think!

(Embarrassed, we try to explain that according to our understanding, the actor submits to the environment more so than usual in Lang's films—to a greater extent being a social being rather than an individual. For example, Dana Andrews totally becomes part of the environment in his Lang films, a journalist corrupted by money or by the business environment.)

LANG: But Dana Andrews plays a different role in these films than in other films!

I already said it a moment ago: when an actor has obtained a certain reputation lots of directors say: I have seen this actor A in this and this movie. This is exactly what I seek to obtain, since I will not pull the same performance out of the actor, which he has already done, in an earlier film. I will now give you another example, *The Big Heat*. In the beginning, Glenn Ford is an ordinary police officer, but during the plot he changes and even though he still is a police officer at the end, he is a completely different person in the beginning. And to get back to Dana Andrews, he is a completely different person in the one movie than the other; he is an actor who is playing his part. Sometimes he gets support from the director—sometimes not. It is as simple as that. You understand!

There are no rules in the movies. You try to find rules, but there are none. I already said earlier: you try to make everything into a mystery. There are no mysteries. I hate you both. . . . Continue!

(Nobody could say this more nicely, more kindly: "I hate you both!" We then continue—with shaky knees.)

Q: *Have you never done a documentary?*
LANG: All my movies are documentaries.

Q: *But they have carefully developed screenplays, etc.: they do not belong to the genre called documentary.*
LANG: Exactly. They have carefully developed screenplays. Period!

(We now ask about Lang's last project, *Und Morgen . . . Mord,* which he worked on in the beginning of the 1960s after *The Thousand Eyes of Dr. Mabuse.* It appears that the other scriptwriter of this planned film is approaching [a reminder that our time is already up: we have been talking for more than an hour and from the beginning we were promised 45 minutes] and that the plans didn't materialize for reasons that Lang does not wish to talk about. Anyway, nobody else got to make it, since Lang kept the copyright to it.)

Q: *Have you had many plans which did not materialize?*
LANG: Everybody has.

Q: *Are there any that you have a hard time giving up?*
LANG: Every one! On the other hand: it has already been 8–9 years since we worked on *Und Morgen . . . Mord,* and today I wouldn't make it even if it were possible.

Lang says something about his subject: if everything continues . . . then the next step is murder. The hands—the famous hands, which they say, appear in many of the movies as the brand name of the director—emphasize and make clear the intended ideas.

Q: *Are you still a pessimist?*
LANG: No—I am an optimist.

Q: *But isn't the thought of fate very strong in your movies?*
LANG: People create their own fate and are responsible for it. The old belief that you cannot escape your fate is only right in the sense that of course it cannot be so, since people themselves are responsible for their fate. But fate is not what the Gods dictate. Fate is what you do, how you treat certain things, how you develop personally.

Q: *In a foreword to the book* Saint Cinema, *you quoted a short sentence in Sanskrit, which contained something about the vision of tomorrow.*
LANG: I remember the quote.

Q: *What is your opinion of the future of the cinema?*
LANG: In my opinion, film is this century's most important art form. It will be different, only this is evident. For my part, I can only say that I do not understand people who do movies about Napoleon. Maybe I am wrong. But I have no interest in movies about Napoleon; it is past history.

(Lang's friend is on his way and this causes a little joke: he asks a waitress to leave a message in the room for "*Schurke* Wuttig" [the crook Wuttig]. We ask again about the documentary.)

Q : *Is it because of the reality aspect of your movies that you call them documentaries?*

L A N G : My movies are about real people. They are not about fantasy products.

(Wuttig, the crook, arrives. Lang pulls away the paper on which we during the afternoon have scribbled down our deep theories and lame questions.)

L A N G : Scram! Get out of here, my children! Goodbye! Never let me see you again before my eyes!

A friendly handshake. *Sight and Sound*'s double agent and *Filmihullu*'s representative disappear out of the picture, partly very happy, partly sad about their blunders. One thing is perfectly clear: that Lang not only has given a personal interview, but also educated us in how you control the situation. In other words, a little sample of how "the world's greatest director" behaves in a situation where you work in a group, just like when making a movie.

Dialogue on Film: Fritz Lang

JAMES POWERS, ROCHELLE REED, AND DONALD CHASE / 1973

QUESTION: *How do you take your coffee?*
FRITZ LANG: Black . . . as my soul.

QUESTION: *Just a minute ago you said you often learned more from bad films than good films and you were telling us why that was so.*
LANG: I learned only from bad films. When a young actor or a writer came to me and asked me, "What can I do to learn to make films?," I was always in a mess because I didn't know what to tell them. And I asked myself how I learned something. Now when I looked at the good films, I always was a very good audience. I was never interested in who the actor was, who the director was or where the cameraman was. I lived with the film. I enjoyed it. It was an adventure. My interest was so full in the film that when I saw a lousy film which I didn't like, there was something which made me say, "Wait a moment, this is not good, this I would have done differently." In my opinion, this is the only way I personally learned. I don't know if another person could do the same thing. You talk to me about myself, you know.

QUESTION: *You said you wondered how students or young filmmakers can learn about films but in the very beginning, there was nobody to learn from, was there?*
LANG: No. You see, I lived in Paris before the First World War started and I

From *Dialogue on Film*, 3.5 (April 1974): 2–11. Reprinted by permission of the American Film Institute.

wanted to become an artist, a painter, and then I went to a movie and this whole thing started to interest me because they were not static pictures which I made when I was painting the canvas, they were moving pictures and I looked at quite a lot of them. Mostly they were adventure pictures.

QUESTION: *Adventure?*

LANG: Yes. Do you know who Arsene Lupin was? Such kind of films, you know, I looked at them and that was for me, not that I had the slightest idea to become a motion picture man, but this interested me as motion pictures and probably there something was created in me, I don't know. I am asked very often how I made my films—mostly when we speak about this naturally I was asked how did you make the first films which you made in Europe, in Berlin. I can only give one honest answer: I made them almost sleepwalking. I had nobody whom I admired so much that I said, "I would like to make a film like this director or like this director."

In those days, I wrote the stories myself. I used four days to write a story, four nights. I remember one day Erich Pommer was asking for something and I hadn't written anything and I said, "Take my word of honor that I'll give it to you in five days." So he asked me for my word of honor and I sat down in the evening with a bottle of French red wine and started that night. In those days, you had for each scene one page so you could interchange whenever you wanted. When you suddenly said, "I need something before," you just put another number on the scene of another page so you could write in four days a film.

QUESTION: *You were in Paris before World War One, studying to be an artist. Was it then that you decided you wanted to make motion pictures?*

LANG: No, I never decided. That came much, much later. (When the First World War broke out), I left Paris with the last train and I was captured on the borderline in Belgium, then the same night we escaped. Probably they were very happy to get rid of us and it was very stupid. Anyway, I was captured because a lady who also was in the last train had forgotten her handbag and I went back to get her handbag with her and they caught me. And probably they were very happy to say, "Leave the door open and let the son of a bitch go." I came back and I had had a hernia. I wouldn't serve as a soldier before I went to Paris and I had the hernia operated on because nobody was thinking about a war at the time, and now, with an operated hernia, I was absolutely ready to go to war. So in the meantime, I worked in a cabaret. It was 1913–14.

QUESTION: *Where was this?*
LANG: Vienna. I fled from Paris and then I had no money—I left every-thing—and I had taken the train to Vienna where my parents lived and there I went, not immediately, to the military. I waited until they called me and I think they called me three or four months later in January or December. But anyway, I made a little money in a cabaret.

QUESTION: *What did you do?*
LANG: A stupid act.

QUESTION: *Singing, talking, a comedy or what?*
LANG: A comedy. But anyway, I met a young man who was a bank clerk and he wrote songs for the same cabaret and he came to me and said, "Why don't we write a film script together?" and I said, "Fine." I had already writ-ten one about the railroads because for me it was so interesting to see the steps of the man in the snow slowly dissolving into the paw of the wolf, you know, and so we both decided we wanted to write films together and fine but I don't know, I didn't like very much what he did. He was a very nice man so I said to him, "I'll tell you one thing. Let me write the scripts and you sell them." So we really sold one and then I had to go to war. I came back, I think it was the third time I was wounded, and I had a sweetheart, she was working in a cabaret, and I didn't have any money. I had 120 Kroner, which in these days was not even $20 a month. I was sitting in a cafe, these kind of Viennese cafes that don't exist anymore.

QUESTION: *Not even in Vienna?*
LANG: Not even in Vienna, not in this way, you know. You came there and you ordered a coffee and with the coffee came two glasses of water and with this you could sit the whole day in your place. You could read all the papers, you could play billiards and you didn't pay for anything. Sitting there—I see it as if it were yesterday on the corner of the billiard table, and I was thinking how I had some decorations, you know, I'd been wounded, and what to do if you have no money and you have a very, very nice sweetheart and you need money. A man came to me and said in an East Prussian dialect, "Excuse

me, Herr Lieutenant, would you be interested to play in a stage play?" I looked at him very odd and said, "Who are you?" And he said, "Oh forgive me, I am the director of a play."

It was a play for the Red Cross, the story of an Austrian lieutenant, he is a wonderful servant. And I said, "So what do you want?" He said, "Well, Mr. Lieutenant, we would like to know if you'd try to play a part in the patriotic Red Cross play?" And sometimes, very seldom, I am at the right moment and I said, "How much do you pay?" I had 120 kroner and I said, "Lieutenant, I'm a wounded Lieutenant living in a hospital with . . ." and he said, "750 kroner." My heart fell from here into my shoes but I said, "That's not very much." And he said, "Well, Mr. Lieutenant, more than a thousand we could not give you." So I made a deal for a thousand. Now I was out of trouble. I had a thousand kroner and a sweetheart. I didn't give a damn about this play. I was never on a stage. What they wanted from me was to play a Prussian officer.

It was in the last year of the war. So we made the first rehearsals and Mr. Ostermeyer said, "Impossible. This man can never play the part we've written." But I had a contract, so they gave me the main part, the Austrian officer, who was wounded and played in the first and the last act. The middle act was where I should have played the Prussian officer who came to help and they stormed the French palace where there was a prisoner of war.

(During this time), I met some people and they called Erich Pommer, who was the head of Decla, probably a spy mission or a political part of the German Army, and he looked at me and I wore a monocle and he said, "This monocle, son of a bitch, I don't want anything to do with it." But they said, "Now look, we promised him we would bring you both together, speak with him." So we came together after a performance, sat together until four or five o'clock in the morning, and then I had the job, in German you call it a dramaturge. You would call it here. . . .

QUESTION: *A writer.*

LANG: Yes, a script doctor. And he promised me—now don't forget I was an Austrian officer and he belonged to the German Army, you know, and they could do whatever they wanted—he promised me that I wouldn't have any trouble. I should get a month or two month's vacation because I couldn't go into the war any more with the wounds and with my bad eyes and he would give me a vacation for two months. The German government would make every step so that I would get out of the Army and serve as a script-corrector/editor at Decla. So, after the play was over, I went to Berlin.

QUESTION: *What was the play called?*
LANG: *Der Heis,* and do you know that the man who played it is still living here?

QUESTION: *Let's go back to the years prior to the war when you were in Paris and you saw your first motion pictures. Was their fascination for you and your interest in them more as a technological phenomenon than an aesthetic one?*
LANG: No . . . take what I'm telling you now with a grain of salt. I ran away from home when I was 18 or 19; anybody who wants to be somebody should run away from home. I could tell you funny adventures which I had which take hours and hours but what is important is I lived in Brussels and then I went to Paris and then the whole Mediterranean and I went up to Bali and then I came back on a ship. I would have to lie if I had to tell you what I did on the ship—I don't know. Then I landed in Marseilles, back again.

QUESTION: *You mean you went to Bali in the South Seas?*
LANG: Yes, from Paris through the whole Adriatic Sea over from Cairo and then to Bali and then back. I know one thing. I lived from making postcards and selling them.

When I came back, I lived in Paris. I didn't have much money, just to buy the most necessary things, and I always liked martinis. So I had a drink. I went to a bar and said, "Give me a dry martini," and I drank half of it and it wasn't so dry. So he changed it to a little less dry. I had at least one and a half martinis for the price of one. But I'm looking around and there was a very nice girl sitting with an elderly man. I went over to them and said, "Would you mind if I make a sketch?" When it was finished, I looked at it and showed it to her. "Oh, it's wonderful," she said and I said, "Here is a present for you." She said, "Thank you." Do you know what she did? [Folds a piece of paper] . . . and put it in her bosom. Then the man with her usually said, "How much do I owe you?," and I said, "It's up to you." I usually got ten or twenty francs.

Anyway, I'll tell you something that is important for somebody who wants to become a director. I always liked people. I was interested in people. Look, a director should know when he sees it how prostitutes behave but he should also know how a queen behaves, a cook behaves; he should also know what is practically the same, how a high financier behaves. Like a housewife behaves. A director is one who has not to study people but in a certain way he has to love them. And when I say love them, I mean understand them, understand why they do certain things. This is very important for the director. And naturally, when I went on all these big travellings, speaking with sailors and speaking with rich girls, and poor people and poor girls, I learned a lot of things.

QUESTION: *From that understanding of these various types of people comes a compassion for them. Do you find that contemporary films lack that kind of deep understanding of the people they portray?*

LANG: I don't see very many films nowadays. From time to time I look at films—the next film I have to look at is *State of Siege* but I saw a film about a girl and a man, an elderly lover who for no reason whatsoever. . . .

RESPONSE: The Getaway.

LANG: *The Getaway. Getaway* is a film today which preaches commit murder, commit crime, and we'll have a happy life ever after.

RESPONSE: *A happy life and lots of money too.*

LANG: You have no happy life without money, unfortunately. Have you seen *Deep Throat?* Look, let me for a moment be very Catholic. I'm a born Catholic and very puritan, and so many people say to me, it's impossible, this picture. I am opposed to this film for a very simple reason. First of all, it is not film as art. But there's something else. If two young people, a boy and a girl, go in together, now what they do when they are alone is only their business, right? So one day they may find out, look, there's another way to make love to each other. I go down on you and you go down on me, whatever you want, right? Something that for them is very beautiful if they find it out by themselves, if it comes out of their passion for each other. But they come and see it for the first time in a motion picture and say, "Oh, let's try that." For me, the whole thing is a crime against youth.

QUESTION: *Because it deprives them of the discovery they would make themselves?*

LANG: It is a crime against youth. Exactly a crime as *The Getaway.*

QUESTION: *But which in the long run is really more harmful:* The Getaway *or* Deep Throat? *Assuming that people will imitate the action on the screen.*
LANG: Probably in the wrong way, *The Getaway*. But it's very possible that the whole sex life of two young people can be gone to hell. I don't know. . . .

QUESTION: *You're just speculating?*
LANG: No, I'm not. I'm thinking about what I did in motion pictures and what other people did in motion pictures, you know, and I think about certain things.

I stopped making films here 1956 or '57 because I foresaw the downfall of the motion picture industry. It's something very peculiar. We talk and we hear so much about the spy business of Mr. Nixon, right? When you made a film for an independent producer or a major company, do you know there were always spies around you which reported every step you did?

I'll give you an example. In the last film which I made here—I came to the conclusion actually in the last three or four films which I made here—that the average citizen breaks the law as often as criminals do but they do it in such a way that it is not an official crime. Do you know what I mean? I wanted to make a serious film showing how average bourgeois made certain things. The last film I made was called *Beyond a Reasonable Doubt.* When Dana Andrews in desperation has killed the girl who made his life unhappy, it was a crime out of despair. When the woman he loves, who was played by [Joan] Fontaine, in the end turns him over to the law, she does it out of selfish reasons because she wants to marry another guy. Correct? Now this film started with an execution of a man and do you know, an audience is very peculiar. Have you seen a film of mine called *Scarlet Street?* Eddie Robinson and Joan Bennett and Dan Duryea. Duryea did not commit a crime but he is sent to the electric chair and dies for a crime which Eddie Robinson has done. Do you know that only one reviewer ever wrote about this case? They accepted it because he was such a nasty son of a bitch.

QUESTION: *Do you mean Duryea was so nasty they accepted the fact that he should die?*
LANG: Yes, he was a nasty son of a bitch. He was a pimp. He was everything nasty. He never committed a crime.

QUESTION: *So the critics just accepted that it was all right that he die?*
LANG: And so did the audience. I get a lot of fan letters and never one fan letter said, "Look but he is an innocent man going to the chair. How could you do that?"

QUESTION: *That was the point though, wasn't it?*
LANG: Isn't that funny? You never thought about it. Be honest.

RESPONSE: *No, not in those terms.*
LANG: Now, spies. I had been to Sing Sing, to Folsom, to San Quentin and the cage in which he lived, remember, was absolutely built according to how prisoners who were going to the chair lived 48 hours or 24 hours before their death. So the producer came to me and said, "Fritz, make it really correct and very gruesome." I said, "No, look . . . you will have trouble with the main office." He said, "No, no, that's my business." I did not show the death of the man. I showed how he was bound to the chair and how they pulled the switch but I didn't see him do anything like this [gestures], you know. I shot the whole sequence and then I went back to another sequence which played in Condemned Row and suddenly the producer came and started to yell, "What are you thinking? What are you doing? That is not the USA 1956. What's going on? Why do you show such a horrible scene?" A spy had come from the main office. The main office had not called me but had called the producer and given the producer hell. "What do you think? Do you think we can sell such a picture?" So the producer comes to me.

We had a hell of a fight with each other and I said, "Look, there's only one possibility. If you want that this film should be finished, walk out of here. If you don't walk out, I'll walk out. I don't give a damn anymore." So I finished the film and I had a very close friend, Gene Fowler, Jr., and he knew exactly how I would cut the film and when the film was over, I said goodbye. The producer says, "But you can't go. You can't leave me alone." I said, "You son of a bitch. I don't want to have anything to do with you anymore or the American motion picture industry," and I walked out and never made a film in the United States anymore. Same business which you have now, if you like, with the government. The spy. So what. Nothing.

RESPONSE: *So Gene Fowler Jr., edited the picture then but he knew what you wanted.*

LANG: He edited. He worked on many of my films and I liked him very much and he knew exactly what I wanted. We had talked about it and I told him why I didn't want to finish. It's a peculiar thing, making motion pictures.

RESPONSE: *You must have worked with producers who facilitated your work sometime in your career.*
LANG: Look, a producer can be a great fellow.

QUESTION: *If he leaves you alone?*
LANG: No, if he helps. Offhand, I didn't find anyone. Offhand, I would say I didn't find any producer here in town. Zanuck gave me mostly a free hand. I had wanted a discussion with him. He said, "You should have made a close up here." I said, "I can still make it." "So why didn't you make it immediately?" So I said, "Mr. Zanuck, I want to ask you a question. Sometimes you dictate a letter to your secretary and then she reads it to you, you dictate it a second time, and is it always correct?" He said, "No, sometimes I have to change it." "But from me you wanted it immediately, it is perfect."

RESPONSE: *Was this in reference to a specific picture you did for Zanuck? Was it* Man Hunt *that he made the comment about?*
LANG: No, it wasn't. It was *Western Union.*

QUESTION: *How did it happen that you became involved in doing Westerns?*
LANG: I left Germany because I couldn't stand the Nazi ideas and the Nazi regime and I went to Paris. I made one film there and then I came here. I was a year at MGM and then I couldn't get a job. And in this one year I had nothing to do. I travelled around the country in my car, I spoke to every man, gas station attendant, whatever. I lived with the Navajos and I learned a lot. Then I made *The Return of Frank James.* I had done some research and I had, I thought, a lot of knowledge. I always thought that Westerns are a certain religion of the American people and I treated some like this. The funny thing was, after I finished *Western Union,* I got a letter from old-timers in Flagstaff who wrote, "Dear Mr. Lang, we saw *Western Union* last night and it's the only film that depicts the West as it really was." How was this for a European director? The old-timers were wrong, naturally, but the film lived

up to their wishes, to what they wished the West would have been. I tried to build legends with human beings, that's all.

QUESTION: *At the time you came to the United States, there naturally were a great many German, Austrian and Hungarian actors and actresses who came at the same time. Why didn't you use more of those European actors? Is it that you wanted not to recreate Europe but you wanted to do American films? So therefore it would not be logical that you would use all these Europeans. . . ?*

LANG: Yes, but look, I can't remember that I ever used a European actor as an American but when I made *Hangmen Also Die,* I used a lot of Germans. I wanted to explain to an American audience what it means if a country is overrun by foreign soldiers, by foreign governments, by foreign powers, with absolutely other ideals as political ideals. Therefore, as it plays in Czechoslo-vakia, I made all the Czechs Americans and all the Germans Germans. I had a great fight—not a great fight but a fight with Bertolt Brecht who wanted me—you know what a quisling is? A quisling is a man who collaborates with the enemy. I had a quisling among the Czechs and Bertolt Brecht, who was responsible for the script, suggested a very good actor, Oskar Homolka. I said, "I can't use him because he must be an American. If he has a German accent, everybody will say, 'Oh, naturally he's sympathizing because somewhere he has a German mother, grandfather, or some relative.'" Brecht never could understand it, never. And there I used European actors. I did the same thing in my first anti-Nazi film. It started with an attempted assassination of Hitler. . . .

QUESTION: Man Hunt?
LANG: *Man Hunt.* Afterwards in London, the Nazis are played by Germans.

RESPONSE: *But what I meant was, if my point is correct, you wanted to make American films.*
LANG: Naturally.

RESPONSE: *For instance, when you made* Liliom *in Paris, you used French actors, when you came to America, you used American actors.*
LANG: Do you know Lotte Eisner? She wrote a book about Ferenc Molnar and she liked him very, very much. When she came here, she said, "You

know, it's very funny. When I see now the Molnar films which you made in Europe, they are all European characters." Whereas your American films are only American characters." When I came to this country, I stopped speaking German. I didn't speak a word of German.

QUESTION: *How did you come to make* Man Hunt?
LANG: It was very peculiar. I am told that John Ford turned it down for political reasons. I don't know why but Kenneth Macgowan, who was the associate producer, offered it to me and I liked it very, very much. I jumped at the idea because it was the first time that I could try to make the American audience understand the Nazi regime.

QUESTION: *Why was the budget so small on* Man Hunt? *You had a terrific cast, a terrific crew and a great story.*
LANG: I may have a clue to that. When John Ford turned the picture down and Darryl Zanuck gave it to me, Darryl said, "Don't show too many swastikas, we don't like that." For me, it was the first time that I could really show what the swastika meant, you know, and I showed it as often as I could. Zanuck never said anything but maybe, because of this, he didn't want to spend. Don't forget, practically everything was made on the lot. Remember the chase with the dogs in the water? It was all made on the lot.

QUESTION: *Of all your films, which is your favorite?*
LANG: *Liliom* I always liked very much. Today, I almost like *Liliom* best of all. *Liliom, Scarlet Street, M,* and *Fury.*

QUESTION: *What was your relationship—or how did you handle your relationship—with the crew?*
LANG: Look, I made a rule to be the first on the set in the morning. The rule is that you should start your first shot at 9 o'clock. I consider the crew very close to me because we are working together. I mean, if someone pushes the cart on which the camera stands and he knows he has to stop exactly on one point for a certain reason, if he doesn't understand why, he may go too far, he may not go far enough. So I was always the first one at the studio at 7 o'clock. And do you now why? For a very simple reason. Look, sometimes you have to go into overtime. If necessary—and you usually should—you send your main actor home because if a woman gets up at 5 or 6 o'clock and

is made up and starts to shoot at 9 o'clock, the close ups which are made at 5 or 6 o'clock that evening can't be very good anymore, that's natural. So you send her home and then you work maybe one hour later. I don't want to hear from the crew, "Naturally, Mr. Lang, you come at 9 o'clock in the morning. It's very easy for you to work one hour or two longer." But when I come at 7 o'clock and work with my crew and sit with my crew and have a cup of coffee with my crew, then they could never say this. I never had trouble with anyone.

QUESTION: *Would you comment on the way in which you like to work with actors?*
LANG: I think you have to work with an actor as you would work with yourself. You have to explain to him how you see the character that he has to put on the screen. You cannot use him. Maybe he is right and you have to think it over. Maybe he is wrong. There's something which you should get out from an actor, something which is under his skin, something which he himself maybe doesn't know exactly. I hate—and I never did it—(to tell an actor how to play a role). I don't want to have 25 little Fritz Langs running around. I have too much respect for an actor.

There's one actor, whose name I don't want to mention, who constantly tells inventions about me. I don't know why—I was told he made two of the best pictures of his life with me—but he tells the most absurd stories. He wrote it a long time ago that I came with crocodile tears in my eyes to beg him to play a part. I like crocodiles much too much. The last time he said something, some weeks ago, he said that I had him and the actors, whom I like very much, sitting a whole day. Everybody who knows motion pictures knows how stupid this is. A whole day because I was shooting a cup of coffee with a spoon and I changed the spoon because I wanted the spoon moved here and I wanted the spoon moved there.

QUESTION: *What was it like to work with you?*
LANG: If anybody knows exactly what he wants, it's probably very hard to work with him because he knows exactly what he wants.

QUESTION: M *was a turning point for many people and it was a classic—it is a classic film. How did it come about? Did you know Lorre before that? Did you know Brecht before that?*
LANG: It had nothing to do with Lorre. I was married to Thea von Harbou.

I had made, as you know, *Die Nibelungen, Metropolis, Woman in the Moon.* Big films, crowds and so on. I got tired of this kind of film and I was thinking of simpler stories. I was talking with Thea von Harbou. What was the most, I'm trying to find the right word now, abominable, the most, not horrible . . . the greatest crime which we reject? We decided, let's write some nasty son of a bitch stories. And we started to write and one day I came to her and I said, "Listen darling, I think we should change this scene. Let's make a film about a child murderer. A child murderer who is forced by a power within him to commit a crime which he afterwards resents very much." And then we made this film.

Those days there were lots of horrible crimes in Germany, there was a mass murderer in the Rhineland, and many reviewers said that this was the inspiration, which is not true. The film was finished long before this mass murderer. At the Berlin Scotland Yard I saw many murders; not murders direct but the result of many murders. One case I will never forget—a small shop where a woman was murdered, and the murderer cut her throat and the blood just dropped over the counter in an open sack of flour, and the blood dropping into this sack of flour, white flour, I will never forget in my whole life. Another one was in a big apartment house where they found chopped-off hands on a plate under the bed of the murderer where he was cooking something; there was only one room in the apartment. There was a man on the borderline of Germany and Czechoslovakia who killed travelers and made sausages out of them and sold them to an audience and they liked them very much. It was really a horrible time, you know.

Peter Lorre I saw first on the stage. Well, anyway, he came to Berlin and he was in two plays and I saw him and my idea was to cast the murderer aside from what Lombroso has said what a murderer is: big eyebrows, big shoulders, you know, the famous Lombroso picture of a murderer. And so I used Peter Lorre, who nobody would think to be a murderer. I had a big fight with Peter. In the kangaroo court scene, which I shot at the Staaken Zeppelinhalle, he didn't want to come because he was playing at night in *Squaring the Circle.* He had rehearsals of *Squaring the Circle* and I had to force him. I said, "Look, I will bring an injunction against you because I have a contract with you," and so he came and we shot the last scenes and we didn't talk until it brought on a great success, and then we talked again.

QUESTION: *But that was his first great success, that film?*
LANG: Yes.

RESPONSE: *He was not known. . . .*
LANG: Well, he was known in the theater, you know. I remember one
thing. There was a German reviewer, he's dead by now, who wrote about this
film, "How can one write about a picture by a man who has no honest outlook about what's going on in the world?" There was also something that
was very funny. Thea von Harbou and I—you know, there was big censorship
in Berlin—we sat two hours in front of the room where the censors were
looking at the film. We weren't sitting there as one who has done something,
we didn't have to be ashamed, and yet you look there like a schoolboy worrying if you get a good note or not. And finally they came out and they said,
"Mr. Lang, this film has practically everything about which we disagree and
which we cannot accept but it is done with such integrity that we don't want
to make any cuts."

QUESTION: *Was it a great success from the beginning?*
LANG: From the beginning. Contrary to destiny, you know.

QUESTION: *And did that kind of film determine some of your future work?*
LANG: No, don't forget I tell you, it's very peculiar because in this film
there's no love story and I'll tell you what happened. I had made a film called
Woman in the Moon, contrary to the man in the moon, hey. When I had
made *Woman in the Moon,* I was sick and tired of films with big masses and
so on. I have to tell you one thing—*Woman in the Moon* was made in my own
company but the release was UFA, and UFA sent an executive to this country
just to hear the first sound films. He came back and asked that I should make
a sequence, probably the starting of the rocket, with sound and I said no
because in my opinion it could have broken the rhythm of the whole film.
The whole thing was silent and then suddenly he wanted a piece with sound
to come in and this was for me. . . . So UFA canceled my contract. My lawyer
said to me if I want to win, I had to live up to my contract, meaning I had to
give all the people that I had on contract in my private company—the actors,
the cameraman, the architect, I don't know, nine or eleven people—to UFA
if UFA wanted them, and UFA thought that they could starve me out, which
they couldn't.

After nine months, we came to an agreement. In the meantime, a man
came to me, very elegant, young, but he had a very peculiar reputation and
in those days I wouldn't have given him my hand. He wanted to ask me if I

would like to make a film with him and I said no, and he came, and he came, and he came, and he came and he came. I didn't want to make any films any more; I wanted to become a chemist. And he came again, and I said, "Let me tell you something. I will make a film for you but you have no rights except to give me the money for what the film costs. You will have no rights to subject, no rights about cutting, no rights about casting." He accepted this. Otherwise *M* would never have been made, because it has no love story, nothing.

QUESTION: *You mentioned that Bertolt Brecht worked on one of the films that you did. You didn't have continuous association with Brecht; you were in this country before he was, long before he was, and he had a very difficult time here financially, did he not?*

LANG: Marthe Feuchtwanger and I and Lilly Latté [Mr. Lang's long-time associate] collected money to help get Brecht over. The European Film Committee or such a thing brought him here and he had enough money. He worked, I think, in one thing with Leon Feuchtwanger.

When Heydrich was assassinated in 1942, I had an idea to make a picture about it, and I asked Brecht if he would like to. "Look," I said, "I don't see any reason why someone should a dead man who was a great poet make bad. I don't care what he said about me." And Brecht said, yes, he would like to make this film with me and we sat together for five days and lined out a story. I didn't want to make any more films under a year-long commitment to any company; I was free-lancing, and there was a European man here named Arnold Pressburger who wanted to make a film with me. And I said, "Brecht, how much do you want to have for this script?," and Brecht said, "Do you think $3,000 is too much?"

Because he couldn't speak English, I said let me see. I knew what I could do and I came back and Brecht said, "How was it?" I said, "Yes, he wants the film. What would you say if I said $5,000?" "Oh," he said, "That would be wonderful, really?" I said, "No, you will get $7,500," and he was very happy. Now we had to search for a man who could work with him, who could speak German very well and be a good writer, and we found John Wexley, who had written *The Last Mile* in New York, and we didn't know it that he was in the Communist Party. Brecht was never in the Communist party. And after five days Brecht did something which spoiled everything. He came to me and said, "Fritz, I'm not working anymore." I said, "Why not?" He said, "Wexley tells me that Pressburger pays him $10,000." I said, "Yes, it's correct." He said, "But if gets $10,000, I want to have $10,000 too. I don't work otherwise." I said, "Okay, let me talk to Pressburger. That's blackmail."

I went to Pressburger and it took me three or four hours, and I said, "Look, $2,500—what the hell." Let me make a long story short. Finally, I convinced him and then they worked together. In the meantime, I was working with the cameraman and one day Pressburger called me. He said "Fritz, something horrible happened." I said, "What happened?" He said, "We have made a mistake. We have to start a month sooner than we expected." Now I had a script over 220 pages and they both weren't finished. Brecht and I had an idea in '42 that Hitler could never win the war and we wanted scenes of the prisoner camps.

These scenes were written much longer and the whole script was unfinished and it was already 220 or 250 pages and you know, in those days, we couldn't make a film that was so long, we didn't have the money. I took another young writer and without saying anything to Brecht or Wexley, I started to cut. I cut naturally not the story but I had to cut most things of the prison camp. Now, I told you before that Brecht wanted me to . . . In his diary, he suddenly claims that I promised him that his wife, Helene Weigel, would play a Czech girl, which is stupid because I told him from the beginning on that I would use only American actors as Czechs . . . anyway, I cut it down as much as possible and we started to shoot. Brecht never came to the set. He was hurt. Again, in his so-called diary, it says Pressburger and Lang don't want to give me the right of the author, or some such thing.

To make a long story short, Wexley claimed that much of the film is from him and very little from Brecht, which is stupid and wrong because there are so many scenes that can only be by Brecht which are so typically Brecht that nobody else could have invented them. It came to an arbitration. Pressburger said I will not speak for Brecht because he blackmailed me for $2,500, so Eisler and I, we spoke for Brecht, and Brecht was there, he sat between me and Eisler. And the arbitration decided the following thing: We will give Mr. Brecht the rights to the author idea of Mr. Lang and Brecht, but the author of the script we will give to Mr. Wexley because Mr. Brecht has always said that he will go back to Europe and he doesn't need it whereas Mr. Wexley stays here and he will need it.

We couldn't do anything. I said, "Look, I will step back—the whole idea is from Brecht." Nothing of this is in his diary but now comes a funny thing.

Wexley could never use anything because he was a Communist and then came the McCarthy trials. Today, if anybody asks, I say the script is from Brecht.

I was the only one who gave Brecht a chance, and Brecht worked on it and I am very happy about it. Brecht could probably never understand that you *work* for an audience. He wanted to push his ideas on an audience. In my opinion, I like audiences. I was always opposed to the American line, "An audience has the mentality of a 16-year-old chambermaid." If this would be true, I would be ashamed to work for such an audience. I like audiences, but I don't think you should give an audience something fifty steps ahead of them. I asked myself—why is the first work of a writer, of a screenwriter, or of a playwright almost always a success. Because he still belongs to an audience. The more he goes away from the audience, the more he loses contact, and what I tried to do my whole life long was I tried not to lose contact with the audience.

But does this mean ?

Fritz Lang Remembers

GENE D. PHILLIPS / 1975

HIGH ABOVE BEVERLY HILLS, beyond Benedict Cañon Drive, Fritz Lang lives in a splendid, secluded home overlooking Los Angeles. Lang's place in film history is equally high. His departure from Germany in 1933 in the wake of the rise of Hitler has been cited as marking the end of the Golden Age of German Cinema; and four decades after he left Germany, in 1973, Lang's spirit so pervaded the Sorrento German Film Encounter of young German film makers that it awarded him a special prize for his achievement as the best German film director.

Now an octogenarian, Lang is still very much an imposing figure and speaks with a ring of authority in his voice grounded in a lifetime of experience. At the same time he is gracious, good-humored, and patient in providing an interviewer not only with fresh anecdotes about his career but with additional details concerning incidents that he has talked about before. Listening to Lang reminisce, one is put in touch with one of the genuine pioneers of motion picture history who has had a lasting influence on the development of the medium. For, as the industry grew, he grew with it and helped it to become an art form by becoming a film artist himself. As one cinema historian has put it, the movie industry will never again see giants like Fritz Lang.

GP: *Let's begin by talking about your early life since there is very little written about it. You were born December 5, 1890, the son of a Viennese architect who wanted you to be an architect too.*

From *Focus on Film,* 20 (Spring 1975): 43–51. Reprinted by permission of Gene D. Phillips.

FL: I ran away from home to become a painter and went first to Brussels and then to Bruges and there I saw my first film. I forget what the title of it was—it was a film about the French Revolution or some such thing. Then I went to Paris and travelled through Marseilles and on to Asia Minor, the South Seas, Africa, China, Japan, and Russia for almost a year. I lived by painting postcards and drawing cartoons for newspapers. Then I went back to Paris and started to work there in a private art school. Then the First World War broke out and I left Paris on the last train and escaped to Vienna. When I came back to Austria in 1914 I was drafted into the Austrian Imperial Army and in 1915 I was sent to war.

GP: *At the Front you were wounded and decorated.*
FL: I was shot in the shoulder in Italy and went back to Vienna. I was rather unhappy because as a lieutenant I didn't have enough money to live on. Then one day I was sitting in a café in my uniform (there were several decorations on it) and a man came up to me and offered me a job, and I asked him very haughtily who he was. His name was Peter Ostermeyer and he was a director of the Red Cross Theatre. The play which he was producing was about an Austrian lieutenant who was captured by the French and then was saved by his servant (every officer had a man who helped him). I asked him what I would be paid and he said 750 kronen. Now as a lieutenant I was getting only 120 kronen, so you can imagine what this meant to me. Sometimes—very seldom—I get a bright idea, so I said to him, "That is very little," and he responded that he couldn't pay me more than 1,000! So naturally I agreed. Then he developed another problem: he was planning for me to play a German officer who appeared only in the Second Act, but because of my Viennese dialect he had to give me the main part.

GP: *How did you make the transition from the stage to working in films?*
FL: The play met with some success and I met someone with whom I had worked before writing scripts who introduced me to Erich Pommer, who had his own production company, Decla-Bioscop. When Pommer first saw me he looked at the monocle which I was wearing (because my right eye has always been not as good as my left) and said, "I don't want to have anything to do with that son-of-a bitch. I don't like his looks." But since he had already promised to talk with me, we met one evening after the show and we talked

together until 4 a.m. He gave me a job in the script department as a script doctor.

G P: *I understand that you worked on several scripts in this period but were some-times dissatisfied with the way that they were filmed.*

F L: In 1919 I told Erich Pommer that I wanted to direct my first film; it was my own script and it was called *Halbblut (Half Breed)*. I still wrote some screenplays for other directors, however, such as *Pest in Florenz (Plague in Florence)*, which was directed by Otto Rippert the same year. I next directed *Der Herr der Liebe (The Master of Love)*. Then I did *Der Goldene See (The Golden Lake)*, the first part of a projected four-part series of features with the overall title of *Die Spinnen (The Spiders)*, and *Harakiri*, whose plot was based on the famous opera "Madame Butterfly."

G P: *It was then that you were offered the direction of* The Cabinet of Dr. Cali-gari.

F L: It was first given to Erich Pommer, not to me, and Erich wanted me to do it. So I read it over and said, "Erich, an audience will not understand an expressionistic film of this kind with distorted perspectives, etc., unless you devise a scene at the beginning of the film in which two people talk in a normal way in a realistic setting so that the audience is aware from the outset that the story is being told by a madman." Erich accepted this idea but he had to take the film away from me because the exhibitors wanted to have the second part of the *Spiders* series. So instead of shooting *Caligari* I made *Das Brillanten Schiff (The Diamond Ship)*, which turned out to be the last part of the series to be filmed.

G P: *At this point you left Decla-Bioscop.*

F L: I was upset about the whole situation and when I got an offer from the Joe May Company my one-year contract with Erich Pommer was over, so I took it. I first wrote scenarios for Joe May's company, and it was there that I met my later wife, Thea von Harbou, who was also writing scripts for Joe May. She had written a book called *Das Indische Grabmal (The Hindu Tomb)* and together we wrote a film script based on it which was very long and so was to be filmed in two parts, to be presented on successive evenings. Joe May, his wife, and his daughter read it and were very enthusiastic about it. I was supposed to direct it, but eight days later Mrs. Von Harbou came to me and said, "Look, I have very bad news for you. Joe May says that you can't direct the picture because he wouldn't be able to get enough money to make such a big film if the director is as young as you are." The truth is that Joe May wanted to direct the picture himself.

GP: *Interestingly enough, you were to make a sound version of this story in 1958, but at this time May directed the silent version and had you direct* Das Wandernde Bild (The Wandering Image).

FL: Erich Pommer offered to rehire me and Thea von Harbou said, "I will help you write a screenplay especially for you to direct"—*Der Müde Tod (Weary Death),* which was to become known abroad as *Destiny.* That was my first big success—but not right away. When it was first shown in Berlin the newspaper critics, for reasons that I have never been able to figure out, tried to kill the picture. One of them said the film made the viewer weary of watching it. After two weeks it was withdrawn from the cinemas in Berlin; but it went on to open to the most unbelievable reviews in Paris and elsewhere. One of the Paris critics said, "This is the Germany that we once loved"—this was right after World War One, remember. Then the film was re-released in Germany and became a world success. Everything in life has a sunny side. Douglas Fairbanks, Sr. bought the American rights to the picture for $5,000 but he had no intention of releasing it there. He liked the technical effects and he had them copied for his famous film, *The Thief of Bagdad.* Naturally, because he had more money and greater technical facilities at his disposal, he improved on the tricks and made them better then we were able to do.

I never travelled around meeting other directors. I wasn't haughty in this respect. It is just that all my life I have been so involved in my work that I guess one could say in general that, whenever I had to balance my private life and my profession, my profession always won out.

GP: *Your next big success in Germany was* Dr. Mabuse, der Spieler (Dr. Mabuse, the Gambler).

FL: It was a thriller about an arch-criminal and the public liked it for that. Nevertheless, it was also a picture of how crime was rampant in Germany after the First World War. The film reflected the demoralised atmosphere of Germany at the time, with the despair and vice attendant on the loss of the war. It was the kind of atmosphere in which a man like Mabuse could thrive.

I saw the master criminal after World War One as a version of the superman which Nietzsche had created in his writings.

G P : *In his book* From Caligari to Hitler *Siegfried Kracauer suggests that your film of the Siegfried legend in the two parts of* Die Nibelungen *also incorporated the idea of the superman, and that its pageantry foreshadowed that of the Nazi rally in Leni Riefenstahl's* Triumph of the Will *(1935).*

F L : I would like to make a remark about this book. In my opinion this book is wrong about a lot of things and it has done a lot of damage, I feel, particularly among young people. When I made my films I always followed my imagination. By making *Die Nibelungen* I wanted to show that Germany was searching for an ideal in her past, even during the horrible time after World War I in which the film was made. At that time in Berlin I remember seeing a poster on the street which pictured a woman dancing with a skeleton. The caption read: "Berlin, you are dancing with Death." To counteract this pessimistic spirit I wanted to film the epic legend of Siegfried so that Germany could draw inspiration from her past, and not, as Mr. Kracauer suggests, as a looking forward to the rise of a political figure like Hitler or some such stupid thing as that. I was dealing with Germany's legendary heritage, just as in *Metropolis* I was looking at Germany in the future and in *Frau im Mond (Woman in the Moon)* I was also showing Germany in the age of the rocket-ships.

G P : Die Nibelungen *as the first film made by UFA, the federation of film studios in Berlin. How did you find working with Erich Pommer when he became the production chief of UFA?*

F L : Erich Pommer in my opinion was the only real producer that I ever worked with in my life. He always discussed things with me instead of just issuing commands from his office. In fact we never said "You *must* do this or that" to each other throughout our entire lives. He came to me while I was making the second part of *Die Nibelungen* and said, "I was thinking about the scene in which the Huns come over the hill. It will cost a lot of money for all of the extras that you want to use. Is it really necessary?" I told him that I would think the matter over and the next day I said to him, "Look, we can't compete with American films when it comes to these massive scenes anyhow; so let's drop this scene from the shooting schedule." "I have been thinking it over, too," Erich said to me, "and I think we should go ahead and shoot the scene just the way that you envisioned it." Tell me one American producer who would react that way. UFA had us take the picture to the United States for release there because it was a tremendous success all over Europe, but we did not meet with the same kind of success in America. After all, what do people in Pasadena know about Siegfried fighting with dragons?

G P :   *But your trip to the U.S. gave you the inspiration for* Metropolis, *did it not?*
F L :   Erich and I were considered enemy aliens and for some such reason we couldn't land in New York on the day that the boat docked there but had to wait until the following day to disembark. That evening I looked from the ship down one of the main streets of New York and saw for the first time the flashing neon signs lighting up the street as if it were daytime. This was all new to me. I said to myself, what will a big city like this, with its tall skyscrapers, be like in the future? That started me thinking about *Metropolis*.

G P :   Metropolis *enhanced your reputation both in Germany and abroad.*
F L :   But after I finished the film I personally didn't much care for it, though I loved it while I was making it. When I looked at it after it was completed I said to myself, you can't change the social climate of a country with a message like "The heart must be the go-between of the head (capital) and the hands (labor)." I was convinced that you cannot solve social problems by such a message. Many years later, in the Fifties, an industrialist wrote in the *Washington Post* that he had seen the film and that he very much agreed with that statement about the heart as go-between. But that didn't change my mind about the picture.

G P :   *Yet young people today take the film very seriously.*
F L :   In the later years of my life I have made it a point to speak with a lot of young people in order to try to understand their point of view. They all hate the establishment and when I asked them what they dislike so intensely about our computerised society they said, "It has no heart." So now I wonder if Mrs. Von Harbou was not right all the time when she wrote that line in *Metropolis* a half century ago. Personally I still think that the idea is too idealistic. How can a man who has everything really understand a man who has very little?

G P :   *I believe that Stanley Kubrick paid tribute to* Metropolis *in naming his 1968 film* 2001 *because your film takes place in the year 2000.*

FL: That never occurred to me, especially since I don't recall that any specific year is ever mentioned in *Metropolis*. In any event another thing that I
didn't like about the film afterwards were scenes like the one in which a
worker is pictured having constantly to move the hand of the giant dial. I
thought that that was too stupid and simplistic an image for a man working
in a dehumanising, mechanised society. And yet years later when I was
watching the astronauts on television I saw them lying down in their cockpit
constantly working dials just like the worker in my film. It makes you
wonder.

GP: Woman in the Moon, *your last silent film, was also a science fiction
story.*
FL: My technical advisers on this film were Willy Ley, who is dead now, and
Professor Oberth, who became a Nazi. Ley, however, became a rocket expert
in the United States. I am told that some of the people who saw the moon
landings said that it was exactly as I showed it in my film—the early part of
the film showing the launching of the rocket expedition and their landing
on the moon, not the later parts of the story, of course.

GP: Woman in the Moon *came right at the dawn of the sound period.*
FL: When I finished it, UFA wanted me to add sound to portions of it—
sound effects for the rocket going off, etc. One of their executives had been
in New York and had seen the first sound picture there and was very enthusiastic about it. I, on the other hand, felt that sound would kill the style of the
film. So UFA told me that they would break their contract with the Fritz Lang
Film Company. My lawyer said to me that I had to live up to all of my obligations to UFA, otherwise I couldn't win my case. This went on for seven
months and I had to give up to UFA my chief actress, my three architects,
and several other people. I was very disgusted with film making and wanted
to become a chemist. Just at this time an independent producer who did not
enjoy a very good personal reputation constantly came to me asking me to
make a picture for him. I always turned him down until finally I said to him,
"I'll make you a proposition: I will make a picture for you provided that you
have nothing to do with it but give me the money to make it. You will have
no right to cut anything or to change anything; the film must be finished
and exhibited to audiences exactly as I made it." This film was *M*.

G P :   M *was your first sound picture and many think it your masterpiece.*
F L :   It is difficult for me to choose which is my best film, but I like *M*. I discovered Peter Lorre, who had been working in improvisational theatre before he came to Berlin where I saw him, and I chose him for the key role of the child murderer in what was to be his very first film.

G P :   *Did you have any problems working with him?*
F L :   The only difficulty that I had with him was that he insisted that he couldn't whistle. Now in general I am not interested in the music that is used in a movie. Having a musical background for a love scene, for example, has always seemed like cheating to me. But the mournful whistling of the murderer in *M* was crucial since it helped establish his sinister character. My wife offered to whistle on the soundtrack for Lorre but it·didn't seem to me to fit properly. Then the cutter volunteered and he was not right either. I am a musical moron who can't carry a tune but I decided to dub the whistling myself. It was off key and turned out to be just right since the murderer himself is off balance mentally. This was a lucky accident which I couldn't have planned; so, you see, I don't take credit for everything that turns out right in my pictures.

G P :   *After the Nazis banned your last German film,* The Last Will of Dr. Mabuse, *you left Germany and made one film in France,* Liliom. *before being signed by David O. Selznick to come to Hollywood.*
F L :   I was under contract to MGM for a whole year without having gotten a project launched. At the end of the year the studio wanted to end the contract. Eddie Mannix, who was the representative of L. B. Mayer, liked me and I said to him, "Look, Eddie, I was the most famous director in Europe and you just can't kick me out without my even making one picture." He asked me what property I would like to make and I told him that I had found a four-page synopsis of a story by Norman Krasna about lynch law and mob rule, and he accepted the idea. So Bartlett Cormack and I wrote the screenplay.

G P :   *You have usually worked on the scripts of your films, though you rarely have received screen credit for this.*
F L :   I began my career in films as a scriptwriter and have always collaborated on the scripts that I was to direct, except when my agent failed to get such a

clause in my contract. I think of the director as the basic creator of a film. Dudley Nichols, a wonderful man and a fine screen writer, always said that the script was the blueprint for the film and that it was up to the director to fill it out. But once shooting had started I never made any substantial changes in the script. I might change a line that an actor couldn't express properly, but I never changed an idea.

G P : *What was your daily routine when you were shooting?*
F L : At the end of the day around 6 p.m. I would look at the rushes from the previous day's shooting. I would arrive home around 8 p.m. and have dinner. Afterwards I sat down at my desk and worked over the scenes for the next day. When you have a seven-page scene to direct you take the script and work out the camera set-ups and blocking on the plan of the set that you have in front of you. You decide how many shots you will take from each camera angle and arrange to do them all together before going on to the next camera set-up because the lighting has to be adjusted each time you shift your camera angle. The next day I would then rehearse the actors until each one knew what to do and then I would begin shooting. The two hours that I spent each evening in this kind of preparation saved two hours on the set next day and consequently could cut as much as a week or more off the shooting schedule.

G P : *Producers should have been grateful for this. Why, then, did you have difficulties with some of them? In a recent interview, for example, Joseph L. Mankiewicz, the producer of your first American film,* Fury, *said that he sold Louis B.
Mayer on having you direct "his" film and that you did not get along with him. I
am sure there is more to the story.*
F L : I wonder sometimes if it serves any purpose to rake up these old arguments. Still, one likes to have the facts straight. To begin with, I was a co-
founder of the Screen Directors' Guild and therefore a black sheep in the eyes
of executives like L. B. Mayer. As for *Fury,* Mr. Mankiewicz came late to the
project. It was I who chose the subject and worked on the script before shooting began, as I pointed out a moment ago. During the course of shooting he
became the producer. I encountered a great lack of cooperation from various
quarters while I was making that picture. In the evening I would check out a
new set before I went home only to find the next morning that it had been
dismantled, allegedly because some of the parts were needed elsewhere in

the studio. If I needed a car with four doors, I got one with two doors—or vice versa. Finally, when we finished shooting the film, Mr. Mankiewicz wanted us to change the ending. Can you imagine Spencer Tracy, after finishing his stirring speech to the judge, immediately turning away to hug his girl? Mr. Mankiewicz, however, got his way.

G P : *How was* Fury *received by the public? Since MGM considered you a "black sheep," did they promote the picture properly?*
F L : The studio was sure that *Fury* was going to be a flop. When Mr. W. R. Wilkerson, the publisher of the *Hollywood Reporter,* asked a studio executive if MGM had any new pictures of interest, the latter said no. Mr. Wilkerson pressed the executive to let him attend a sneak preview of *Fury* and he was told, "Don't bother to go and see it. It's a terrible movie and it's all the fault of that German son-of-a-bitch with the monocle, Fritz Lang. Let's play poker instead." But Wilkerson knew of my reputation in Europe and insisted on going to the preview. When the preview was over it was clear that the film was a great success and Mr. Mankiewicz asked everyone that he saw in the foyer of the theatre if they really thought it was a good picture. I had gone over to the Brown Derby restaurant with Marlene Dietrich after the preview and Mr. Mankiewicz came in a bit later. When he came up to me I did a stupid thing: he offered me his hand and I did not shake it.

G P : *Does it really bother you when a producer or someone else that you have worked with makes less-than-kind remarks about you in an interview?*
F L : It used to, but a friend of mine told me that you cannot work in this business for a long time without making some enemies. What someone says about you today will be forgotten tomorrow by most people who read it, my friend pointed out; so there is no point in making an issue of it. Besides I have from time to time received recognition for my work and that makes it easier for me to forget the unpleasant things.

G P : *One accolade that you received was from some old-timers out West who registered their surprise that a European director could capture the authentic flavor of the Old West in pictures like* Western Union.
F L : The answer to that is simple. I never believed for a moment that the Old West as pictured in the Western movies which I saw ever existed. The legend of the Old West is the American counterpart of the Germanic myths like that

which I embodied in *Die Nibelungen.* A director of any nationality, therefore, can create this legend on the screen that we know as the Old West since it is something that people have built up in their imaginations. What probably impressed those gentlemen who wrote to me, I suppose, were the little realistic touches that I put into a film like *Western Union.* Such as when Randy Scott pats his horse on the back to reassure it, or when Scott flexes his fingers, which are still healing from some burns, before he goes into a gun battle to see if they are all right. That is the kind of thing real cowboys do.

G P :   *During the Second World War, you made several anti-Nazi movies, such as* Man Hunt *and* Ministry of Fear, *the latter based on Graham Greene's novel. Greene has told me that he was disappointed that the psychological dimension of his novel was not more evident in the film. How did you feel about the script?*
F L :   I have always admired Graham Greene, and when I came back to Hollywood from New York, where I had signed the contract, and read the script, I did everything I could to get out of making that picture; but Paramount wouldn't cancel the contract. That was one of the times that my agent had failed to get a clause in my contract that allowed me to work on the script.

G P :   *In addition to your war films, you also made some thrillers in the Forties like* Woman in the Window. *That was a screenplay that you did work on.*
F L :   As the story originally stood, a lonely man, a professor (Edward G. Robinson), meets an attractive girl and goes home with her. He has no affair with her; in fact he may never have even considered that possibility. Suddenly her boyfriend comes in and attacks the professor who kills the man with a big pair of scissors while defending himself. Because he is an involuntary murderer, everyone in the audience at this point would have wanted him to get off. Then another man (Dan Duryea) tries to blackmail him and he kills this fellow too, and finally commits suicide. I personally felt that an audience wouldn't think a movie worthwhile in which a man kills two people and himself just because he had made a mistake by going home with a girl. That's when I thought of having him wake up after he had poisoned himself to discover that he had fallen asleep in a chair at his club. As he leaves the club he recognises the hat-check boy as the blackmailer in his dream, the porter as the man he killed in the girl's apartment, etc. He stands looking into a store window at the portrait of a woman when another girl comes up and asks him to go with her, just as Joan Bennett had done at the

beginning of the picture. Robinson is scared and runs away shouting, "Not on your life!" So I was able to end the film on a healthy laugh instead of just grimly winding up a story with three deaths in it.

G P :   Scarlet Street *had the same trio of stars as* Woman in the Window: *Joan Bennett, Edward G. Robinson, and Dan Duryea. Did you have censorship problems with the movie because Duryea, who had been conning Robinson with Bennett's help, goes to the chair for killing her—when in reality Robinson did it?*
F L :   The studio was worried about that, but I pointed out that Robinson is punished more by living with his guilt than he would have been by going to jail. At the end of the film he is a man driven by the Furies, at his wit's end. Interestingly enough, not one review complained that an innocent man had to go to the chair for a crime he did not commit. But the reason that no one commented on it is possibly not because they were aware that he had done a lot of other things that would have justified his death, but because they simply did not like his character. If this is so one wonders if the morals of the average moviegoer have eroded over the years.

G P :   *Why is* Scarlet Street *your favorite among your American films?*
F L :   I cannot really say why, any more than I could tell you earlier why I liked *M*. Somehow a certain film just seems to click, have all the right touches, and turn out the way I hoped that it would. This is difficult when there are obstacles to one's creative freedom.

G P :   *The greatest obstacle to your working in America was, of course, when you were blacklisted during the era of Senator Joe McCarthy and the Un-American Activities Committee.*
F L :   I was on the list, but I was never a member of the Communist Party, though I had friends who were. Someone from the American Legion went to the front office and said, "We have no proof that Lang is a Communist, but we know that he has fiends who are. We suggest that you investigate him before you let him make another picture for you." The front office doesn't investigate people; the easiest way out was just not to let them work any more. So I didn't get a job for a year and a half. Then one day Harry Cohn, the top executive at Columbia, said to me, "Fritz, is there any truth in this business about your being a Red?" "On my word of honor there isn't," I replied. With Cohn's support I was hired by an independent producer to

make *The Blue Gardenia,* and then Cohn asked me to make *The Big Heat* at Columbia.

G P : *It has been suggested that your films often deal with the duality of human nature, man's capacity for good and evil, and that this has never been more vividly displayed than in* Scarlet Street *and* The Big Heat: *one side of Gloria Grahame's face is permanently disfigured by Lee Marvin when he throws hot coffee in her face in the latter film.*

F L : I knew perfectly well at the time that you can throw coffee at someone and not leave a scar at all. So I put in a shot showing the coffee overboiling on the stove before Marvin picked up the pot. That made it more believable.

G P : *I have often wondered if you were drawn to doing* While the City Sleeps *because it deals with a homicidal maniac, as did* M.

F L : *While the City Sleeps* was actually based on a real murder case somewhere in Chicago; I read in the papers that the killer wrote on a mirror, "Catch me before I kill more." That is what drew me to the story.

G P : *Your last American film before visiting Germany again was a picture called* Beyond a Reasonable Doubt. *Is there a connection between* M *and that film in terms of the anti-capital punishment theme?*

F L : The theme of my later films in America is that not everyone who does wrong is considered a criminal by society or themselves. In *Beyond a Reasonable Doubt* you have a woman (Joan Fontaine) who finds out that her lover once killed his mistress, but she doesn't turn him in until she falls in love with someone else. What would you call behavior like that? Ultimately I don't like to dwell on the thematic implications of my films, to explain what they mean. Sometimes they have a very personal meaning for me and I have never given an interview about my personal life. All I have to say I have said in my films and they speak for themselves.

INDEX

Visconti, Luchino, 147
von Bagh, Peter, ix, xii, xiii, 146
von Baky, Josef, 86
von Braun, Wernher, 60
von Harbou, Thea, vii, xi, 9, 14, 34, 53, 55, 69,
    72, 78, 86, 88, 92, 98–99, 123, 169–70, 171,
    177–78, 180, 182
von Twardowsky, Hans, 74, 109–10

Wagner, Fritz Arno, vii
Wald, Jerry, 118, 142
Walker, Alexander, 77
Walk in the Sun, A, 116
Wallington, Mike, 146–48
Wallis, J. H., 111
Wanger, Walter, vii, 104, 113
Waram, Percy, 111
war films, 59
Warner Brothers, 114–15, 119
Warren, Robert Penn, 64
Wegener, Paul, 91
Weigel, Helene, 173
Weill, Kurt, vii, 93, 105

Weinberg, Herman G., 50, 51, 54, 66, 68, 73,
    76
Welles, Orson, 23
Wells, H. G., 71
Welsch, Howard, 116
Westerns, 19–20, 21, 25–26, 57, 59, 63, 97–98,
    127, 151, 184–85
Wetvoll Prize, 51
Wexley, John, 109, 172–74
Wiene, Robert, 91
Wilder, Billy, 27
Wilkerson, W. R., 184
Winchester '73, 56–57, 64, 89
Wollen, Peter, x
Woman on the Beach, 96
Wyler, William, 27

Young Torless. See *Der Junge Törless*

Zanuck, Darryl F., 63, 87, 106, 107–08, 116,
    142, 166, 168
Zola, Emile, 88, 119
Zuckmayer, Carl, 53

CONVERSATIONS WITH FILMMAKERS SERIES
PETER BRUNETTE, GENERAL EDITOR

The collected interviews with notable modern directors, including

Robert Aldrich • Pedro Almodóvar • Robert Altman • Theo Angelopolous • Bernardo Bertolucci • Jane Campion • George Cukor • Brian De Palma • Clint Eastwood • John Ford • Jean-Luc Godard • Peter Greenaway • John Huston • Jim Jarmusch • Elia Kazan • Stanley Kubrick • Spike Lee • Mike Leigh • George Lucas • Michael Powell • Martin Ritt • Carlos Saura • John Sayles • Martin Scorsese • Steven Soderbergh • Steven Spielberg • Oliver Stone • Quentin Tarantino • Lars von Trier • Orson Welles • Billy Wilder • Zhang Yimou